BIMALA DEVI DASI

Śrīla Prabhupāda-līlāmṛta, Volume 5

LET THERE BE A TEMPLE

In Vṛndāvana there is a place where there was no temple, but a devotee desired, "Let there be a temple and *sevā,* devotional service." Therefore, what was once an empty corner has now become a place of pilgrimage. Such are the desires of a devotee.

—*from the Bhaktivedanta purports to Śrīmad-Bhāgavatam*

Śrīla Prabhupāda-līlāmṛta, Volume 5

LET THERE BE A TEMPLE

India / Around the World
1971–1975

A Biography of His Divine Grace A. C. Bhaktivedanta Swami Prabhupāda

Founder-Ācārya of
The International Society for Krishna Consciousness

Satsvarūpa dāsa Goswami

THE BHAKTIVEDANTA BOOK TRUST
Los Angeles · London · Paris · Bombay · Sydney

Readers interested in the subject matter of this book are invited by the Bhaktivedanta Book Trust to correspond with the Secretary.

Bhaktivedanta Book Trust
3764 Watseka Avenue
Los Angeles, California 90034

First Printing, 1983: 10,000 copies

Printed in the United States of America

Library of Congress Cataloging in Publication Data

Gosvāmī, Satsvarūpa Dāsa, 1939–
Let there be a temple.

(Srila Prabhupada-lilamrta ; v. 5)
Includes index.
1. A. C. Bhaktivedanta Swami Prabhupada, 1896–1977. 2. Hindus—India—Biography. 3. International Society for Krishna Consciousness. I. Title. II. Series.
BL1175.A14G67 1983 294.5'512'0924 [B] 83-6411
ISBN 0-89213-119-5

Contents

Foreword

Volume V of *Śrīla Prabhupāda-līlāmṛta* covers the time from March of 1971 to April of 1975. During this period, Swami Bhaktivedanta traveled extensively, overseeing the rapid expansion of ISKCON.

Although Swami Bhaktivedanta's American and European disciples had already been introduced to Indian food and dress along with *Vaiṣṇava* devotion, they had not yet learned how to live in India. This volume depicts the struggles of those devotees and of Swami Bhaktivedanta as he teaches them to live and do business and build temples in India, among Indians.

Events moved quickly. Devotees were thrust into positions of leadership for which they had little preparation. They were asked to negotiate land purchases while dealing with crafty businessmen, to build magnificent temples without being cheated, and to find their way through the Indian legal system. Sometimes they confronted open arms and sometimes suspicion, and they met with varying degrees of jealousy among the caste *gosvāmīs* in Vṛndāvana. Western devotees accustomed to a comfortable standard of living found themselves living on land infested with rats, mosquitoes, and even snakes. They chanted and preached, but also protested and fought for their cause in as diplomatic a way as possible. Occasionally a devotee's responsibility would be too great, and he would have to give it up. But by the end of this volume, due to the constant guidance of Swami Bhaktivedanta, ISKCON had become successful at the three sites so important to the Swami's vision for ISKCON in India: Vṛndāvana, Bombay, and Māyāpur.

Like the previous volumes, this is a human story. It is the story of a Vaiṣṇava *guru*, as understood by his disciples. Events that might on the surface be subject to detrimental interpretation are not ignored but are presented along with their transcendental meaning. The story contains anger and frustration as well as joy and exhilaration.

The devotional understanding is important herein, as it was in the previous volumes. Frequently, those who associated with Swami Bhaktivedanta misunderstood his words and acts. But here the author offers us the more mature, interpretive meaning. As the author indicated in the Introduction to Volume III, "Although the activities of Śrīla

Prabhupāda may appear ordinary, they have an internal meaning.'' It is this internal meaning which serves as the interpretive framework for the life of Swami Bhaktivedanta—in this volume and throughout the entire work. While that meaning is always present, to the ordinary biographer it is seldom self-evident.

Those readers who have been fascinated by the first four volumes of Swami Bhaktivedanta's biography will be fascinated by this volume as well. Like the others, it provides rich data for understanding the growth of a religious movement new to Westerners. It provides documentation more extensive than that available for any other such movement. For the historian of religions, it offers more evidence for the significance of sacred time and sacred space as a motif in religious experience.

Of particular significance is that this volume shows ISKCON to be not merely a ''new'' religion concentrated on the two coasts of North America, but a movement deeply rooted in India while reaching throughout the world. It is an Indian religious movement in that it originated in India and continues to live and grow in modern India.

Dr. Robert D. Baird
Professor, History of Religions
School of Religion
University of Iowa

Preface

After the disappearance of His Divine Grace A. C. Bhaktivedanta Swami Prabhupāda from this mortal world on November 14, 1977, many of his disciples saw a need for an authorized biography of Śrīla Prabhupāda. The responsibility of commissioning such a work rested with the Governing Body Commission of the International Society for Krishna Consciousness. At their annual meeting in 1978, the GBC resolved that a biography of Śrīla Prabhupāda should be written and that I would be the author.

According to the Vaiṣṇava tradition, if one aspires to write transcendental literature, he must first take permission from his spiritual master and Kṛṣṇa. A good example of this is Kṛṣṇadāsa Kavirāja Gosvāmī, the author of Lord Caitanya Mahāprabhu's authorized biography, *Śrī Caitanya-caritāmṛta.* As Kṛṣṇadāsa Kavirāja has explained:

> In Vṛndāvana there were also many other great devotees, all of whom desired to hear the last pastimes of Lord Caitanya.
>
> By their mercy, all these devotees ordered me to write of the last pastimes of Śrī Caitanya Mahāprabhu. Because of their order only, although I am shameless, I have attempted to write this *Caitanya-caritāmṛta.*
>
> Having received the order of the Vaiṣṇavas, but being anxious within my heart, I went back to the temple of Madana-mohana in Vṛndāvana to ask His permission also.

This transcendental process is further described by His Divine Grace Śrīla Prabhupāda in his commentary on the *Caitanya-caritāmṛta* as follows:

> To write about the transcendental pastimes of the Supreme Personality of Godhead is not an ordinary endeavor. Unless one is empowered by the higher authorities or advanced devotees, one cannot write transcendental literature, for all such literature must be above suspicion, or in other words, it must have none of the defects of the conditioned souls, namely mistakes, illusions, cheating, and imperfect

> sense perception. The words of Kṛṣṇa and the disciplic succession that carries the orders of Kṛṣṇa are actually authoritative.... One must first become a pure devotee following the strict regulative principles and chanting sixteen rounds daily, and when one thinks he is actually on the Vaiṣṇava platform, he must then take permission from the spiritual master, and that permission must also be confirmed by Kṛṣṇa from within his heart.

So to say the *Śrīla Prabhupāda-līlāmṛta* is an authorized biography does not mean that it is a flattering portrait commissioned by an official body, but that it is an authorized literature presented by one who is serving the order of Kṛṣṇa and *guru* through the disciplic succession. As such, *Śrīla Prabhupāda-līlāmṛta* is not written from the mundane or speculative viewpoint, nor can ordinary biographers comprehend the significance and meaning of the life of a pure devotee of God. Were such persons to objectively study the life of Śrīla Prabhupāda, the esoteric meanings would evade them. Were they to charitably try to praise Śrīla Prabhupāda, they would not know how. But because *Śrīla Prabhupāda-līlāmṛta* is authorized through the transcendental process, it can transparently present the careful reader with a true picture of Śrīla Prabhupāda.

Another important aspect of the authenticity of *Śrīla Prabhupāda-līlāmṛta* is the vast amount of carefully researched information that I am able to focus into each volume. The leading devotees of the Kṛṣṇa consciousness movement, in addition to giving me permission to render this work, have also invited the world community of ISKCON devotees to help me in gathering detailed information about the life and person of Śrīla Prabhupāda. The Bhaktivedanta Book Trust, Prabhupāda's publishing house, has given me his collection of letters, totaling over seven thousand; and scores of Prabhupāda's disciples have granted interviews and submitted diaries and memoirs of their association with Śrīla Prabhupāda. Aside from his disciples, we have interviewed many persons in various walks of life who met Śrīla Prabhupāda over the years. The result is that we have a rich, composite view of Śrīla Prabhupāda, drawn from many persons who knew him in many different situations and stages of his life. The Acknowledgments section in this book lists the persons who are cooperating to bring about *Śrīla Prabhupāda-līlāmṛta.*

Despite the authorized nature of this book and despite the support of my many well-wishers, I must confess that in attempting to describe the glories of our spiritual master, His Divine Grace A. C. Bhaktivedanta Swami Prabhupāda, I am like a small bird trying to empty the ocean by carrying drops of water to the land. The picture I have given of Śrīla Prabhupāda is only a glimpse into his unlimited mercy, and that glimpse has only been possible by the grace of *guru* and Kṛṣṇa.

Satsvarūpa dāsa Goswami

Acknowledgments

Editor: Maṇḍaleśvara dāsa
Research Chief: Baladeva Vidyābhūṣaṇa dāsa
File Manager and Compiler: Gaura Pūrṇimā dāsa

The Gita-Nagari Press Supervisors: Maṇḍaleśvara dāsa, Gaura Pūrṇimā dāsa
Editorial Assistant: Bimalā-devī dāsī
Production Manager: Gaura Pūrṇimā dāsa
File Consultants: Aṣṭa-sakhī-devī dāsī, Rukmiṇī-devī dāsī, Prāṇadā-devī dāsī
Compositors: Nārāyaṇī-devī dāsī, Gaura Pūrṇimā dāsa, Prāṇada-devī dāsī
Layout: Sādhana-siddhi dāsa
Copy Editor: Bimalā-devī dāsī
Inhouse Proofreader: Gaura Pūrṇimā dāsa
Typists: Ācārya-devī dāsī, Nārāyaṇī-devī dāsī

* * *

BBT Coordinator: Śrīla Rāmeśvara Swami
Copy Editor/Proofreader: Kṣamā-devī dāsī
Indexer: Kīrtana-rasa dāsa
Proofreader: Rādhā-vallabha dāsa
Sanskrit: Gopīparāṇadhana dāsa
BBT Archives: Parama-rūpa dāsa, Nitya-tṛptā-devī dāsī

Special thanks to our ISKCON centers in Baltimore, Boston, Ireland, Philadelphia, Trinidad, Vancouver, and Washington, D.C., for their contributions to pay for the printing of this volume.

Introduction

One day in June of 1977, Śrīla Prabhupāda sat in his garden at the Krishna-Balaram Mandir in Vṛndāvana, India, conversing with a few devotees. Although for months he had been manifesting external symptoms of ill health, he still enjoyed sitting here with his disciples, while aromatic jasmine blossoms scented the air and the fountain gently splashed. He had been discussing various topics, including how modern, godless civilization was a society of two-legged animals. Speaking of life in India as he had known it as a child, he described a simpler way of living, and he began recalling some of his childhood experiences.

At his birth, he said, an astrologer had predicted that at age seventy he would leave India and establish many temples. Prabhupāda said he hadn't understood this prediction for many years, but that by Kṛṣṇa's grace he had gone to America (at the age of seventy) to execute the order of his spiritual master. In America, the result of his preaching had given him great hope, and he had obtained permanent residency there, expecting not to return to India.

One of Śrīla Prabhupāda's disciples present, Tamāla Kṛṣṇa Goswami, spoke up. "Do you regret having come back to India?"

"No," Śrīla Prabhupāda replied. "My plan was to stay in America, but Kṛṣṇa's plan was different. Therefore when I was coming back I was speaking to Dvārakādhīśa [the Kṛṣṇa Deity in ISKCON's Los Angeles temple]. I said to Dvārakādhīśa, 'I came here to preach. I don't know why You are dragging me back.' So I was unhappy to leave, but Kṛṣṇa had His plan."

Śrīla Prabhupāda went on to say that by following Kṛṣṇa's plan of leaving Vṛndāvana and then, after preaching in America, coming back to Vṛndāvana, he had gained the most wonderful temple, the Krishna-Balaram temple in Vṛndāvana.

"You always came out victorious," Tamāla Kṛṣṇa said. "I have never seen you defeated. In Bombay, for example, it seemed to be an impossible situation."

"Yes, no one was interested," said Śrīla Prabhupāda. "Who could see that such a big project would come up?"

"Only you could see that," said Tamāla Kṛṣṇa. "You and Rādhā-Rāsavihārī [the Kṛṣṇa Deity at ISKCON's Bombay temple]."

"But still I was determined."

"They should write a book about that," said Tamāla Kṛṣṇa.

"It is history," Śrīla Prabhupāda added. "That is worth writing about. Māyāpur also."

This present volume of *Śrīla Prabhupāda-līlāmṛta* is an attempt to fulfill Prabhupāda's desire that a book be written about the struggles undergone for establishing a wonderful temple for Kṛṣṇa in Bombay, as well as in Māyāpur and Vṛndāvana. It is a history worth writing about.

This history is worth telling not only to Śrīla Prabhupāda's intimate followers, but to the whole world. After all, it is for the benefit of people everywhere that Śrīla Prabhupāda struggled against great obstacles to establish these three important ISKCON temples—in Bombay, in Vṛndāvana, and in Māyāpur. For Śrīla Prabhupāda, "temple" meant not only a building but a center of highest learning, an institution for teaching the science of God. He saw that people were mad after material progress with little interest in understanding their spiritual identity; they identified themselves with the material body. Centers of spiritual learning and culture, therefore, were of prime importance in liberating people from their bodily identification.

Śrīla Prabhupāda's plan had been to transplant the seedling of India's spirituality in the West and then to return the healthy plant to its native soil, where the teachings of Lord Kṛṣṇa had become confused by persons misrepresenting Vedic culture. In reawakening India's own culture, Śrīla Prabhupāda wanted especially that there be wonderful temples of Kṛṣṇa consciousness, temples for everyone's benefit.

This story, *Let There Be A Temple,* is worth telling in that through it we learn of the mind and actions of a pure devotee of the Lord. We cannot expect to imitate such a great, empowered devotee as Śrīla Prabhupāda, but we can read about his activities in this volume, and that will inspire us, and show us how, by persistence, hard work, and patience, we can become successful in our attempts to regain our forgotten Kṛṣṇa consciousness and become pure devotees of the Lord.

This history is worth writing about also because to hear of Śrīla Prabhupāda's activities is naturally very relishable. Hearing about the activities of Lord Kṛṣṇa's pure devotee is as relishable and purifying as hearing about Lord Kṛṣṇa Himself. Simply by reading and appreciating *Śrīla Prabhupāda-līlāmṛta* we will purify our hearts and advance in spiritual enlightenment.

Although *Let There Be A Temple* focuses primarily on Śrīla Prabhupāda's establishing of three major temples in India, this volume also describes his varied activities as the world-traveling leader of his burgeoning International Society for Krishna Consciousness. As related in preceeding volumes of this series, Śrīla Prabhupāda wanted the Kṛṣṇa consciousness movement on every continent, in every city, in every town and village. So although Śrīla Prabhupāda's establishing of his three main Indian centers provides the theme for the present volume, the reader will also find Śrīla Prabhupāda actively representing Lord Kṛṣṇa and the disciplic succession in Los Angeles, Nairobi, New York, Melbourne, Paris—all over the world.

CHAPTER ONE

Calcutta
March 1971

It was midnight. Śrīla Prabhupāda sat on a pillow behind his low desk, his light the only one on in the building. All the other devotees were in bed. On the desk before him rested the dictating machine and a volume of *Śrīmad-Bhāgavatam* with Bengali commentary. A small framed picture of his spiritual master, Bhaktisiddhānta Sarasvatī, sat between two small vases of roses and asters. On the floor beyond the desk was the broad mat covered with white cotton fabric, where a few hours before, devotees and guests had sat.

But now he was alone. Although usually he retired at ten, rising three or four hours later to translate, tonight he had not rested, and his *Bhāgavatam* lay closed, his dictating machine covered.

He had sent two of his disciples, Tamāla Kṛṣṇa and Bali-mardana, to purchase land in Māyāpur. Six days had passed, however, and still they had neither returned nor sent word. He had told them not to return until they had completed the transaction, but six days was more than enough time. He was anxious, thinking constantly of his two disciples.

A breeze arrived, carrying the fragrance of *nīm* trees through the open window. The night was becoming cool, and Prabhupāda wore a light *cādar* around his shoulders. Absorbed in thought, leaning against the white bolster pillow, he paid little attention to the familiar sights in his room. A clay jug with drinking water sat beside him, and a potted *tulasī* plant sat upon a small wooden pedestal. The electricity, off most of the day and night, was now on, and moths and other insects hovered around the bare bulb overhead. A lizard patrolled the ceiling, occasionally darting forward near the light to capture an insect.

Why were Tamāla Kṛṣṇa and Bali-mardana taking so long? It had been more than just a wait of six days; he had been trying to obtain land in Māyāpur for years. And this time the prospects had been excellent. He had clearly instructed Tamāla Kṛṣṇa and Bali-mardana, and by now they should have returned. The delay could mean a complication, or even danger.

The land they were trying for was a nine-*bīgha* plot on Bhaktisiddhānta Road, less than a mile from the birthsite of Lord Caitanya Mahāprabhu. The Sek brothers, Muslim farmers who owned the plot, had been asking a high price. Only recently had a Calcutta lawyer familiar with Navadvīpa been able to seriously negotiate a fair price. The Sek brothers had settled for 14,500 rupees, and Prabhupāda had authorized withdrawal of the funds from his bank in Krishnanagar. Thus Tamāla Kṛṣṇa and Bali-mardana had left for Māyāpur, while Prabhupāda had remained in Calcutta, carrying on with his affairs but thinking often of the activities of his disciples in Māyāpur. Their mission was very important to him, and he kept them in his mind, personally blessing them with his concern.

Prabhupāda wanted an ISKCON center in Māyāpur; it was a desire that had increased within him as his movement had increased throughout the years. He could easily visit or live in Māyāpur; that was no problem. But he needed a place for his disciples. His spiritual master had ordered him to preach in the West; and now with the success of his Kṛṣṇa consciousness society, the Western Vaiṣṇavas required a center in Māyāpur where they could reside and worship and receive the immense benefit of the holy *dhāma.* Bhaktisiddhānta Sarasvatī had stressed the great importance of Māyāpur, and some of his *sannyāsī* disciples had temples there. Why shouldn't the International Society for Krishna Consciousness also be able to take shelter of Māyāpur?

Since birth, Prabhupāda had been aware of the significance of Lord Caitanya and His *dhāma,* Śrī Māyāpur. He had grown up in Calcutta, where everyone knew of Lord Caitanya, and because his father, Gour Mohan De, had been a pure devotee of Lord Caitanya, from childhood he had sung the Bengali songs of Gaura-Nitāi and Their pastimes in the land of Gauḍa. He had imbibed deeply the teachings and pastimes of Lord Caitanya, especially after meeting his spiritual master in Calcutta in 1922.

Lord Caitanya had spent His first twenty-four years in Māyāpur and Navadvīpa. Yet since His manifest pastimes there almost five hundred years ago, the places of those pastimes had been obscured, the Lord's birthsite lost, and His teachings confused and misused. Despite the disciplic line of pure devotees from Lord Caitanya, not until the advent of Bhaktivinoda Ṭhākura, the father of Bhaktisiddhānta Sarasvatī, did Lord Caitanya's *saṅkīrtana* movement and pure teachings begin to emerge. Bhaktivinoda Ṭhākura published many books and preached to reestablish the intellectual, moral, and spiritual integrity of Caitanya Vaiṣṇavism. He researched and explored the land of Navadvīpa, ascertaining the exact birthsite of the Lord. Citing Vedic evidence, he established that many previous incarnations of Viṣṇu had enacted pastimes in Navadvīpa.

Not only did Bhaktivinoda Ṭhākura document Navadvīpa's past glory, but he also foresaw its glorious future, when a religion based on the teachings of Lord Caitanya would emerge and spread throughout the world, and when European and American Vaiṣṇavas would throng to Navadvīpa to join their Bengali brothers in chanting "Jaya Śacīnandana!"* The time would come, Bhaktivinoda Ṭhākura wrote, when in the land of Navadvīpa on the plain of the Ganges a magnificent temple would arise, proclaiming to the world the glories of Lord Caitanya.

Bhaktisiddhānta Sarasvatī, carrying out the desires of his father and preceptor, Bhaktivinoda Ṭhākura, had formed the Gaudiya Math for propagating the teachings of Lord Caitanya and the glories of Navadvīpa-dhāma. He had induced a wealthy disciple to spend his fortune for erecting a temple at Lord Caitanya's birthsite in Māyāpur, and he had constructed a *kīrtana* hall commemorating the place of Lord Caitanya's *kīrtanas.* He had also constructed his own residence in Māyāpur. He had built temples throughout India—sixty-four in all—but because he wanted the English-speaking world especially to take to Lord Caitanya's movement, he had emphasized as first priority the publishing and distributing of Kṛṣṇa conscious literature.

Śrīla Prabhupāda, sitting in his room in the Calcutta temple, shared the great vision of Bhaktisiddhānta Sarasvatī and Bhaktivinoda Ṭhākura. Yet to enact this great vision he had to take practical steps, and he was content to take them in the most humble way. A devotee should not simply daydream, expecting Kṛṣṇa to accomplish everything with "miracles."

Prabhupāda, however, was not dreaming idly. Working for years alone in India, he had held his plan of going to the West, and Kṛṣṇa had at last fulfilled that desire. In America, in whatever circumstances and with whatever small facility Kṛṣṇa had provided, he had preached. And slowly, step by step, he had met with success, realizing his vision of a worldwide society of devotees. Always he had kept his greater vision in mind, as every step forward had given him deeper satisfaction and had brought him closer to fulfilling his mission.

---

*"All glories to Lord Caitanya, the son of Śacī!"

Prabhupāda sometimes told the story of a poor potter who dreamed of expanding his business and becoming fabulously rich. As the potter slept one night, he dreamed of how much land and how many houses he would have and of how he would have a beautiful wife. When the potter considered that perhaps the wife would quarrel with him, he became angry and said, "If my wife fights with me, I will *kick* her!" And kicking, he broke the only two pots in his stock and was reduced to nothing.

Whether chanting or writing or reading or preaching, Prabhupāda had been absorbed in his plans for spreading Kṛṣṇa consciousness and fulfilling the dream of the past *ācāryas.* Now he was anxious to complete the next step, and for this he was waiting up past midnight, meditating on his two disciples and their important mission.

As Prabhupāda sat, rapt in thought, the only sounds were the usual sounds of the night: mice within the walls, a *brahmacārī* snoring on the veranda, and in the distance the night watchman making his rounds, his stick striking the street. There were no cars, and only an occasional wooden ricksha clattered along the potholed street.

Prabhupāda wondered if perhaps his boys had been robbed. Before sending them off, he had shown Tamāla Kṛṣṇa how to carry money around his waist in a makeshift cloth money belt. But it had been a great deal of money, and robberies were not uncommon around Navadvīpa. Or perhaps there had been some other delay. Sometimes in land negotiations involving large sums of money, the court would require that a clerk record the denomination and serial number of every note exchanged. Or perhaps the train had broken down.

Suddenly Prabhupāda heard footsteps on the stairs. Someone opened the outer door and now walked along the veranda just outside. A soft knock.

"Yes, who is it?" Prabhupāda asked. Tamāla Kṛṣṇa entered and prostrated himself before Śrīla Prabhupāda.

"So," Prabhupāda asked, "what is your news?"

Tamāla Kṛṣṇa looked up triumphantly. "The land is yours!"

Prabhupāda leaned back with a sigh. "All right," he said. "Now you can take rest."

* * *

London
August 1971

Prabhupāda had asked the Indian high commissioner for the United

Kingdom to petition Prime Minister Indira Gandhi to attend ISKCON's upcoming cornerstone-laying ceremony in Māyāpur. Already Prabhupāda had instructed all his G.B.C. secretaries to attend the ceremony, and he had asked the devotees to invite many prominent citizens of Calcutta. Writing to his disciples in India, he said that if they could not get Indira Gandhi to come, they should at least get the governor of Bengal, Sri S. S. Dhavan.

Meanwhile, Prabhupāda was meeting in London with several of his disciples experienced in architecture and design; he wanted them to draft plans for his Māyāpur project. Nara-Nārāyaṇa had built Ratha-yātrā carts and designed temple interiors, Raṇacora had studied architecture, and Bhavānanda had been a professional designer, but Prabhupāda himself conceived the plans for the Māyāpur buildings. He then told his three-man committee to provide sketches and an architect's model; he would immediately begin raising funds and securing support in India for the project. To the devotees who heard Prabhupāda's plans, this seemed the most ambitious ISKCON project ever.

While taking his morning walks in Russell Square, Prabhupāda would point to various buildings and ask how high they were. Finally he announced one morning that the main temple in Māyāpur should be more than three hundred feet high! Māyāpur's monsoon floods and sandy soil would create unique difficulties, he said, and the building would have to be built on a special foundation, a sort of floating raft. A civil engineer later confirmed this.

The first building, Prabhupāda said, should be a large guesthouse, four stories high, and his design, although not strictly conforming to any one school of architecture, resembled most that of Rajasthan. He wanted a pink-and-rust colored building with many arches and a wide marble veranda on each floor except the ground floor. The building should run east-west, so that the sun would pass lengthwise over it and not shine directly into the building's broad front. Southerly breezes would cool the guesthouse in summer. The building should be equipped with electric fans and lights, modern toilets and showers, and the rooms should be furnished, spacious, and well ventilated.

This guesthouse should be built as soon as possible, Prabhupāda said; then other buildings would follow. He wanted residential buildings for five hundred devotees, a large *prasādam* hall seating several thousand, a kitchen complex, and a *gośālā* (a shelter for the cows that would pasture in nearby fields). In time ISKCON would acquire adjoining land and develop parks, with flower gardens, trees and shrubs, fountains, walkways, and arbors.

The main building, the colossal Mayapur Chandrodaya Mandir, was to be no less than three hundred feet high and costing perhaps tens of millions of dollars. Prabhupāda's description astounded the architects as well as the devotees; it sounded grander than the United States Capitol or St. Peter's Cathedral. The temple's central dome would house a three-dimensional model of the universe. The design, however, would be based on the Vedic description and would depict not only the material universe but also the spiritual universe.

Entering the main hall, a person would look up and see the planets situated just as *Śrīmad-Bhāgavatam* describes, beginning with the hellish planets, then the middle planets, wherein the earth is situated, then the heavenly planets of the demigods, and then Brahmaloka, the highest planet in the material world. Above Brahmaloka, the observer would see the abode of Lord Śiva, and above that the spiritual sky, or *brahmajyoti.* Within the spiritual effulgence of the *bramajyoti* would be the self-illuminating Vaikuṇṭha planets, inhabited by eternally liberated souls. And highest of all would be the supreme planet of Kṛṣṇaloka, where God in His original eternal form enjoys His pastimes with His most confidential devotees.

The temple would also house a miniature palace in which the Deities of Rādhā and Kṛṣṇa would reside, surrounded by silks and pillars of silver, gold, and jewels. The Mayapur Chandrodaya Mandir and the Māyāpur city would be ISKCON's world headquarters.

And why such a fabulous architectural wonder as this in such an obscure part of the world? The answer, Prabhupāda explained, was that Māyāpur was actually not obscure; it seemed so only from the mundane perspective. To mundane vision, that which was central *seemed* remote. The soul and the next life seemed remote, while the body and immediate sense gratification seemed central. By establishing the Temple of Human Understanding in Māyāpur, Śrīla Prabhupāda would be directing the materialistic world's attention back to the true center.

Any sincere visitor would be charmed by the beauty of ISKCON's Māyāpur project and would perceive that here indeed was the spiritual world. And the devotees living in Māyāpur, by remaining constantly immersed in singing Hare Kṛṣṇa *kīrtana* and discussing the philosophy of Kṛṣṇa consciousness, would be able to convince any intelligent visitor that the teachings of Lord Caitanya Mahāprabhu were the highest truth. The devotees would explain the philosophy of the Absolute Truth, which would enable visitors to comprehend actual spiritual truth beyond sectarian religious dogma. Furthermore, the continuous Hare Kṛṣṇa *kīrtana* and the blissful devotees engaged in a wide variety of services to Lord Kṛṣṇa would demonstrate that *bhakti-yoga* was the simplest, most direct process for meditating on the Supreme Personality of Godhead. While staying in ISKCON's Māyāpur city, a person would quickly become a devotee of the Lord and begin chanting and dancing in ecstasy.

Śrīla Prabhupāda was demonstrating how the world could be spiritualized by linking material things with the Supreme Personality of Godhead, Kṛṣṇa, through *bhakti-yoga.* And why shouldn't such spiritual feats surpass the achievements of the materialists?

Prabhupāda was sorry to learn through the Indian high commissioner that the prime minister could not attend the cornerstone-laying ceremony in Māyāpur. Yet he took it as Kṛṣṇa's desire. He said he would invite a prominent Vaiṣṇava to officiate, or he might do it himself. "On the whole," he wrote, "it was Lord Caitanya's desire that a Vaiṣṇava shall lay down the cornerstone instead of asking some material man or woman to perform the holy work."

The monsoons came, and the Ganges spilled over her banks, flooding the entire ISKCON Māyāpur property. Acyutānanda Swami had built a straw and bamboo hut where Prabhupāda was soon to stay, but the waters rose until Acyutānanda Swami had to live in the bamboo rafters. He wrote Prabhupāda that had it not been for Bhaktisiddhānta Road,* the damage would have been extensive. Prabhupāda replied,

> Yes, we were saved by Srila Bhaktisiddhanta Road. We shall always expect to be saved by His Divine Grace Srila Bhaktisiddhanta Saraswati Goswami Maharaj Prabhupada. Always pray to His Lotus Feet. Whatever success we have had in preaching Lord Chaitanya's mission all over the world is only due to His mercy.

* * *

*The elevated road that runs before ISKCON's property and the birthplace of Lord Caitanya, serving as a dike against the Ganges.

New Delhi
November 10, 1971

The car pulled out from the crowd in front of the airport terminal. Prabhupāda, sitting in the back seat, his bamboo cane against his knee, his hand in his bead bag, talked with his Delhi disciples. As the car moved through the broad avenues of New Delhi Prabhupāda removed two knee-length flower garlands from around his neck and placed them beside him on the seat. It was midday, and the November climate was pleasant. Prabhupāda had arrived from Calcutta just in time for the ten-day ISKCON *paṇḍāl* festival, beginning the next day.

One of the devotees mentioned how fitting it had been that the mayor of New Delhi, Mr. Hans Raj Gupta, had greeted Prabhupāda at the airport. Prabhupāda smiled.

In his speech before Mayor Gupta and a gathering at the airport, Prabhupāda had explained India's duty of performing welfare work for the rest of the world. He had also described how, at age twenty-five, he had met his Guru Mahārāja and had then received the order to carry Lord Caitanya's message to the English-speaking world. Explaining why he had waited until he was seventy before going West, he had remarked, "I was trying to become a successful tool for preaching Lord Caitanya's message." Hundreds of thousands of preachers were needed now, as the Kṛṣṇa consciousness movement was spreading throughout the world. "And the black men are also dancing," Prabhupāda had said. "And they are asking the Indian people, 'Why you and the swamis do not give us this sublime method?' "

Delhi was the third Indian city Prabhupāda had visited since his return from Africa a month ago. His first stop, Bombay, had begun roughly. Śyāmasundara had neglected to carry Śrīla Prabhupāda's inoculation card, so immigration officials had denied Prabhupāda entry into India, quarantining him at the Bombay airport hospital for ten days.

Confined to a suite with an adjoining veranda overlooking a garden, Prabhupāda had resigned himself to a more limited sphere of activity. Still, each morning after breakfast he had conducted a dialogue with Śyāmasundara about certain leading Western philosophers: Śyāmasundara would present a particular philosophy, and Prabhupāda would discuss it in light of the Vedic view. Then, with only one day left before the end of the ten-day quarantine period, the inoculation card had arrived, and Prabhupāda had been released.

Immediately he had left for Calcutta and a series of *kīrtana* and lecture programs at Desh Priya Park. He had stayed in Calcutta two and a half weeks, appreciating the location of the ISKCON temple at Albert Road in the heart of what had once been the *sāhab* (European) section. "Now I am bringing the *sāhabs* back to the *sāhab* quarter," Prabhupāda had said, "but this time they are all coming as Vaiṣṇavas. You should never give up this place."

Some of the Calcutta devotees had complained to Śrīla Prabhupāda that the temple was being mismanaged and that, due to insufficient income, their diet was inadequate. When Prabhupāda had questioned the temple leaders, one devotee had replied, "Śrīla Prabhupāda, I was simply trying to execute your will."

"Is it my will," Prabhupāda had asked, "that all the devotees should be disturbed?"

He had settled the differences, arranged for an improved diet, and had even recommended a democratic election of temple officers. But he had also explained that because Kṛṣṇa consciousness was such an important mission, the devotees should cooperate, even if there were discrepancies. The material world is like an ocean, he had said, and there would always be waves.

During this visit to Calcutta, Prabhupāda had also spoken of his plans for Māyāpur. Nara-Nārāyaṇa had built a scale model of the building ISKCON would construct on the newly acquired property, and Prabhupāda had shown it to all his guests and had asked them to help. Seeing Prabhupāda's absorption in this project, Girirāja had volunteered to help in any way required. "It seems the two things you want most," Girirāja had said, "are for the books to be distributed and to build a temple at Māyāpur."

"Yes," Prabhupāda had said, smiling. "Yes, thank you."

When Prabhupāda arrived at the home of Mr. Ram Niwas Dandaria in New Delhi, a waiting reporter interviewed him.

"I understand," said the reporter, "that by 'Kṛṣṇa' you mean some eternal principle."

"I do not mean a principle," Prabhupāda replied. "I mean a person like you and me." Prabhupāda was explaining Lord Kṛṣṇa as the Supreme Person when suddenly sirens began sounding.

"Blackout! Blackout!" cried the reporter and others in the house. War between Pakistan and India had been imminent for weeks, and air raid drills and warnings were now commonplace in Delhi.

"Sir"—the reporter spoke tensely in the darkened room—"this is the presence of reality. We are being threatened by this fight with Pakistan. The siren is the ugly reality coming for us."

"We are always in the ugly reality," Prabhupāda said, "—twenty-four hours a day. Suppose there is no blackout? Still, if you go in the street, there is no guarantee that you will get home. In this way, you are always in the ugly reality. Why do you say only this blackout? This is just one of the features of this ugly reality. That's all."

Reporter: "Yes, but at the moment..."

Prabhupāda: "You do not realize that you are in ugly reality twenty-four hours a day? *Padaṁ padaṁ yad vipadām.* There is danger at every step."

Reporter: "I know, sir, but this is collective, national danger. Have you anything to offer us as a remedy?"

Prabhupāda: "Kṛṣṇa consciousness is our only remedy. Take to this process, and you will be happy."

Reporter: "Sir, I think someone should go to the Yahya Khan [the president of Pakistan]."

Prabhupāda: "What benefit will you derive by going to Yahya Khan?"

Reporter: "Someone is out to kill me."

Prabhupāda: "But suppose Yahya Khan does not kill you? Will you be safe? Then what is the use to go to Yahya Khan? You will die today or tomorrow. If you want to save yourself, then go to Kṛṣṇa. That is our proposition. Even if you go to Yahya Khan, and he does not fight, then you mean to say that you will live forever? What is the use of flattering Yahya Khan? Flatter Kṛṣṇa, so that you may be saved perpetually. Why don't you do that?"

Reporter: "I was only thinking in terms of collective security. I can see your point..."

Prabhupāda: "You should know that you are always in danger."

Reporter: "Yes, sir, we agree. The late Einstein said the same thing..."

Prabhupāda: "That is our position, and Kṛṣṇa says, 'I will save you.' Therefore, let us go to Kṛṣṇa. Why go to Yahya Khan?"

Reporter: "Simply because he is disturbing us, that's all."

Prabhupāda: "Your mind is always disturbing you all the time, because it is always with you. Your body is always with you. Are you not suffering from bodily pains? Why don't you go to Yahya Khan to cure your pains? You are always in danger. Why don't you realize that?"

Reporter: "We realize that this is a national disaster."

Prabhupāda: "These are symptoms. People are trying to give a patchwork cure for the disease. *We* are giving the supreme cure. This is the difference. No patchwork cure will help you. You need a complete cure.

janma karma ca me divyam
evaṁ yo vetti tattvataḥ
tyaktvā dehaṁ punar janma
naiti mām eti so 'rjuna

The cure is no more repetition of birth and death. That is what we want. That is the benefit of Kṛṣṇa consciousness. *Yaṁ prāpya na nivartante/ tad dhāma paramaṁ mama.* If you go to Kṛṣṇa, then you don't come back again to this material world."

Reporter: "Sir, mine was a very hypothetical question. Suppose a hundred pure, saintly, Kṛṣṇa conscious people are meditating or discussing together, and someone comes along and drops the bomb—"

Prabhupāda: "Those who are Kṛṣṇa conscious are not afraid of bomb. When they see a bomb coming, they think that Kṛṣṇa desired the bomb to come. A Kṛṣṇa conscious person is never afraid of anything. *Bhayaṁ dvitīyābhiniveśataḥ syāt.* One who has the conception that something can exist outside of Kṛṣṇa is afraid. On the other hand, one who knows that everything is coming from Kṛṣṇa has no reason to be afraid. The bomb is coming—he says, 'Ah, Kṛṣṇa is coming.' That is the vision of the devotee. He thinks, 'Kṛṣṇa wants to kill me with a bomb. That is all right. I will be killed.' That is Kṛṣṇa consciousness."

When the reporter asked if the Vaiṣṇava would die without fighting, Prabhupāda said that the Vaiṣṇava would fight, but only under the direction of Kṛṣṇa, and he cited Arjuna and Hanumān as examples. He continued to explain Kṛṣṇa consciousness as the only solution. The blackout ended.

A few of Prabhupāda's disciples had organized the New Delhi *paṇḍāl* program like the public festivals Prabhupāda had already introduced in India. Tamāla Kṛṣṇa, Tejās, and Guru dāsa had enlisted the help of important Delhi men, including the mayor and members of New Delhi's Management and Reception Committee. These persons had granted permission and issued letters of introduction to others, whom the devotees had then approached for donations.

The devotees found everyone they met sympathetic to Śrīla Prabhupāda. They respected him, especially after meeting him. Some disagreed philosophically, yet all were impressed by Prabhupāda's converting Westerners to Hindu *dharma* and God consciousness, and they had genuine respect for Prabhupāda's worldwide propagation of the teachings of *Bhagavad-gītā.*

Prabhupāda had great stature among the Indians as a *sādhu.* Speaking only on the basis of the scriptures, he exhibited full surrender to Lord Kṛṣṇa. He was above politics and sectarianism; he was fully spiritual and commanded respect. Everyone, regardless of personal philosophies or practices, seemed to accept him as a true representative of Indian culture, a genuine *sādhu* and *guru.*

Among the distinguished persons who agreed to appear as guest speakers during the ten-day festival were Sri Hans Raj Gupta, mayor; H. Bachchan, a famous Hindi poet; Sri Syama Caran Gupta, chairman of the Delhi Metropolitan Council; Sri C. B. Agarwal, a famous orator; Sri Vipin Candra Misra, magistrate of the Delhi High Court; Dr. Atma Ram, a renowned scientist; Colonel B. R. Mohan, ex-mayor and industrialist of Lucknow; Sri L. N. Sakalani, a prominent industrialist; Sri Aditya Nath Jha, the lieutenant-governor of Delhi; Sri Jagjivan Ram, Indian defense minister; and His Excellency James George, the Canadian high commissioner. Guru dāsa had also had friendly conversations with the U.S. ambassador to India, Kenneth Keating, who had repeatedly expressed his respect for the Kṛṣṇa consciousness movement. Ambassador Keating regretted that he would be out of town during the function.

The devotees had secured an excellent location at the L.I.C. Grounds in Connaught Place, the heart of New Delhi's commercial district. There they had arranged for a large tent and outdoor lighting for the ten-day festival. On opening day the program started at six A.M. with a *kīrtana* and an *ārati* before the newly arrived Deities of Rādhā and Kṛṣṇa, white marble Deities from Jaipur enthroned upon a flower-bedecked altar on the large stage. Attendance was sparse at first, but picked up when after a noon *kīrtana* and *ārati* devotees began distributing Kṛṣṇa *prasādam.* The evening program started with a *kīrtana,* which continued enthusiastically, building to an ecstatic climax as Śrīla Prabhupāda entered.

For the pious people of Delhi, the evening Hare Kṛṣṇa festival was a momentous occasion. Since the location and the hour were ideal and admission was free, the crowd had grown to tens of thousands, many having come specifically to see the young American Vaiṣṇavas.

At Prabhupāda's arrival hundreds of people surged forward to touch his feet and receive his blessings, as a ring of disciples escorted him through the crowd. Prabhupāda, wearing a gray wool *cādar,* his "swami hat" pushed back casually on his head, moved calmly forward toward the stage with natural, aristocratic poise. He sat on the *vyāsāsana,* and the audience quieted.

New Delhi's mayor, Sri Hans Raj Gupta, spoke first. He had met Śrīla Prabhupāda in the early 1960s when Prabhupāda had approached him for a donation to publish the first volume of *Śrīmad-Bhāgavatam.* Mayor Gupta, recognizing Prabhupāda as "someone sincere and near to God," had helped, and Prabhupāda had later presented him with complimentary copies of the first two volumes of his *Śrīmad-Bhāgavatam.* Mr. Gupta was impressed by Prabhupāda's success in spreading Vaiṣṇavism in the West, and as he introduced Śrīla Prabhupāda, he expounded on the Kṛṣṇa consciousness philosophy he had read in Prabhupāda's *Bhāgavatams.*

He said, speaking in Hindi, that as mayor of Delhi for five years he had many times welcomed important visitors and delivered addresses, but such functions were usually only formalities. This was not, however, the case with Śrīla Prabhupāda, he said, since no one he had ever known could compare with him. He praised Prabhupāda for doing "an immense amount of good work in India and the whole world." Said Mayor Gupta, "He has also given me love and affection, and I am more affected by that than anything else."

Then Prabhupāda spoke. When he began by asking whether the audience preferred him to speak in Hindi or English, many called out for Hindi, a few for English. But Prabhupāda announced, "I am going to speak in English, because my disciples, being Americans and Europeans, have joined me. They are following me, and they must understand. If I speak in Hindi they cannot follow. So I am going to speak in English."

"Ladies and gentlemen," Prabhupāda continued, "I thank you for your kindly participating in this Kṛṣṇa consciousness movement. Just now we will vibrate one transcendental song, *Jaya Rādhā-Mādhava Kuñjabihārī.* As you know, Kṛṣṇa's eternal consort is Śrīmatī Rādhārāṇī, the pleasure potency of Kṛṣṇa. Kṛṣṇa is the Supreme Personality of Godhead. When He wants to enjoy, He exhibits His pleasure potency, which is known as Rādhārāṇī."

After chanting *Jaya Rādhā-Mādhava* Prabhupāda expounded the science of Kṛṣṇa for half an hour, quoting *Bhagavad-gītā* on why Kṛṣṇa comes to the material world, how the *jīva* souls are transmigrating from one body to another, birth after birth, and how human life is the opportunity for the *jīva* souls to revive their love of Kṛṣṇa.

"This is religion," Prabhupāda said, "—simply surrender to Kṛṣṇa. Become a Kṛṣṇaite.... It doesn't require a church. It doesn't require a mosque. It doesn't require anything. But wherever you sit down, you can chant Hare Kṛṣṇa. This is the easiest method."

Following Śukadeva Gosvāmī, the ancient speaker of *Śrīmad-Bhāgavatam,* Prabhupāda condemned a materialistic life spent "working hard like the hogs or dogs," without self-realization. He emphasized that India had a treasure house of knowledge, which Indians should distribute all over the world. Unfortunately, the Indians were forgetting their real duty.

In conclusion Prabhupāda said, "So there are many things to be spoken in this connection of the Kṛṣṇa consciousness movement. I am trying to present this to you in the next ten days. This is the beginning. I shall request you to come here. We don't charge any fees. We are depending on Kṛṣṇa. If Kṛṣṇa likes, He will benefit us. We are completely surrendered to Kṛṣṇa. If He likes, He can maintain us. If He likes, He can kill us. We don't mind. We have no business. We have no separate interest. We request you to come and join this movement. It is not sectarian. We have many Hindus, Christians, Jews, Muhammadans, and Sikhs also all over the world who are now in Kṛṣṇa consciousness. We are preaching one word, *Kṛṣṇa,* one scripture, *Bhagavad-gītā,* and one *mantra,* Hare Kṛṣṇa. Chant Hare Kṛṣṇa, Hare Kṛṣṇa, Kṛṣṇa Kṛṣṇa, Hare Hare/ Hare Rāma, Hare Rāma, Rāma Rāma, Hare Hare. Thank you very much."

Prabhupāda attempted to leave the stage, and again the crowd rushed forward to touch his lotus feet. Although Prabhupāda's disciples were already convinced of his greatness, that greatness took on a vivid reality at times like this, when they heard him speaking so powerfully and saw him surrounded by throngs of worshipers.

As Prabhupāda proceeded to his car, he remained calm and humble, but the disciples surrounding him tensed to protect him from being jostled by a frantic crowd. Yet despite the devotees' sincere attempts, individuals in the crowd would manage to break through, diving between the devotees' legs to throw themselves before Prabhupāda.

"Do you know why they are worshiping me?" Prabhupāda said, turning to the disciples near him. "It is because I am free from sex desire."

Śrīla Prabhupāda in Delhi,
November 1971.

The Delhi *paṇḍāl*, November 1971.

Devotees carry Śrīla Prabhupāda on a palanquin in Vṛndāvana in 1971, overlooking Varṣāṇā, the birthplace of Śrīmatī Rādhārāṇī (*above*).

Śrīla Prabhupāda takes the devotees on a tour of Vṛndāvana, November 1971 (*above*). On *parikrama* (holy procession) through the streets of Vṛndāvana, November 1971 (*left*).

Śrīla Prabhupāda in Visakhapatnam, February 1972 (*right*). The ground-breaking and cornerstone-laying ceremony, Juhu, Bombay, March 1972 (*below and bottom right*).

Śrīla Prabhupāda and Karandhara dāsa meet with Dai Nippon executives to discuss the printing of Prabhupāda's books, Tokyo, April 1972 (*top left*). Śrīla Prabhupāda awards *sannyāsa* to Hridayananda, Satsvarūpa, Rupānuga, and Bali-mardana, May 1972 (*middle left*). Devotees glorify Śrīla Prabhupāda with homages and *kīrtana* at his Vyāsa-pūjā (birthday ceremony) in New Vrindaban, September 1972 (*bottom left*).

Śrīla Prabhupāda takes a morning walk with a few disciples during the construction of the Mayapur Chandrodaya Mandir, 1973 (*top*). Śrīla Prabhupāda performs an initiation ceremony in the temple room of the Mayapur Chandrodaya Mandir (still under construction), 1973 (*above*).

Śrīla Prabhupāda at the London Ratha-yātrā, July 1973.

Śrīla Prabhupāda meets with guests in his quarters at Bhaktivedanta Manor, summer 1973.

Śrīla Prabhupāda speaks with devotees on the lawn at Bhaktivedanta Manor, summer 1973.

Śrīla Prabhupāda offers first *āratī* to Śrī Śrī Rādhā-Paris-īśvara after Their installation in Paris, August 1973.

The *āratī* during the installation of Śrī Śrī Rādhā-Gokulānanda at Bhaktivedanta Manor, on Janmāṣṭamī, 1973.

The *kīrtana* following the Deity installation.

Devotees chant in ecstasy while on *parikrama* during the Māyāpur festival, March 1973.

Śrīla Prabhupāda arrives in Geneva, May 31, 1974.

Śrīla Prabhupāda is greeted by the mayor of Geneva.

Śrīla Prabhupāda takes his morning walk near the Eiffel Tower, June 1974.

Lecturing before student radicals at La Salle Pleyel, Paris, June 1974 (*above*). Śrīla Prabhupāda and the devotees outside the newly acquired Schloss Rettershof, Frankfurt, June 1974 (*right*). Śrīla Prabhupāda on a morning walk with Baron von Dürkheim in Frankfurt (*below*).

īla Prabhupāda chants through the streets at the Melbourne
tha-yātrā, June 1974 (*above*). Prabhupāda and his disciples chant
d dance before ten thousand people at the San Francisco Ratha-
trā, July 7, 1974 (*below*).

A morning walk on Venice Beach, Los Angeles (*above and right*). During a visit to Dallas in July 1972, Śrīla Prabhupāda instructs young Dvārākadhīśa in forming the letters of the Sanskrit alphabet (bottom).

Śrīla Prabhupāda holds informal meetings on the roof of his quarters in Bombay, summer of 1974 (*above and left*). The cornerstone-laying ceremony for the grand temple in Bombay (*below*).

The completed projects in Bombay (*top*), Vṛndāvana (*middle*), and Māyāpur (*bottom*).

For ten consecutive nights Śrīla Prabhupāda lectured at the *paṇḍāl.* In many of his lectures he would speak of *dharma* (religion) in connection with the Kṛṣṇa consciousness movement.

"The Kṛṣṇa consciousness movement is the topmost *yoga* system. It is very scientific. Don't think it is a sentimental movement. It is authorized, supported by the Vedic literatures. And actually it is becoming effective. Religion is surrender to God. These boys and girls have taken to this real religion. This movement is so important, and we are giving everyone a chance to make this life successful. Therefore our humble request is that you take to Kṛṣṇa consciousness.

On the fifth evening, after Justice Misra had referred to religion in his introduction, Śrīla Prabhupāda defined the word in his lecture. "*Religion* means constitutional position. In the English dictionary *religion* is described as faith. But by Vedic definition religion cannot be changed like faith because it is the law given by the Lord. Only surrender unto the lotus feet of Kṛṣṇa is *dharma.* That is Kṛṣṇa's verdict. One should not have any ulterior motive in approaching God.

"Why not surrender immediately? Be intelligent. Real religion means to surrender immediately. Why should you wait for many, many births? We request all of you to try to understand this process of Kṛṣṇa consciousness very seriously. Take to it, and you will become happy."

Śrīla Prabhupāda saw the Indian people abandoning their *dharma* for materialism, and he spoke strongly, pointing out their great mistake and urging them to rectify it. "If you actually want to advance your nation, India, then you must take to the culture of Kṛṣṇa consciousness. This will glorify your country. You cannot compete with the Western world in the field of technology. It is impossible. The Western countries are meant for that purpose, for advancing technology. But you are meant for a different purpose. Your special advantage is that you have been born in this land of Bhārata-varṣa after many, many births and after performing many pious activities.

"India is very poverty-stricken, so wherever I go I am told I come from a very poor country. India advertises this image—our ministers beg from other countries. We are accepted as a beggars' culture. At the Berkeley University one Indian student protested the studying of the Hare Kṛṣṇa movement. He was the only student to protest. He said, 'Swamiji, what benefit is made by accepting this Hare Kṛṣṇa movement?' In another place a girl asked me, 'Swamiji, what is God?' So I asked her, 'Are you Indian? You should be ashamed of being called an Indian, because you ask what is God, although you come from India, the land of God.' India is the land where Lord Kṛṣṇa appeared. So although you may be born Indian, if you have no *dharma,* what is the difference between you and the animals?"

One night while Prabhupāda was speaking, an American hippie in the audience approached the stage. He had long, wild blond hair and wore a vest and high leather boots. A miniature framed picture of Viṣṇu, Brahmā, and Śiva hung on a chain around his neck. When the boy tried to climb up on the stage, some of the devotees pushed him back, but Śrīla Prabhupāda intervened. He had a devotee bring a cushion and place a microphone in front of the boy. Then Śrīla Prabhupāda said, "Yes?"

"Have you realized yourself?" the young man demanded. "Have you realized the soul in the innermost depths of your being?"

"Yes!" Śrīla Prabhupāda replied.

At first the man was taken aback, but then he again challenged, "Now you tell me another thing. When was the *Bhagavad-gītā* written?"

"Now you answer *my* question," Śrīla Prabhupāda said. "What is the process of receiving knowledge from the *Bhagavad-gītā*?"

"No," the young man retorted, "you tell *me*—when was the *Bhagavad-gītā* written? In your lecture you said five thousand years ago, but according to other swamis, it was written only fifteen hundred years ago. Answer my question. I asked you first!"

Śrīla Prabhupāda raised his voice angrily. "I am not *your* servant, I am Kṛṣṇa's servant. You must answer my question!"

A heated argument began, with the hippie yelling at Śrīla Prabhupāda and Śrīla Prabhupāda arguing back. Finally, the devotees removed the boy from the stage.

The incident confused the audience. Many people began to leave. "Why did your Guru Mahārāja become angry?" some of them demanded from the devotees. "He should have answered the man's question." Some of the civic leaders supporting the *paṇḍāl* program also became upset, fearing Śrīla Prabhupāda had made an unfavorable impression on the public. Those who were devotional, however, remained in their seats to hear further what Prabhupāda had to say.

To the devotees it was inconceivable. Why had Prabhupāda, in the middle of his talk, invited a crazy hippie onto the stage, given him a microphone and a seat, and then argued with him to the point of yelling and shouting? And all before an audience of twenty thousand!

Bhavānanda: *One man who had helped organize the* paṇḍāl *protested,*

"Oh, Swamiji has gotten angry. This is not good." But Śrīla Prabhupāda seemed to have done it purposefully. He had spoken for a long time that evening on how to understand the Bhagavad-gītā, *and then he had this hippie brought on the stage. It was bewildering to us. We couldn't figure it out.*

Girirāja: *Śrīla Prabhupāda was actually using the entire incident to illustrate the process of understanding* Bhagavad-gītā. *After the man left, Prabhupāda completed his lecture by stating that one must approach Kṛṣṇa or Kṛṣṇa's representative with a submissive attitude, by serving and inquiring, not simply asking challenging questions. The whole incident had illustrated this point.*

Yadubara: *Many in the audience misunderstood the incident. It caused a split. But those who understood what Śrīla Prabhupāda had done could see that this hippie was a rascal, and this had been a time for transcendental anger against his nonsensical opinions.*

Tejās: *After everything was over, Prabhupāda told us, "Just as the* gopīs *were lusty for Kṛṣṇa, Arjuna would also get angry for Kṛṣṇa. So it is not bad that a devotee becomes angry for Kṛṣṇa." But many people in the crowd could not understand this point—how a devotee is not impersonal. The Indians are used to seeing impersonalist* yogīs *who express no emotion. The audience was mostly impersonalists.*

The last night of the *paṇḍāl* program, Śrīla Prabhupāda spoke privately with James George, the Canadian high commissioner.

Mr. George: "You have attracted so many Canadians and Americans."

Prabhupāda: "I have not attracted them. Kṛṣṇa has attracted them."

Mr. George: "True."

Prabhupāda: "Kṛṣṇa is all-attractive. I am simply presenting the means of being attracted. That is my business. It is similar to the way a magnet attracts iron. If the iron is rusty, however, then magnetic force cannot attract. Therefore, my business is to remove the dirt. This process is *ceto-darpaṇa-mārjanam,* cleasing the heart.

"At the present moment every one of us is in a consciousness of thinking, 'I am this body.' Because you were born in Canada, you are thinking you are Canadian. Because I was born in India, I am thinking I am Indian. And because he was born in America, he is thinking he is American. None of us are American, Canadian, or Indian. We are living entities."

Mr. George: "I have no problem following all of that. How, though, is this change of consciousness to be brought about, for example, in the West? This, I take it, is your mission."

Prabhupāda: "There is no question of East and West. It is philosophy—it is science. In mathematics, for instance, two plus two equals four. This is equally understandable in the West as well as the East. It is not that two plus two in the West is five, and two plus two in the East is three. Two plus two is equal to four everywhere.

"The first knowledge, then, that must be understood by human society is that we are not these bodies. It is very common knowledge. From this point, our spiritual knowledge can advance. If we do not know what spirit is, then what is the question of advancing in spiritual knowledge?"

After their conversation, Mr. George accompanied Prabhupāda to the stage and introduced him to the crowd.

"For several years I've been wanting to meet this swami and see what it was about him that was affecting so many of our young people in Canada and North America. I was very happy this evening to come in response to your kind invitation, and especially to meet Swamiji. I think, as he himself said to me a short time ago, there is something really happening. Whether he is doing it or it is being done through him, as he said, it is beside the point. But there is something happening, and everyone who doubts that should be here tonight to see this. It is happening, not only here in Delhi, but it's happening in Toronto and Cleveland and Los Angeles and New York and all sorts of places. What is it? I don't know how he would answer that question. For me, at a deeper level what is happening is the awakening of a search."

In his lecture, Śrīla Prabhupāda compared the material body to a machine operated by a driver, the soul. And he spoke of the soul's natural position as servant of Kṛṣṇa. Addressing Mr. George, Prabhupāda concluded his speech.

"Here our honorable high commissioner of Canada is present. I request that since you have come to our country, please try to understand this philosophy. I have traveled in your country, in Canada, also, and as you have already mentioned, we have got five branches, in Montreal, Toronto, Vancouver, Hamilton, and Ottawa. So the boys are struggling. They are distributing culture, these books, and I am getting very encouraging reports. Many young men are also coming. It is a very scientific movement. So I request you to inform your government to give these boys facility to inject this Kṛṣṇa consciousness movement in your country. Thank you very much. Hare Kṛṣṇa."

*   *   *

After the successful ten-day *paṇḍāl* festival—seven hundred thousand had attended—Śrīla Prabhupāda took his disciples on a short excursion to Vṛndāvana. His preaching tours had taken him to such places as Amritsar, Surat, Indore, Gorakhpur, Allahabad, and Benares, but never to Vṛndāvana. With so many of his disciples gathered in Delhi for the festival, Prabhupāda considered it an opportune time to travel to nearby Vṛndāvana.

They set out in two vehicles, Śrīla Prabhupāda and four others in Mrs. Kamala Bakshi's Ambassador and forty devotees following in a rented bus. Prabhupāda remained silent during the ride out of the city, past the factories and through the agricultural fields, groves, and villages along the Delhi–Agra Road en route to Vṛndāvana. When, after a couple of hours, they approached the outskirts of Vṛndāvana, Prabhupāda directed the driver of his car to a village and into the center of the small town to a sweet-water well. Here Prabhupāda and his party drank, took a breakfast of fresh fruit, and then continued on their way. Just before reaching Chatikara Road, which leads directly into Vṛndāvana, Prabhupāda's car broke down.

Tejās: *After Prabhupāda's car broke down, he rode the rest of the way with us on the bus. Our relationship with Prabhupāda was very reverential, although we were in the most intimate situation, staying with him and traveling in a bus with him. Prabhupāda never said anything about it. In those days we were actually very much like a family—Prabhupāda knew everyone, and everyone knew Prabhupāda and would talk to him—but still we were very reverential.*

In Vṛndāvana a Mr. G. L. Saraf accommodated Prabhupāda, his secretaries, and the women in the party at his home, Saraf Bhavan. The rest of the devotees stayed in a nearby *dharmaśālā.*

Prabhupāda had come to Vṛndāvana for more than just a pilgrimage; he had come to try and secure land for ISKCON. When in 1967 he had come to Vṛndāvana from America, he had come to recuperate, but on recovering his health he had looked for a place in Vṛndāvana for his disciples. He had tried to establish an "American House," a center where his disciples could live in Vṛndāvana's ideal atmosphere and receive training in Kṛṣṇa conscious culture and then go out and preach. But after two months of little prospect for establishing his American House, he had left.

This time, however, Prabhupāda was coming to Vṛndāvana as that city's famous ambassador to the world, renowned for propagating the glories of Rādhā-Kṛṣṇa and Vṛndāvana in the West. The success of the Hare Kṛṣṇa movement was being widely publicized in India, as Prabhupāda and his band of foreign disciples traveled from city to city holding *kīrtanas,* lecturing from *Śrīmad-Bhāgavatam,* and telling of Kṛṣṇa consciousness in the West. So when Prabhupāda arrived in Vṛndāvana with forty disciples, the entire town heralded his presence.

The municipality of Vṛndāvana arranged a formal reception, attended by prominent local citizens and *sādhus.* A spokesman for the city praised Śrīla Prabhupāda and his accomplishments. "O great soul! Today we, the inhabitants of Vṛndāvana, known as Brijabāsīs, all combinedly offer our humble welcome to Your Holiness in this holy place of Vṛndāvana, and in doing so we feel very proud.... For many years you stayed in the Rādhā-Dāmodara temple and worshiped Her Majesty Śrīmatī Rādhārāṇī in a meditative mood, and thus you now have the transcendental vision to deliver the entire world. As proof of your perfection, we can see these foreign devotees before us, and we feel very proud to see how you have transformed them into such pure devotees.

"O great preacher of Vedic culture, formerly a great many swamis went to foreign countries, but now you have wonderfully preached the *saṅkīrtana* movement and the sublime philosophy of *bhakti* cult in the Western countries, and that is the only means for giving peace and prosperity to all people of the world in this age. For preaching religion and culture, your holy name will remain ever dazzling.

"To speak frankly, we feel a very intimate relationship with you, and we feel perfect satisfaction at this time in the privilege to present you this address of welcome. We take it for granted that you are one of us in Vṛndāvana. We are sure that wherever you travel, you must carry with you the impression of Śrī Vṛndāvana-dhāma. The culture, religion, philosophy, and transcendental existence of Śrī Vṛndāvana-dhāma travel with you. Through the great message Your Holiness carries, all the people of the world are now becoming very intimately related with Vṛndāvana-dhāma. We are certainly sure that through your preaching alone the transcendental message of Vṛndāvana will spread all over the world. May you be crowned a success in these noble activities."

Then Śrīla Prabhupāda spoke, beginning by explaining how the International Society for Krishna Consciousness is trying to establish *daiva-varṇāśrama,* or a God-conscious social order, with universal application.

"We should not consider that Kṛṣṇa is Hindu or Indian. Kṛṣṇa is for all. These foreigners are taking to Kṛṣṇa consciousness by understanding that Kṛṣṇa is for all. They are not accepting a form of religious principles, like Hindu or Muslim or Christian. These are designated religions. If I am calling myself a Hindu, this is not my religion—this is my designation. Because I happen to take birth in a Hindu family, therefore I call myself a Hindu. Or because I take birth in a particular land, I call myself Indian or American. But our Kṛṣṇa consciousness movement is not for such designated personalities. This Kṛṣṇa consciousness is *sarvopādhi-vinirmuktam.* When one becomes free from all designations, he can take to Kṛṣṇa consciousness. As long as one is Hindu or Muslim or Christian, there is no question of Kṛṣṇa consciousness.

"So these boys and girls, or ladies and gentlemen, who have joined me, they have given up their designations. They are no longer Americans or Canadians or Australians. They are thinking of themselves as eternal servants of Lord Kṛṣṇa. Without this, there is no question of liberation from the material contamination. As long as there is material contamination, we have to devise these social orders and spiritual orders, according to *śāstra*—as *brāhmaṇa, kṣatriya, vaiśya, śūdra, brahmacārī, gṛhastha, vānaprastha,* and *sannyāsa.* These are all material designations. But this Kṛṣṇa consciousness movement is for becoming transcendental to these material designations, and these boys, these foreigners, they are being taught in that light.

"When I started my propaganda in New York, 26 Second Avenue, that time only half a dozen boys were coming and hearing. That hearing means I was singing, chanting Hare Kṛṣṇa *mantra,* and reading some verses from *Bhagavad-gītā,* and they were patiently hearing. Because I know if someone patiently hears the holy name of Kṛṣṇa or about His pastimes, then—*śṛṇvatāṁ sva-kathāḥ kṛṣṇaḥ*—Kṛṣṇa purifies him from within.

"So, actually it so happened with these boys and girls. I say boys and girls, because in the Western countries there is no distinction. They are given equal liberty. In our country there is still discrimination. I mean to say, grown-up boys and girls are not allowed to mix together, although it is going on now. But in European countries there is no such restriction. So there was no possibility of making any distinction between the boys and the girls. So many of them are attending. I was chanting in Tompkins Square Park, and these boys and girls used to surround me and dance and chant Hare Kṛṣṇa *mantra.* Some of them became a little advanced and purified and came forward, 'Swamiji, please accept me as your disciple.'

"So my condition was that anyone who wants to become my disciple must be free from the four kinds of sinful activities: illicit connection with women, meat-eating, intoxication, gambling. In this way, on this condition, these boys and girls were accepted as my disciples. According to *pañcarātrikī viddhi,* when they are fairly advanced they are given the sacred thread, *upanayana-saṁskāra,* following the path and instruction of my Guru Mahārāja, His Divine Grace Bhaktisiddhānta Sarasvatī Gosvāmī Prabhupāda. According to *śāstra,* they should not be considered as coming from families of *mlecchas* and *yavanas*—they should not be considered like that—because they are now purified. That is also mentioned by Śukadeva Gosvāmī in the *Śrīmad-Bhāgavatam,* and you know of it:

kirāta-hūṇāndhra-pulinda-pulkaśā
ābhīra-śumbhā yavanāḥ khasādayaḥ
ye'nye ca pāpā yad-apāśrayāśrayāḥ
śudhyanti tasmai prabhaviṣṇave namaḥ

How to become purified? By taking shelter of a bona fide spiritual master. So they are all purified according to the *pañcarātrikī viddhi,* and many of them have got this sacred thread."

Prabhupāda continued explaining the holy name's power to elevate anyone, regardless of birth, and he cited Haridāsa Ṭhākura who, despite his Muhammadan birth, was accepted as the *ācārya* of chanting the holy name. Prabhupāda also discussed the dynamics of the Kṛṣṇa consciousness movement, telling how, according to Rūpa Gosvāmī's principle of *yukta-vairāgya,* the International Society for Krishna Consciousness was using material things in the service of Kṛṣṇa.

"In the Western countries they are very luxuriously situated. My disciples are giving me residential quarters even a governor could not imagine. I remember one night some time back I was a guest in a Lucknow government house. At that time the governor was Biswanath Das, and he was personally known to me. So I remember the kind of luxurious apartment where I had the opportunity to lie down one night. But they, my disciples, are giving me all this. So we cannot reject that, because that is the standard of living in America. You cannot say, 'No, I shall not lie down in this nice apartment. I shall lie down in the street. I am a *sannyāsī.*' Then nobody will respect me. There in America the standard of living is like that. Therefore, Rūpa Gosvāmī says that you should not be attached to that, but for the service of Kṛṣṇa if you have to use such things, you should receive it.

"People are engaged in the service of *māyā,* but we want to engage everything in the service of the Lord. That is the Kṛṣṇa consciousness movement. So we are using airplanes, we are using dictaphones, we are using teletype machine. Even for cleansing our floor, we are using a machine. This is the system. In each and every center we have got new cars. We cannot do without them. In Europe and America practically no gentleman walks in the street. It is the system there. So we have to use it, but we should not be attached to it. Our attachment should be only for Kṛṣṇa, and for Kṛṣṇa's service we can accept anything. That is the Kṛṣṇa consciousness movement."

Prabhupāda concluded his address by asking for land. He wanted to establish a temple for his society in Vṛndāvana.

Afterward, a Mr. S., a motor parts salesman and resident of Vṛndāvana, offered Prabhupāda a plot of land his family had been saving for some worthy religious purpose. Prabhupāda smiled. Although he had only just arrived in Vṛndāvana, already Kṛṣṇa was providing an opportunity for establishing his ISKCON center. Prabhupāda thanked Mr. S. for offering this service to Lord Kṛṣṇa. By his donating land, the Kṛṣṇa consciousness movement would increase, and the donor, Mr. S., would benefit.

Prabhupāda was aware that behind the formal reception and ceremonial words of Vṛndāvana's prominent citizens dwelt a deeper feeling of reserve and even suspicion, especially among the caste *gosvāmīs,* the proprietors of Vṛndāvana's major temples. While accepting Śrīla Prabhupāda's foreign disciples as devotees (of a sort), many Vṛndāvana residents nevertheless felt reluctant to accept the foreign Vaiṣṇavas as *brāhmaṇas, sannyāsīs,* and *pūjārīs.* This misunderstanding was due to a traditional Hindu concept: only those born in caste *brāhmaṇa* families could become *brāhmaṇas.*

Prabhupāda, however, followed exactly in the footsteps of Bhaktisiddhānta Sarasvatī, who had freely accepted anyone, regardless of sex or social position. When in 1932 Bhaktisiddhānta Sarasvatī had led more than one thousand followers in a Vṛndāvana pilgrimage, certain prideful caste *brāhmaṇas* had denied the pilgrims entry into the temples. The pilgrims had been harassed by rock throwers and boycotted by shopkeepers. Bhaktisiddhānta Sarasvatī had then met with *brāhmaṇas* of Vṛndāvana and had scripturally proved to them that the soul, being transcendental, was free from designation and that anyone who became a Vaiṣṇava automatically qualified as a *brāhmaṇa.* The prejudices, however, had remained.

Prabhupāda also followed Śrīla Bhaktisiddhānta in denying that the *gosvāmī* title could be inherited. *Gosvāmī* meant one who controlled the senses, and the title could not be adopted simply because one was born in a family of so-called *gosvāmīs*.

The original *gosvāmīs* were the six Gosvāmīs of Vṛndāvana: Śrī Sanātana, Śrī Rūpa, Śrī Raghunātha Bhaṭṭa, Śrī Jīva, Śrī Gopāla Bhaṭṭa, and Śrī Raghunātha dāsa Gosvāmīs, all of whom were in the renounced order and were, therefore, without issue. Almost five hundred years ago, these six Gosvāmīs had discovered the places of Kṛṣṇa's Vṛndāvana pastimes and had built the first big temples in Vṛndāvana. They had appointed married disciples to carry on the Deity worship in their temples, and now the descendants of those original priests were claiming exclusive rights as temple *gosvāmīs* in Vṛndāvana. Prabhupāda had written in *The Nectar of Devotion* about his spiritual master's struggle in this matter:

> ... after the disappearance of Lord Caitanya's great associate Lord Nityānanda, a class of priestly persons claimed to be the descendants of Nityānanda, calling themselves the *gosvāmī* caste. They further claimed that the practice and spreading of devotional service belonged only to their particular class, which was known as Nityānanda-*vaṁśa*. In this way, they exercised their artificial power for some time, until Śrīla Bhaktisiddhānta Sarasvatī Ṭhākura, the powerful *ācārya* of the Gauḍīya Vaiṣṇava *sampradāya*, completely smashed their idea. There was a great hard struggle for some time, but it has turned out successfully, and it is now correctly and practically established that devotional service is not restricted to a particular class of men.

Prabhupāda therefore opposed the caste *gosvāmīs'* ideas of birthright. And the caste *gosvāmīs* feared Prabhupāda's movement, since it threatened their hereditary social preeminence. Yet on this occasion of Prabhupāda's triumphant return after preaching Vṛndāvana's glories to the Western world, no one protested his attempts to establish a temple. Those who disagreed remained silent or even offered flowery praise.

The land was in Ramaṇa-reti. Prabhupāda noted that the property on the outskirts of Vṛndāvana was located on busy Chhatikara Road, a main thoroughfare into Vṛndāvana and a traffic route to Agra and the Taj Mahal. The land was also adjacent to the Vṛndāvana *parikrama* path, where millions of pilgrims passed annually, circumambulating Vṛndāvana and visiting its temples and holy places.

Ramaṇa-reti (literally "charming sand") was mostly forest, with a few *āśramas* and abandoned fields. Celebrated as a favorite spot of Kṛṣṇa's, where He and His brother Balarāma and Their cowherd boyfriends had played five thousand years ago, Ramaṇa-reti abounded in transcendental love of God, which is the special atmosphere of Vṛndāvana.

Although various city officials had casually mentioned that the city might donate land, Prabhupāda took more seriously Mr. S.'s offer. Mr. S. explained that although other *sādhus* had been asking for the land, he and his wife had not yet decided; they wanted to give it to a group who would build a Rādhā-Kṛṣṇa temple there as soon as possible. When Prabhupāda assured Mr. S. he would do so, Mr. S. vowed that the land was now Prabhupāda's.

Prabhupāda had heard such promises before, and they had often proved false. But considering this offer serious, he appointed disciples to remain in Vṛndāvana to draw up a deed with Mr. S.

Meanwhile, Prabhupāda took his disciples on a pilgrimage to many of the important holy places of Vṛndāvana: Varṣāṇā (the birthplace of Śrīmatī Rādhārāṇī), Gokula (the place of Kṛṣṇa's earliest pastimes), Rādhā-kuṇḍa, Govardhana, and Vṛndāvana's major temples. At Govardhana Prabhupāda told the devotees not to step on Govardhana Hill or pick up any of the rocks: Govardhana Hill was nondifferent from Kṛṣṇa. Also at Govardhana Prabhupāda took the devotees to a little temple, where he showed them Kṛṣṇa's footprint. The footprint was very large. If Kṛṣṇa's foot had been that big, the devotees marveled, then He must have been eight feet tall. "Yes," Prabhupāda said. "They were much bigger then."

Near Govardhana, at Bindu-sarovara, a lake commemorating the place where Rādhā and Kṛṣṇa first met, the devotees swam while Prabhupāda bathed from buckets of water in the nearby field. Later, while Prabhupāda took *prasādam*, the devotees tried to chase away a few stray dogs by throwing stones and yelling, but Prabhupāda stopped them. "Leave them alone," he said, and he began throwing the dogs *prasādam* from his plate.

At Varṣāṇā, the birthplace of Rādhārāṇī, the devotees carried Prabhupāda on a palanquin up the many steep steps to the temple. On the top of the hill, he looked toward a distant hill. "Just over there," he said, pointing, "Kṛṣṇa used to come down that hill. Rādhā would come down this hill, and They would meet in the middle. There was a forest there. So this is a very special place, because it is the meeting place of Rādhā and Kṛṣṇa."

In each holy place Prabhupāda would sit down, hold a *kīrtana*, and come before the Deity and offer obeisances. Then he would briefly describe the pastimes of Kṛṣṇa related with the particular place.

Dīnadayādri: *The Indians at the holy places were always hounding Prabhupāda for money. They assumed that his disciples, being Americans, were rich, so they wanted money. Prabhupāda would give something, but there were so many that as soon as he would give to one, half a dozen others would crowd around him, preventing him from walking by. In some of the temples they wouldn't let us enter.*

Prabhupāda then took his group to the place beside the Yamunā where Kṛṣṇa had shown His mother all the universes within His mouth. Touching the water, Prabhupāda said, "It is too cold for an old man like me. But you take a bath. I'll put a few drops on my head." He directed the women to a separate place to swim, where the Indian women bathed, and the men plunged in and began swimming. They sported in the water as Prabhupāda stood on the bank, watching. Suddenly Prabhupāda put on a *gamshā,* walked to the river's edge, sprinkled some water on his head, and then waded in up to his knees. The devotees were delighted to see him duck beneath the water and begin bathing and splashing with them in the Yamunā.

Śrīla Prabhupāda decided that he would remain in his quarters at Mr. Saraf's home, while his old friend Hitsaran Sharma took the devotees to Vṛndāvana's famous temples. Prabhupāda did, however, make a point of going with his disciples to visit the Rādhā-Dāmodara temple, where he had lived for several years writing *Śrīmad-Bhāgavatam* and *Back to Godhead* magazine before going to America in 1965.

At the Rādhā-Dāmodara temple Prabhupāda told the devotees of his plans for an ISKCON temple in Vṛndāvana, and he suggested to the Rādhā-Dāmodara *pūjārī* that ISKCON use the Rādhā-Dāmodara temple.

"We shall prepare the whole temple nicely," Prabhupāda said, "and we shall make a silver throne for the Deity. Fifty to a hundred men will take *prasādam* here. It will be unique. If you want to, we can do it. Otherwise we can start our own temple somewhere. We are prepared to spend money. If you give us a chance, we'll spend it here. We want to make this a great festival in Vṛndāvana, because it is Jīva Gosvāmī's place. Rūpa Gosvāmī and Jīva Gosvāmī sat here. We have literature, we have books. Everyone is associating with us all over the world."

Yamunā devī dāsī: *His Divine Grace was very frequently giving indication of how much he wanted his rooms at Rādhā-Dāmodara maintained nicely. He was extremely fond of his quarters there. One night during his stay in Saraf Bhavan he agreed that he would stay for one twenty-four-hour period within his rooms at the Rādhā-Dāmodara temple. It was a very exciting event for all of us to look forward to. He selected three or four men to accompany him to spend the night there at the Rādhā-Dāmodara temple.*

Saraf Bhavan was some distance from Sevā-kuñja, where the Rādhā-Dāmodara temple is located. During the very early hours of the morning I walked through the streets of Vṛndāvana and arrived at the Rādhā-Dāmodara temple. Inside of Śrīla Prabhupāda's sleeping room I could see the light coming through the latticed red stone windows and the wooden shutters. Back and forth he was walking and chanting.

Suddenly, very much to my surprise, the wooden shutters burst open, and a shaft of light filled a small corner of the courtyard. Prabhupāda stood in his room under one bare light bulb. When he saw me, he asked, "How have you gotten here?" I said that I had walked. "Oh, this is not good," he said. "It is very dangerous in the street. There are so many wild dogs. And there are dacoits. In this quarter a man will kill even for a loṭa *[waterpot]."*

So there was some chastisement from Prabhupāda on the one hand, but on the other hand he seemed pleased. "So you are chanting japa*?" he said. And I said, "Yes, Śrīla Prabhupāda." He said, "That is very nice. So go to the* samādhi *of Rūpa Gosvāmī and chant there."*

Then around four o'clock other pilgrims were starting to filter in to attend the morning ārati *program. Prabhupāda came out where we were chanting, and he said that this corner at Rādhā-Dāmodara temple was just like the hub of the wheel of the spiritual world—it was the center. He requested that his rooms always be well maintained and that they be cleansed daily.*

Rādhānātha: *I had only met Śrīla Prabhupāda briefly in Bombay, and then I had gone alone to live in Vṛndāvana. I had lived there about six months with the local people, and it was there that I got real attached to Kṛṣṇa consciousness. I used to just live on the bank of the river with all the* bābājīs*—a very simple life. I know it was just by that initial contact with Prabhupāda that that seed was planted.*

One day a big bus full of American devotees having a kīrtana *pulled into Vṛndāvana, and I was thinking, "Oh, here they are again." The first thing I asked was, "Is Prabhupāda coming?" And they said, "Yes, Prabhupāda is here. He will be speaking tomorrow morning."*

I was already attracted to a lot of gurus *in Vṛndāvana—Prabhupāda's Godbrothers and also devotees from other* sampradāyas. *But on the morning when I came for the* Bhāgavatam *class and heard Prabhupāda chanting* Jaya Rādhā-Mādhava, *I just sat there and listened. I had never seen anyone with such a quality of love for Kṛṣṇa. All the great people I had met in India became insignificant when I saw Prabhupāda chanting* Jaya Rādhā-Mādhava. *He was so serious and grave, and the quality of his devotion was so intense. I just couldn't believe it.*

He kept looking over at me every now and then, kind of nodding, because I guess he remembered me from Bombay. Then he spoke, and he was glorifying Vṛndāvana so nicely. He was talking about how wonderful Vṛndāvana is, how spiritual the atmosphere is. And he was talking about how careful the devotees must be to take advantage of the atmosphere.

From that day I started thinking, "This is my Guru Mahārāja"—just because of the way he spoke. His lecture had been so precise and inclusive that it had encompassed every other philosophy and every other teacher I had ever heard. I could see also that Prabhupāda's example was pure, and I could see his disciples were actually giving up sinful life. I used to go to his darśanas *every day, although I was still living on the bank of the Yamunā.*

All the people of Vṛndāvana were glorifying Prabhupāda. They were so proud of him, because the people of Vṛndāvana are attached to Vṛndāvana. They love Kṛṣṇa, and they love Vṛndāvana, because Vṛndāvana is the place where Kṛṣṇa lives. That's their mood. They worship the land of Vṛndāvana. But they would tell me they appreciated Prabhupāda. Most of them would call him "Swami Bhaktivedanta." They would say, "He's the greatest saint, because he is bringing Vṛndāvana all over the world. He is making the glories of Vṛndāvana known to the whole world."

Then one day Prabhupāda and his disciples went to an āśrama *in Ramaṇa-reti. I got there late, just as Prabhupāda was leaving. He was walking the last twenty yards or so to his taxi, and many Brijabāsīs were offering their full* daṇḍavats *in the road. I felt very insignificant, another member of the crowd, and as Prabhupāda walked by me I offered my full obeisances also.*

When I lifted my head to get up, however, I saw Prabhupāda's feet were right there in front of me. I thought, "Oh, my God, Prabhupāda is standing right there." I very slowly looked up, and Prabhupāda was just standing there looking right at me. He looked me in the eyes for a couple of seconds and then said, "So how long have you been here in Vṛndāvana?" I said, "About six months, Śrīla Prabhupāda." He just looked at me again, and he was in a very serious mood, very compassionate, gazing into my eyes. He nodded his head and said, "Do you like it here?" I said, "This is the most wonderful place I've ever been in my life."

Then all of a sudden his serious expression just blossomed into the most beautiful smile. His eyes were glistening radiantly, and he looked at me for about five or ten seconds. It seemed like a real long time—I couldn't believe the mercy he was giving me—and then he just replied, "That is very nice. Vṛndāvana is a wonderful place." And then he walked on.

This was very special for me, because most of the devotees were always telling me I was in māyā *for staying in Vṛndāvana and because I was kind of attached to my own program in Vṛndāvana. I was feeling that the devotees didn't understand, and I was upset with them, thinking that they didn't appreciate the atmosphere. But Prabhupāda's words alleviated all my anxieties toward the Hare Kṛṣṇa movement. It was the most special personal contact. It wasn't* what *Prabhupāda was saying. It was his personal, transcendental concern for me. So then I went to his classes every day and all the* darśanas, *and there was no doubt in my mind. He very much convinced me on every level of Kṛṣṇa consciousness.*

When Prabhupāda left, the devotees told me that I should join and go on parikrama *with them all around India, and they said that Prabhupāda had personally invited me to come. I was unbelievably appreciative that Prabhupāda was so merciful, but at the same time I was very attached to Vṛndāvana. I told them I just wanted to stay here, and if they ever came back I would serve Prabhupāda here, but that I didn't want to leave Vṛndāvana.*

Soon after that, my visa expired. So I had to leave the country. But before I left, the people of Vṛndāvana, especially the bābājīs, *were telling me that Swami Bhaktivedanta had established* New *Vṛndāvana in the West. They said, "If you have to leave Vṛndāvana, you should go to* New *Vṛndāvana. So whatever you do, don't leave Vṛndāvana. New Vṛndāvana and Old Vṛndāvana are the same, because Swami Bhaktivedanta has created Vṛndāvana in the West." They said it with great pride. So I left for New Vṛndāvana.*

Prabhupāda trained his disciples in the etiquette of living in Vṛndāvana-dhāma. "In the holy *dhāma,*" he said, "if one of my disciples drinks from a jug incorrectly and he contaminates that jug, everyone will notice it. Don't be criticized for this uncleanliness, or I will be criticized. It is the duty of the disciple to follow these etiquette habits very austerely. I am putting so much energy into this party in India because I want to train you how to live here."

Prabhupāda wrote his disciples in the West of his successful tour of Vṛndāvana.

> I am currently in Vrindaban with a party of 40 devotees, and we are having daily *parikrama* of the holy places. We shall return to Delhi tomorrow by coach. The officials and residents of Vrindaban have greeted us very nicely, and they are simply astounded to see our SKP chanting with great jubilation through the city streets. The Mayor has publicly proclaimed that I have done something wonderful, and practically speaking, they realize that before I went to the western countries no one there knew about Vrindaban. Now hundreds of visitors and hippies from your country come here to see Krishna's place. The Vrindaban devotees have understood that Vrindaban is now world-famous due to my preaching work, so they are all very much appreciating their home-town Swamiji.

* * *

Delhi
December 1, 1971

Upon his return to Delhi, Śrīla Prabhupāda, along with the forty disciples who had accompanied him to Vṛndāvana, stayed at the Birla Mandir. The host offered Prabhupāda a small house reserved for special guests in the back of the formal gardens.

Meanwhile, political turmoil continued to trouble the nation's capital, as the threat of an all-out war between India and Pakistan increased. Even peaceful Vṛndāvana had been disturbed, being only ninety miles from Delhi and thirty-four miles from Agra, with its large military installation. One night, while Śrīla Prabhupāda had been staying at Saraf Bhavan, the local authorities had ordered a blackout. Śrīla Prabhupāda and the devotees had been confined to their quarters, the electricity had gone off, and everyone had covered their windows with blankets, so that even the candlelight could not be detected.

Nevertheless, despite political agitation and threats of war, Prabhupāda had now come to Delhi to preach. On his second day in the city he visited the American ambassador to India, Kenneth Keating, at the American Embassy.

Śrīla Prabhupāda explained to Mr. Keating the basic philosophy of Kṛṣṇa consciousness: the distinction between the material body and the self, or soul, living within the body. "You have got this striped coat," he told Mr. Keating, "but I cannot address you 'Mr. Striped Coat.' Yet we are actually being addressed like that. We are identifying with this body." And Prabhupāda explained the soul's transmigration through the 8,400,000 species.

"That is very interesting," Mr. Keating commented. "I believe in the transmigration of the soul."

"It is a fact," Prabhupāda said. "Just like this child is transmigrating from one body to another"—he indicated Sarasvatī. "In the same way, when I give up this body I will transmigrate to another body. This is a science.

"I see the American boys and girls, although coming from very rich and respectable families, are turning to hippies. In spite of your arrangement for very big universities, they are becoming frustrated. They are no longer satisfied to live in material opulence. So the present position of human society is dangerous, because everyone is feeling dissatisfied and confused."

"Do you have many Indian followers as well as foreigners?" Mr. Keating inquired.

"Yes, so far as Indians are concerned, everyone accepts Kṛṣṇa as the Supreme Personality of Godhead."

"Well," Mr. Keating added, "I am very impressed with the sincerity of these young American men."

"Everyone," said Prabhupāda, "as soon as he understands the science of Kṛṣṇa consciousness, will accept it immediately."

"When Swami Rajanandaji was here," said Mr. Keating, "I asked him his definition of God, and he thought a minute and said, 'Well, I would say God is the thread which links one good person to another.' I thought that was a very interesting definition."

"This is stated in *Bhagavad-gītā*," Prabhupāda said. "Just like you have a pearl necklace, and it is strung on a thread. So all the pearls are resting on that thread. Everyone is resting in God—not that only good men should be resting on that thread. The definition given by the *Vedānta-sūtra* is perfect: *janmādy asya yataḥ*. 'God is the origin, or source, of everything.' What do you say?"

"I am very impressed," Mr. Keating replied.

"Another definition of God," Prabhupāda continued, "is that He is all-attractive. Everyone has the attractive features of opulence, strength, fame, beauty, renunciation, and wisdom to some extent. You are an ambassador, a representative of your country. So you are attractive. Sometimes somebody comes to me, 'Let me see the Swamiji.' So this attractiveness everyone possesses. But *God* means He who has got all attractiveness in full."

After some time Ambassador Keating apologized and excused himself for an appointment he had to keep. "I am an ambassador, and I have to move from the sublime to the mundane. I appreciate very much your coming."

Śrīla Prabhupāda: "Now I am also coming to the mundane point of view. Next time I come back to the U.S.A. I wish to see the president."

"I can write a letter," Mr. Keating offered. "I will be glad to help you."

Prabhupāda smiled. "You are busy helping the whole world so that peace may come and people may be happy. But instead of being happy, the people of your country are becoming hippies—there is some defect. And here is a chance to rectify that defect: Kṛṣṇa consciousness. So let us do something tangible, scientific, so that people will become happy."

That evening Prabhupāda wrote one of his disciples about the meeting.

> You may be pleased to know that this morning I met here in Delhi with your American Ambassador to India, Mr. Kenneth Keating. He has got very good respect for our Movement, and he has promised to help me to arrange a meeting with your President when I shall return to your country perhaps in the late Spring. I have requested him to help this Movement and that help will save your country from great danger by turning hippies into happies.... let us see what can be done.

The next day, while Prabhupāda was on his morning walk in the streets of Delhi, he asked a devotee to get a paper from a newsboy passing by on a bicycle. Prabhupāda read the headlines: "*Emergency declared; three enemy planes downed.*" He had a devotee read aloud.

> Pakistan launched a massive attack on the western front, bombing seven Indian airfields and crossing the cease-fire line in strength in Poonch.... The Prime Minister in her broadcast late tonight described

> it as a full-scale war launched by Pakistan against India.... Earlier the President had declared national emergency.

The national emergency had international implications, with America cutting off supplies to India and supporting Pakistan, China threatening India, and Russia supporting India.

"This war will not last long," Śrīla Prabhupāda said immediately. "It will soon be finished. And Pakistan will lose."

Later that night he heard Indira Gandhi's broadcast over the radio.

> I speak to you at a moment of great peril to our country and our people.... Today a war in Bangla Desh has become a war on India. This imposes on me, my Government and the people of India a great responsibility. We have no other option but to put our country on a war footing.

Prabhupāda was not alarmed. War was not the only "ugly reality"; birth, death, old age, disease, and so many other material sufferings were inevitable—war or no war. Prabhupāda continued to follow the news, however, and some days Śyāmasundara would purchase for him three or four different newspapers.

After a few days at the Birla Mandir, Prabhupāda and his party moved to a *dharmaśālā* in the Kamala Nagar district of old Delhi. There Prabhupāda delivered what the devotees later referred to as "the blackout lectures." While black-painted newspapers and blankets covered the windows and combat jets flew overhead, Prabhupāda would speak by candlelight to his disciples.

"The propensity to fight is very strong in this age of Kali," he said, "and the population is becoming so sinful that they are trying to accumulate atomic weaponry for ultimate destruction of humanity." Sometimes Prabhupāda would ask a disciple to speak to the group also. No guests were present, since during blackouts no one could walk the streets, and on some nights the police pounded on the door demanding the devotees extinguish even their candles.

"Due to the war in India," Prabhupāda wrote in a letter, "our programs here have been reduced, and there is every night a blackout." Not only in Delhi but in other parts of India his disciples were encountering difficulties in their preaching attempts. In Māyāpur the government had ordered the devotees to leave the area because of its close proximity to Bangladesh.

As Prabhupāda had predicted, however, the war did not last long. On December 17 Prabhupāda read the headlines of the *Indian Express*—"NIAZI SURRENDERS: BANGLA DESH IS FREE. *India Decides on Unilateral Cease-Fire in West.*" Prabhupāda was joyous. He told the devotees confidentially that the reason the war had ended so quickly was because of their massive *saṅkīrtana-yajña* at the *paṇḍāl* a month earlier.

On the very same page that had announced India's victory, however, another headline read, "PM blames USA for war." Indira Gandhi was blaming President Nixon for the war. The American devotees tensed as they walked the streets, sensing the Indians' mistrust, and daily newspaper propaganda only worsened the condition. "There is great propaganda now against America in India," Prabhupāda wrote, "due to the country's stand against India and the war with Pakistan."

Delhi was the seat of much political agitation, and Prabhupāda decided to relocate the devotees who were there with him. Although his disciples were peaceful and far from being politically active, he sent some to Calcutta, while others accompanied him to Bombay. International politics would not stop the oncoming wave of Lord Caitanya's movement.

CHAPTER TWO

From 1965 until 1970 Śrīla Prabhupāda had concentrated mainly on establishing Kṛṣṇa consciousness in America. His plan had been that if the Americans turned to Kṛṣṇa consciousness, the rest of the world would follow. Although his preaching to the English-speaking people had begun in India, some sixty years of singlehanded endeavor there had convinced him that Indians were either too absorbed in politics, too ignorant of their spiritual heritage, or too crippled by poverty to seriously accept Kṛṣṇa consciousness. Therefore he had not been successful.

But in the United States success had come. Clearly, America was the prime field for implanting Kṛṣṇa consciousness. Yet Prabhupāda found the West uncultured and uncivilized. If a trace of civilization remained anywhere, he would often say, it was in India, the heart of the original Vedic culture.

By 1970 he had demonstrated through his extensive traveling and preaching that he intended to establish the Kṛṣṇa consciousness movement not only in the U.S. but all over the world—especially in India. Even accepting that preaching in the United States and preaching in India were equally important, still the preaching in the United States was going well without Prabhupāda's constant, direct management; what he had begun, his American disciples could continue.

But in India Prabhupāda could not allow his disciples to manage ISKCON. He saw how often and how easily the Indians were able to cheat his disciples. Half of ISKCON's work in India was being spoiled, he said, due to his disciples' being cheated. If they put on a *paṇḍāl* program, they might end up paying several times the standard cost. The only way for ISKCON to develop in India would be under Prabhupāda's direct management.

Beginning in 1970 with a small band of American disciples, Prabhupāda had traveled from place to place in India as a model *sannyāsī*, opening a great new field for ISKCON. Now he wanted to construct big temples in India—three in particular: one in Vṛndāvana, one in Māyāpur, and one in Bombay. As early as 1967 he had attempted to make an "American House" for his disciples in Vṛndāvana. Māyāpur, being the birthplace of Lord Caitanya, was especially important; and Bombay was India's major city, "the gateway to India." As with most of Prabhupāda's big plans, even his closest disciples couldn't fully comprehend the scope of his vision. But Prabhupāda knew what he wanted, and he knew it all depended on Kṛṣṇa. Gradually he began to unfold his plans.

Temple construction, he said, was secondary to book publication and distribution. But Kṛṣṇa consciousness must run on two parallel lines, just as a train runs on two rails. One rail was *bhāgavata-mārga;* the other, *pañcarātrakī viddhi. Bhāgavata-mārga* referred to the philosophy of Kṛṣṇa consciousness, hearing and chanting about Kṛṣṇa and disseminating the message of Kṛṣṇa. The second rail, *pañcarātrakī viddhi,* referred to the rules and regulations for worshiping the Deity in the temple. Of the two, *bhāgavata-mārga* was the more important.

Although great liberated souls like Haridāsa Ṭhākura could remain in perfect Kṛṣṇa consciousness simply by chanting Hare Kṛṣṇa constantly, Prabhupāda knew that his disciples, with their restless natures and past sinful habits, needed the special purification of worshiping the Lord in the temple. Therefore, one of his reasons for wanting to establish temples in India was to purify his disciples by giving them elaborate Deity worship.

Temples, however, were also for preaching. "No one listens to a poor man," Prabhupāda would say. And he therefore wanted to construct palatial buildings, to attract the masses to Kṛṣṇa consciousness. Especially he wanted this in India, where the tradition of temple worship still existed. Building temples and worshiping the Deity *was* secondary to publishing and distributing books, but it was not to be neglected. Prabhupāda prepared to give temple construction in Māyāpur, Vṛndāvana, and Bombay as much of his attention as necessary.

* * *

Bombay
November 1971

For a year the devotees had been living at the Akash Ganga address, two apartments on the seventh floor of a building in the heart of Bombay. But Prabhupāda was not satisfied with this. He wanted land in Bombay, to build on and to expand. He was determined. Instead of his usual morning walks, he would take long rides in his car to observe various parts of the city.

Because many of the ISKCON life members lived in aristocratic Malabar Hill, Prabhupāda's disciples thought it a good place for a temple. On several occasions Prabhupāda rode to the top of Malabar Hill and walked around various properties, considering certain large buildings as possible temples. But for one reason or another he judged them all unacceptable.

Then in November, a Mr. N. offered to sell ISKCON five acres in Juhu, practically on the shore of the Arabian Sea. As soon as Śrīla Prabhupāda approached the land, he remembered having seen and considered it years before. In August of 1965, during the weeks just before he had left for America, he had been staying at Scindia Colony. In the evenings he had gone to the home of Scindia Steamship Company owner Mrs. Sumati Morarji in Juhu, where he had read and explained *Śrīmad-Bhāgavatam* for her and her guests. Several times he had passed this very property and had thought what a good location it would be for an *āśrama* and a Rādhā-Kṛṣṇa temple. Although his attention had been absorbed in the task of leaving India, he had still considered the Juhu land. Now he was again in Juhu, reconsidering the same land he had noticed years before. He took it as a reminder from Kṛṣṇa.

The land was overgrown with tall grasses and bushes, and many coconut palms stood throughout. In the back of the property were several tenement buildings. The land bordered on Juhu Road, the main traffic artery back to Bombay, eighteen miles to the south. A broad expanse of beach on the Arabian Sea was a brief walk away.

The location was good—peaceful, yet not remote. Several five-star hotels bordered the nearby beach, and developers were beginning work on other hotels and apartment buildings. When Prabhupāda walked along the beach, he liked even more the idea of buying the land. Rich men had weekend homes on the beach, and thousands of Bombayites would be out enjoying the beach on Sundays. Daily, hundreds of Juhu residents used the long, broad seashore for morning walks before going to work. Almost always people were strolling or gathering there, and yet the beach was clean. The mild waves and open skies were inviting. The locale was ideal not only for hotels, but for a Kṛṣṇa conscious center.

Prabhupāda wanted the Juhu land, and although his disciples continued to show him houses in Malabar Hill, he didn't change his mind. His disciples wanted whatever he wanted, yet they had trouble developing enthusiasm for a property so far from the city and with no available housing or temple facility.

Mr. N., the owner of the five-acre plot, had set a reasonable price and seemed friendly and sincere. Yet risks were involved in such transactions, and in this case, Prabhupāda even found reasons for suspicion. Through his lawyer, he learned that Mr. N. had previously entered into an agreement to sell this same land to the C. Company but had later cancelled the agreement. The C. Company had then filed a suit against Mr. N. for breach of contract. If the Bombay High Court decided in the C. Company's favor, the land would be awarded to them. When Prabhupāda's secretary questioned Mr. N. about this entanglement, Mr. N. assured him the C. Company could not win the suit, but that in any case, ISKCON could withhold a certain portion of their payment until the litigation with C. was settled.

Mr. N. was a well-known figure in Bombay. Formerly the sheriff of Bombay (an honorary judicial police position), he was now publisher-editor of one of the largest daily English newspapers in Bombay. He was wealthy, owning several properties in Juhu and Bombay, and influential—not a man one would want to oppose. To purchase the Juhu land under the present circumstances required boldness.

In late December Prabhupāda met with Mr. and Mrs. N. at their home in the Theosophical Colony in Juhu. Mr. N.'s home was on the beach, and thus the visit afforded Prabhupāda another opportunity to appreciate the value and beauty of Juhu Beach, with its border of palms leaning toward the sea. The Theosophical Colony was a private neighborhood of attractive homes with luxuriant lawns and flower gardens and many exotic birds. Ashoka trees grew on either side of Mr. N.'s driveway, and a line of palm trees, standing just inside the massive stone wall, encircled the property. A gardener opened the gate for Prabhupāda and the few disciples with him.

Mr. N. was a short, stocky man with a receding hairline. His hair was clipped short, and his round face was pockmarked. He appeared to be in his fifties. Mrs. N. had a fair complexion and, unusual for an Indian, wore her hair short. Prabhupāda had brought flower garlands and *prasādam* from the Rādhā-Kṛṣṇa Deities of ISKCON Bombay, and these he offered to Mr. and Mrs. N. Mr. N. invited his guests to sit with him and his wife on the front porch, which faced a picturesque garden.

Śrīla Prabhupāda openly expressed his appreciation of the Juhu land but admitted he had very little money. Mr. N., however, seemed inclined toward Prabhupāda and said he wanted to sell him the property. Quickly they reached a verbal agreement. To Mrs. N., however, the agreement seemed too liberal. But when she objected, her husband overruled her.

Prabhupāda and Mr. N. agreed on a down payment of 200,000 rupees; after making the down payment, ISKCON would immediately receive the conveyance. ISKCON would pay the remaining balance of 1,400,000 rupees later, in regular installments. Prabhupāda negotiated further regarding the down payment, offering to pay 50,000 rupees now and another 50,000 later, at which time ISKCON would be allowed to move onto the land. As soon as they paid the remaining 100,000 rupees, the down payment would be complete, and Mr. N. would give them the deed. Mr. N. agreed.

Śrīla Prabhupāda was always one to think carefully over such business transactions. He had said that if a businessman tells you, "Sir, for you I am making no profit," you should know he is lying. Therefore, even in ISKCON's early days in New York City, when the real estate shark Mr. Price had posed as a well-wisher of the devotees, Prabhupāda had been suspicious. Mr. Price had, in fact, cheated the devotees, despite Prabhupāda's warnings to them. Now, as then, Prabhupāda was suspicious. But he wanted the Juhu land and would take the risk.

Prabhupāda had taken similar chances. At Jhansi in 1953 he had occupied a building, although he had had little legal standing or financial security. And in his first storefront in New York, as well as in his largest building to date, the Watseka Avenue church in Los Angeles, he had moved in without assurance of the monthly payments. Practically the entire success of his movement had come by his taking one risk after another for Kṛṣṇa. When the devotees in Boston had written to Prabhupāda that they had rented a big house for one thousand dollars a month, calculating that they would be able to make the payments by dramatically increasing their *Back to Godhead* sales, Prabhupāda had approved and had even commended their example to others. So if some risks were involved in Bombay, that was only natural.

Once committed to the land, Prabhupāda began to unfold his vision for a grand project in Bombay. On December 22 he wrote to Yamunā,

> Here in Bombay we have got good prospects to purchase a very large land in Juhu for very cheap price, just in the middle of a rich neighborhood. We shall build our camp there and begin constructing a temple immediately, and later on we shall develop a large hotel and school. There is also a chance of getting a nice bungalow in Bombay city also. So in general we shall make our headquarters in Bombay, and also build up Vrindaban and Mayapur.

While devotees around the world delighted to hear Prabhupāda's plan for a Bombay center, devotees in Bombay had mixed feelings. To envision a temple rising from what was little more than a jungle tract was not easy. Nor was it easy to envision the five-star ISKCON hotel Prabhupāda spoke of. The tenement buildings in the rear of the land were fully occupied, and according to Indian law, the tenants could not be removed. If the devotees moved onto the land, they would have to erect temporary housing, maybe even a temporary temple, and the land was mosquito-ridden and teeming with rats. Juhu was a small, almost isolated neighborhood, without wealthy ISKCON supporters. Although Prabhupāda (and land speculators) predicted that Juhu would grow, at present it was only a village of about two thousand. To reside at Juhu would be a drastic contrast to the comfortable Akash Ganga Building in downtown Bombay.

Tamāla Kṛṣṇa explained to Prabhupāda, "We are Westerners. We cannot live like this. We need doorknobs and running water."

"Don't you want to become purified?" Prabhupāda replied.

When the Bombay devotees learned of Śrīla Prabhupāda's response to Tamāla Kṛṣṇa, the words "Don't you want to become purified?" went deep into their hearts. They knew that Prabhupāda was asking them to become more austere, and that it was for their ultimate benefit. They began to regard moving to Juhu as a formidable spiritual challenge rather than a drudgery. Developing the Juhu property was important to their spiritual master, and it was something greater and more wonderful than they at present realized.

Prabhupāda knew he was asking his disicples to make a great sacrifice, but he could not avoid it. To preach Kṛṣṇa consciousness, a devotee had to be prepared to tolerate many difficulties. And whatever difficulties he was asking his disciples to undertake, he was prepared to undertake to a much greater degree himself. On the one hand, he didn't think that living on the undeveloped Juhu property would be too difficult for his disciples, provided they maintained cleanliness and chanted Hare Kṛṣṇa. Yet he knew that because they were Westerners, they would find it hard.

A preacher, nevertheless, had to make sacrifices—not artificially or arbitrarily, but to expand the Kṛṣṇa consciousness movement. Sometimes serving Kṛṣṇa was pleasurable, sometimes difficult. In either case, a devotee had but to do the needful, acting as a menial servant of the spiritual master.

Prabhupāda counseled his Bombay disciples, impressing on them his vision for ISKCON Bombay. Although all of them were ready to follow his decision, some of them had been feeling doubtful and weakhearted.

Seeing their spiritual master's commitment to the project, however, they vowed to give up their separatist mentalities. Prabhupāda then left for Jaipur, for a week's preaching engagement at the Rādhā-Govinda temple.

* * *

Jaipur
January 12, 1972

Jaipur is an ancient city in the state of Rajasthan. Occasionally some of Prabhupāda's disciples would go there to purchase marble Rādhā-Kṛṣṇa Deities for ISKCON temples in India and around the world. The devotees in ISKCON centers in Detroit, Toronto, Dallas, as well as throughout Europe, wanted to install Rādhā-Kṛṣṇa Deities and, with Śrīla Prabhupāda's permission, were ordering *mūrtis* from Jaipur.

On such an errand two women, Kauśalyā and Śrīmatī, had gone to Jaipur in January of 1972 on behalf of the New York City temple. When a government official had discovered Srīmatī wasn't carrying her passport, the officials, suspicious of spies due to the war with Pakistan, had insisted the women stay in town until Śrīmatī's passport arrived in the mail. Meanwhile, the girls had daily visited the Govindaji temple and had sometimes held *kīrtana* in the street in front of the temple. They had had daily talks with P. K. Goswami, who was in charge of the temple, as well as Jaipur businessmen and other respectable citizens (almost everyone in Jaipur regularly visits the beloved Deities of Rādhā-Govinda).

The citizens of Jaipur had been moved by the devotion of Prabhupāda's two disciples, and when one of the men had asked, "What can we do to help your movement?" the girls had replied, "Bring Śrīla Prabhupāda here." Some of Jaipur's prominent citizens had devised a plan to share expenses and responsibilities in arranging a *paṇḍāl* program, and the two women had sent a letter to Prabhupāda in Bombay, inviting him to come and preach. He had agreed.

At Śrīla Prabhupāda's request, devotees from Delhi and other Indian centers came to Jaipur to join him. Prabhupāda took a small room within the Govindaji temple compound, and his disciples moved into a nearby house.

Prabhupāda liked the location. The only disturbance was the many monkeys—large, charcoal-faced monkeys with long curling tails. Climbing through the trees and across the rooftops, they would scamper down unexpectedly to steal whatever they could. The women cooking for Prabhupāda were exasperated by the monkeys' bold forays to steal vegetables from the kitchen, even *capātīs* right off the fire, and they complained to Śrīla Prabhupāda.

"Neither be their friends nor their enemies," Prabhupāda advised. "If you make friends with them, they will simply be a nuisance. If you become their enemies, they will become very vindictive. Just maintain a neutral position."

The monkeys, however, continued to raid the kitchen. Again the cooks complained to Prabhupāda. "Yes," Prabhupāda said, "if you want to stop the monkeys, then this is what you must do. Purchase one bow and arrow, and shoot a monkey on the top of a tree with the arrow. And then when he falls down, take the monkey and hang him upside down by the legs to a branch of a tree. Next to him you also hang the bow and arrow. This will teach them."

Prabhupāda knew that shooting monkeys was illegal in Jaipur, and he did not expect his disciples to actually shoot them. But he delivered the advice with a serious expression. Indirectly he was advising them not to be so upset over a few monkeys.

Prabhupāda and his disciples immediately joined in the intense devotional atmosphere of Jaipur. Since the Rādhā-Govinda temple was under the jurisdiction of Jaipur's royal family, to visit the Deity daily was practically required for all citizens. Morning and evening, crowds of enthusiastic worshipers would come and go, worshiping the forms of Rādhā and Kṛṣṇa on the altar.

These were Rūpa Gosvāmī's original Rādhā-Govinda Deities from Vṛndāvana. Almost five hundred years ago, when a Mogul ruler had attacked the Govindajī temple in Vṛndāvana, the king of Jaipur had arranged for the Deities to come to Jaipur. The worshipers at the Rādhā-Govinda Mandira displayed spontaneous excitement in seeing the Deities. They would come forward, crying, "Jayo! Jayo!" "Govinda! Govinda!" And when the curtains were closing, the people would rush forward to catch a last glimpse of the divine forms. Śrīla Prabhupāda avoided the large crowds before the Deity, keeping to his schedule of rising early and translating the *Bhāgavatam*.

Speaking with Kauśalyā and Śrīmatī, Prabhupāda praised them for having arranged the Jaipur *paṇḍāl* program. "You girls are carrying on Lord Caitanya's movement so nicely," he said. "Just see! Even without husbands, you go on preaching." He said that the Western women were different from Indian women, who simply stayed at home.

Then Prabhupāda discovered that his two women disciples had not actually done a thorough job. Although the *paṇḍāl* program was to begin in two days, no one had arranged for the large tent to be erected. Prabhupāda said it was not a woman's nature to do such organizational work. The women became morose to hear him. When they showed him the flyer they had printed advertising the festival, Prabhupāda became angry. "It is not standard," he said. It did not say "International Society for Krishna Consciousness," but only "A. C. Bhaktivedanta Swami and his foreign disciples."

"What is this!" Prabhupāda shouted.

"What, Śrīla Prabhupāda?" Kauśalyā asked.

"*Foreign!* Why do you say *foreign*? It must be 'American' and 'European'. That is what is attractive, that they are American and European. But you are just a woman. What can I expect?" The two women began to cry and left the room.

With Śyāmasundara's help, Kauśalyā and Śrīmatī had new, corrected flyers printed and returned to tell Śrīla Prabhupāda. But now his mood had changed completely. His anger was gone. He was soft; after all, these disciples had tried their best. In a disarming disclosure, he began to explain that to be a spiritual master was difficult.

"I chastise you," he said, "because it is my duty. *Disciple* is related to *discipline,* so it is my duty to my disciples. Otherwise, I am not upset with anyone. I simply do this to discipline you, because you are my disciples." He consoled them, saying they were sincere and lacked expertise because of poor upbringing. The devotees present felt Śrīla Prabhupāda was wonderfully expressing to them a bit of what he, as spiritual master, felt in training them.

In a great last-minute endeavor, the devotees obtained the *paṇḍāl* and erected it in time for Prabhupāda to begin his program as advertised. On opening day the devotees held a parade through the streets, with Prabhupāda riding in a palanquin, a large embroidered umbrella sheltering his head. Also in the procession were decorated elephants, brass bands, and devotees—Indian, American, and European—performing *kīrtana.*

Śrīla Prabhupāda's first program was in the morning after the *darśana* of Govindajī, so as to catch the huge morning crowd. People would come hurrying into the temple to see Rādhā-Govindajī and then proceed out into the large Hare Kṛṣṇa *paṇḍāl* beside the temple. On the opening morning Prabhupāda performed an *abhiṣekha* ceremony, bathing marble Deities of Rādhā and Kṛṣṇa. He named these Deities, soon to be shipped to the ISKCON temple in New York, "Rādhā-Govinda." After one of Śrīla Prabhupāda's disciples had performed a fire sacrifice, Prabhupāda lectured to the crowd in Hindi. The schedule for the remaining days would be morning and evening lecture, *kīrtana*, and *prasādam* distribution.

* * *

While preaching in Jaipur, Śrīla Prabhupāda was simultaneously reflecting on and, through letters to his disciples, acting on matters in many other parts of the world. Although he participated fully, giving two lectures a day, and although he constantly met and interacted with guests, friends, and devotees, he was also absorbed in thoughts of other places and concerns. He was conducting his movement on many fronts. Wherever he happened to be at present was his "camp," just as a general makes camps in various places while conducting many battles in the overall effort of a war. His preaching in Jaipur, therefore, was only a small fraction of the scope of his worldwide mission.

From Jaipur Prabhupāda wrote his disciples in Calcutta, urging them in their development of the Māyāpur land; he wanted a grand opening ceremony by Lord Caitanya's birthday in March. Unfortunately, the government was restricting foreigners from entering Nadia, because of its proximity to Bangladesh. "Please try very hard to get those permits," Prabhupāda urged his men in Calcutta, "as we must be all assembled there for Lord Caitanya's appearance day." Repeatedly Prabhupāda mentioned his concern over the government's restricting his men.

> I do not think there will be difficulty if we just go there like the ordinary pilgrims and set up our camp there for kirtan continuously. Anyone will see we are only serious devotees of Lord Chaitanya and not Pakistani spies.

Prabhupāda wrote ahead to his disciples in Nairobi, driving them onward with his blessings. "Continue to work very hard for His pleasure and all of you will go back to home, back to Godhead."

To the San Diego temple president, Śrīla Prabhupāda wrote,

> I am very pleased to hear from you that book sales are increasing very fast. I am hearing such good news from all over the Society, and this pleases me more than anything.

And Prabhupāda was often thinking of the land in Bombay. Sometimes he talked about it or mentioned it in a letter to his representatives there. The Bombay land purchase was still not finalized, and Prabhupāda was particularly anxious that his disciples pay the money as agreed and move immediately onto the land.

*　　　*　　　*

Tamāla Kṛṣṇa was Śrīla Prabhupāda's Governing Body Commission secretary for India. Some of the devotees said that actually Prabhupāda was the G.B.C. secretary for India. Although he allowed his secretaries in other parts of the world to manage mostly on their own and to make their own decisions, in India he would scrutinize even small matters and make most of the decisions himself. Still, he counted on Tamāla Kṛṣṇa as his trusted assistant in important dealings. He would send Tamāla Kṛṣṇa from one Indian center to another to help the local devotees with governmental, legal, organizational, or preaching problems.

In Bombay, just prior to coming to Jaipur, Tamāla Kṛṣṇa had asked Prabhupāda's permission to take *sannyāsa*, the renounced order. Śrīla Prabhupāda had awarded *sannyāsa* to only a few men, and he had specified their duties as "traveling and preaching." Taking *sannyāsa*, therefore, not only meant giving up wife and family but also renouncing managerial posts. At the same time as Prabhupāda had set up his Governing Body Commission, he had also initiated several *sannyāsīs*, purposefully not appointing any of them, even though they were some of his most able men, as G.B.C. secretaries. The *gṛhasthas* were to manage the temples as presidents and G.B.C. secretaries, and the *sannyāsīs* were to travel and preach. Śrīla Prabhupāda, therefore, had to carefully consider whether or not to give Tamāla Kṛṣṇa *sannyāsa* and thus lose his G.B.C. secretary for India.

On principle, Śrīla Prabhupāda liked the idea of giving Tamāla Kṛṣṇa *sannyāsa*. If a young man was actually qualified to give up family life and to use his intelligence and energy in preaching Kṛṣṇa consciousness, then Prabhupāda was always ready to encourage it. The world was in dire need of Kṛṣṇa consciousness, and even hundreds of *sannyāsīs* would still not be enough. On these grounds, how could he not appreciate the request of one of his leading disciples to take *sannyāsa*? But first he would test Tamāla Kṛṣṇa's determination.

Tamāla Kṛṣṇa was insistent. Seeing that Prabhupāda would not make a commitment, Tamāla Kṛṣṇa had adopted the tactic of presenting himself before Prabhupāda early in the morning without saying a word. In Bombay he had entered Prabhupāda's room, led the *maṅgala-ārati* before the Deities, and then sat silently before Śrīla Prabhupāda.

Knowing the mind of his disciple, Prabhupāda could understand that Tamāla Kṛṣṇa was not only determined but obstinate. After several days of tolerating Tamāla Kṛṣṇa's silent insistent presence every morning, Prabhupāda had finally agreed to consider seriously the request.

Prabhupāda was also concerned with Mādrī-devī dāsī, Tamāla Kṛṣṇa's wife. She was an attractive, intelligent girl who had given her life to Kṛṣṇa consciousness, and Tamāla Kṛṣṇa, by his own choice, had married her only a year ago. Spiritually, Mādrī was Śrīla Prabhupāda's daughter, and Prabhupāda wanted to protect her from undue disturbance. Even as householders, Tamāla Kṛṣṇa and his wife had been renounced, traveling with Prabhupāda throughout India, with little time or facility for private life as husband and wife.

Tamāla Kṛṣṇa had been in Bombay when Śyāmasundara had informed him that Prabhupāda had mentioned in a letter to Brahmānanda Swami in Africa that Tamāla Kṛṣṇa might take *sannyāsa*. Spurred on, he had left his wife in Bombay and joined Prabhupāda in Jaipur. On leaving, however, Tamāla Kṛṣṇa had asked Mādrī for his personal copies of the first three volumes of *Śrīmad-Bhāgavatam*, signed by Śrīla Prabhupāda. Mādrī had become suspicious. She had asked why he wanted them. "I just want to read them," Tamāla Kṛṣṇa had answered. But she had suspected the worst: "No, you're not coming back." But assuring her that he would definitely be returning, he had left for Jaipur.

Once with Śrīla Prabhupāda, Tamāla Kṛṣṇa again resumed his silent insistence. Whenever there would be an open meeting in Prabhupāda's room, the G.B.C. leaders would usually sit in a privileged position near Prabhupāda, so as to best receive direct instruction. Tamāla Kṛṣṇa, however, would simply sit outside the door. The first time he did this,

Prabhupāda looked up and said, "Tamāla Kṛṣṇa, you are sitting outside? That is very nice," and the other devotees took it that Prabhupāda was praising his disciple's humility.

When on one occasion Prabhupāda addressed Tamāla Kṛṣṇa as "Tamāla Kṛṣṇa Mahārāja," the devotees were startled. The women devotees in Jaipur, being close friends with Mādrī, became angry at what they took to be Tamāla Kṛṣṇa's duplicity.

Although Prabhupāda had not given permission, Tamāla Kṛṣṇa went ahead with his plans, even to the point of preparing his *sannyāsa-daṇḍa* and dying his clothes. The women were outraged; Mādrī was not even there to represent herself. All together the women went to see Śrīla Prabhupāda, who patiently and sympathetically heard their presentation.

Then Prabhupāda called for Tamāla Kṛṣṇa and said, "Your wife is my daughter, my disciple, and I have to think for her also. So I do not know how I can do this, because she will be in great difficulty." Tamāla Kṛṣṇa argued, but Prabhupāda pacified him and asked him to be patient. The *sannyāsa* issue had become a topic of controversy among the devotees in Jaipur. The men were rooting for *sannyāsa,* and the women were opposed. Prabhupāda, however, remained grave.

Throughout the week-long festival large crowds continued to come for Prabhupāda's morning and evening lectures. Prabhupāda would chant prayers from *Brahma-saṁhitā* and then lecture in Hindi. Not only did the citizens of Jaipur honor Prabhupāda, but they honored his disciples also. Here, more than in most other Indian cities, the devotees were treated not as foreigners or outsiders but as *sādhus.* "This whole city is made of devotees of Rādhā-Govindajī," Prabhupāda commented. The police chief, who visited often, was cordial and respectful. As Prabhupāda and his disciples went from place to place in Jaipur during the day, policemen would salute them, halting traffic to let them pass. People invited Śrīla Prabhupāda to their homes, and they treated him like a king.

Prabhupāda had also asked several women devotees to carefully observe the Deity worship in Jaipur. They informed him they had observed that every night the Deities were dressed in night clothes and that Their clothes were also changed at two other times, in the morning and in the afternoon. The women told Prabhupāda how a priest offered the Deities scented oils on cotton-tipped sticks, which the priests would later offer, along with flower garlands from the Deities, to the incoming worshipers in exchange for fresh garlands. These devotional practices were standard, Prabhupāda said, and could be introduced throughout ISKCON.

Each evening Prabhupāda spoke at the *paṇḍāl*, and often a respectable Jaipur citizen would introduce him. When the queen of Jaipur introduced him one evening, she expressed her devotional sentiments for Prabhupāda and his movement.

After lecturing each evening, Prabhupāda would stay for a slide show of ISKCON's activities around the world. One night during the slide show, Śrīla Prabhupāda called Tamāla Kṛṣṇa over beside his *vyasāsana.* "Taking *sannyāsa* will be difficult now," he said softly. "Your wife will suffer too much." He sat back a moment while Tamāla Kṛṣṇa took in what he had said. Then Tamāla Kṛṣṇa leaned forward and said with determination, "One way or another, Śrīla Prabhupāda, she's going to suffer. Either she'll suffer now when I take *sannyāsa*, or if I take *sannyāsa* later on, she will be just as unhappy. There will never be a time when she'll want me to. So since the feeling is going to be the same, it might as well come now. Free me. She'll get over it."

Prabhupāda said no more, but he remained thoughtful. Later that night after the *paṇḍāl* program, he called for his *sannyāsī* disciples, Subala, Madhudviṣa, Gargamuni, and Devānanda, and for his personal secretary, Śyāmasundara. Gathering them together along with Tamāla Kṛṣṇa, he said, "Tamāla Kṛṣṇa wants to take *sannyāsa*. So what is your opinion? Should he take or not?"

Everyone agreed he should. Finally, Prabhupāda consented. "You will have to prepare things," he said.

"Things are prepared already," Tamāla Kṛṣṇa said.

"Then," said Prabhupāda, "tomorrow morning we must have the ceremony."

The next morning Prabhupāda performed a special ceremony in the *paṇḍāl*, lighting the sacrificial fire and offering Tamāla Kṛṣṇa the *sannyāsa-daṇḍa.* The women were angry with Tamāla Kṛṣṇa, but it was too late.

After the ceremony Prabhupāda called Tamāla Kṛṣṇa Mahārāja to his room. "You have given up a very good wife and a high position. Therefore I am giving you the title Gosvāmī. Now you have to be in the same mood as the Gosvāmīs, being able to preach all over the world and accept disciples." Suddenly Prabhupāda began to laugh. "I have been testing you," he said, "to see whether or not you were determined. So what will you do?"

"I thought I would go with my *daṇḍa,*" said Tamāla Kṛṣṇa Gosvāmī, "and, without anybody else, simply wander from city to city in India and preach about Kṛṣṇa, without any vehicle or anything, just like Lord Caitanya did."

"Very good," Prabhupāda said. Tamāla Kṛṣṇa Mahārāja offered obeisances and walked out.

Scarcely an hour later, however, Prabhupāda called him back. "This is not a very good proposal," he said. "If you want to do something, you should have some assistants and facilities at your disposal." Prabhupāda then assigned a couple of *brahmacārīs* to go with Tamāla Kṛṣṇa Mahārāja for preaching. He also gave his new *sannyāsī* his first assignment. Immediately after Jaipur, Prabhupāda was planning to go to a festival in Nairobi, Africa, yet in Ahmedabad another program awaited him. "You go on my behalf to Ahmedabad," said Prabhupāda.

At Tamāla Kṛṣṇa Gosvāmī's *sannyāsa* initiation, Śrīla Prabhupāda had given him the *sannyāsa-mantra,* a verse that describes the surrendered, devotional attitude of the Vaiṣṇava *sannyāsī.* Vaiṣṇava *sannyāsa* emphasizes engaging one's body, mind, and words in ecstatic service to Kṛṣṇa, as distinguished from the *sannyāsa* of the impersonalists, who speculate on Brahman or sit alone in silent meditation. The Vaiṣṇava *sannyāsī,* by taking shelter of the lotus feet of Kṛṣṇa, crosses the ocean of nescience and brings others across with him.

As Śrīla Prabhupāda was demonstrating, a Vaiṣṇava *sannyāsī* should travel all over the world, working with all his might to reclaim the fallen souls on behalf of Lord Kṛṣṇa. Vaiṣṇava *sannyāsa* meant coming to places like Jaipur and preaching. It meant worshiping Govindajī in the temple, and it meant sending Rādhā-Govinda to be worshiped by the devotees in New York City. It meant allowing women an equal opportunity to become pure devotees in Kṛṣṇa consciousness. And it meant separating a man from his wife for the higher purpose of *sannyāsa.*

Śrīla Prabhupāda, although beyond the *varṇāśrama* designation of *sannyāsa,* was nevertheless the best *sannyāsī* and the creator of many other *sannyāsīs,* whom he instructed to follow in his footsteps. He said his *sannyāsīs* should do even more than he—make more followers, publish more books, and establish more ISKCON centers.

* * *

Bombay
January 24, 1972

On returning to Bombay, Prabhupāda was disappointed to find that the devotees had neither paid Mr. N. nor moved to Juhu. Madhudviṣa Swami, whom Prabhupāda had put in charge, frankly admitted his inability to accept the responsibility for such a difficult project. The disciple Prabhupāda had originally deputed to handle such affairs was Tamāla Kṛṣṇa Mahārāja. But now that he had taken *sannyāsa*, he had renounced his G.B.C. duties for traveling and preaching, and Prabhupāda was without a manager for Bombay. Already Prabhupāda was doing most of the managing, but he couldn't do everything—he couldn't stay constantly in Bombay.

Searching for a veteran disciple to manage Juhu, Prabhupāda thought of Brahmānanda Swami, who was still preaching in Nairobi. Prabhupāda decided to fly to Africa and invite Brahmānanda Swami to come and manage Bombay. He wanted to act swiftly, so that ISKCON could take possession of the land. Even if Mr. N. changed his mind later, once the devotees were living on the land, getting them to leave would be very difficult for him.

Śrīla Prabhupāda planned to fly to Nairobi immediately, and he wanted to carry large Rādhā-Kṛṣṇa Deities with him. The Deities he had previously sent to Nairobi had been broken in shipping, so this time Prabhupāda brought with him strong-bodied Madhudviṣa Swami to carry the thirty-six-inch marble Deities. With special permission from the airlines, Prabhupāda boarded, followed by Madhudviṣa Swami, who held in his arms the one-hundred-pound Deity of Kṛṣṇa. After setting Kṛṣṇa in place beside Prabhupāda's seat, Madhudviṣa Swami left the plane and came back carrying Rādhārāṇī.

Prabhupāda passed most of the flight debating with Madhudviṣa Swami, who took the position of the impersonalist. Prabhupāda would always defeat him. "This is how you become a preacher," Prabhupāda said. "You must be able to take both sides of the argument and defeat your adversary. This is what Lord Caitanya would do."

Since Prabhupāda's first visit to Nairobi four months ago, Brahmānanda Swami and a few American devotees had rented a house near the city. They had recruited some African devotees but had not yet developed the temple and *āśrama*. Barely able to maintain their own simple program, they were unprepared to receive Śrīla Prabhupāda properly.

Typical of Prabhupāda's stay in Nairobi was his arrival: no one was at the airport to meet him. The devotees were not even sure if Prabhupāda was coming. Prabhupāda's secretary had phoned Brahmānanda Swami that Prabhupāda was willing to come to Kenya but that Brahmānanda Swami should try to arrange a meeting with the president and schedule a big *paṇḍāl* festival. Brahmānanda Swami, however, had never received a clear message of *when* Prabhupāda was coming.

At the airport Prabhupāda and Madhudviṣa Swami carefully put the Rādhā-Kṛṣṇa Deities into a taxicab and rode with Them to the address of the ISKCON center. Prabhupāda rang the doorbell, and when Brahmānanda Swami opened the door and saw his spiritual master, he cried out, "Prabhupāda!" and bowed down.

"What happened?" Prabhupāda asked, standing beside Rādhā and Kṛṣṇa. "Why no one came to pick us up at the airport?" Brahmānanda Swami was unable to reply.

No sooner did Prabhupāda arrive than his assistant, Madhudviṣa Swami, became bedridden with hepatitis. Prabhupāda had left his regular secretary, Śyāmasundara, in India to work on a legal case concerning the Māyāpur land, so he was now without a personal assistant.

In Nairobi Prabhupāda followed his usual schedule of bathing in the afternoon and then putting on fresh clothes, but one day after his bath he found that no clothes were ready. When he asked for them, Brahmānanda Swami explained that the African servant had washed them and put them on the line to dry. But when Brahmānanda Swami had gone to get them, they hadn't been there; apparently someone had stolen them from the clothesline. Prabhupāda tolerated the inconvenience without any display of emotion.

That evening, when the devotees of ISKCON Nairobi gathered in the temple to hear Prabhupāda speak from *Bhāgavad-gītā*, Prabhupāda saw the different items of stolen clothing on the African boys; one boy wore the *kurtā*, another the top piece, and another the *dhotī*. Prabhupāda pointed this out to Brahmānanda Swami, who immediately took the boys out and retrieved the clothing from them. When Brahmānanda Swami returned the clothes, Prabhupāda didn't seem to take the offense seriously, but only laughed.

Prabhupāda did not laugh, however, at the Nairobi devotees' bad cooking.

When they served him white maize mush, he called it pig food, and the hard, white chickpeas, he said, were suitable only for horses. Then Harikṛpā, a black devotee from America, went to the kitchen, boiled some vegetables, and served them to Prabhupāda without any spicing. Prabhupāda called it dog food. "You are still an uneducated African," he told Harikṛpā. And he went into the kitchen to cook for himself. Almost a dozen devotees joined him, watching him cook a complete meal of *dāl,* rice, *capātīs,* and *sabjī.* He cooked enough for all the devotees, and everyone was satisfied. Bad cooking and stolen clothing, however, continued to be problems during Prabhupāda's week-long stay in Nairobi.

Brahmānanda Swami found that Prabhupāda was mostly absorbed in his Bombay project. "The only reason I've come," Śrīla Prabhupāda told Brahmānanda Swami, "is to get you for this." Once he asked Brahmānanda Swami, "Which is the most important city in India?"

"Calcutta?" Brahmānanda replied.

"Calcutta?" Prabhupāda looked at him oddly. "Don't you know Bombay is number one? Delhi is number two, and Calcutta is number three."

Prabhupāda encouraged Brahmānanda Swami to return with him and take charge of the Bombay project. This Bombay project, he said, would be unique within ISKCON, incorporating the religious with the cultural in a gorgeous temple, international hotel, theater, and diorama exhibition. Seeing Prabhupāda's strong desire, Brahmānanda Mahārāja agreed to somehow relinquish his Nairobi responsibilities to others and help in Bombay.

In yet another way Prabhupāda's visit to Nairobi connected with his Bombay project. When Brahmānanda Swami and Cyavana showed Prabhupāda the Nairobi Hilton, a modern building with twin round towers, Prabhupāda liked the design and wanted to give it to his architect for the Bombay hotel and temple.

Prabhupāda, Brahmānanda Swami, Bhāgavata, and an African devotee were walking in Nairobi's public gardens. On being introduced to Prabhupāda, the African had inquired, "If I want to, can I get married?"

"Oh, yes," said Prabhupāda.

"But Prabhupāda," the boy continued, "if you want to get married in our community, the boy has to pay money to the father of the bride."

This was exactly opposite the Vedic system, Prabhupāda replied, wherein the father of the bride presents a dowry to his son-in-law. Hearing this, Prabhupāda's new disciple looked worried. He asked, "Then, will you give me money when I want to get my wife? Because I'm not working now, I'm just working for you. When I want to get my wife, will you give me money?"

Prabhupāda shook his head. "You don't worry about all of this," he said "—whether you'll get a wife, or whether you will get money, or this, or that. Later on, when it is time for you to get married, I will bring one American girl, and you will marry her."

Wherever Prabhupāda turned in his fledgling Nairobi temple, he found neophyte disciples and discrepancies. Walking into the *brahmacārī āśrama*, he found books, boards, and paint cans scattered about the room. When he said things should be kept more neatly and orderly, the temple commander, Harikṛpā, replied, "Prabhupāda, I try to tell them, but these boys don't listen to me."

Prabhupāda bent down and picked up some pieces of wood. "If they don't do it," he said, "then you should do it! Put these over here." And Prabhupāda began engaging all the men present. Within five minutes the room was neat.

The World Hare Kṛṣṇa Movement Festival at Nairobi's City Stadium was a combination success and failure. Although Brahmānanda Swami had managed to see many highly posted government officials and diplomats, many of whom had promised to attend the festival, none of them actually appeared—except for Mr. Y. Komora, Kenya's director of education. But an audience of several hundred attended *kīrtana*, heard Prabhupāda's speech, and took *prasādam*.

Although the devotees had invited the leading Kenyan citizens to enhance the glorification of Kṛṣṇa, their honored guest, Mr. Komora, used the opportunity to speak in praise of Kenya. Nevertheless, he spoke highly of Prabhupāda and the Kṛṣṇa consciousness movement. Regarding *Bhagavad-gītā*, he said, "Your learned founder has made this great book available in the English tradition with an erudite commentary."

Śrīla Prabhupāda also attended other engagements in and around Nairobi. He told his Nairobi disciples that in preaching to the Africans they should stress the chanting of Hare Kṛṣṇa by holding public *kīrtanas*. Lord Caitanya, he said, spoke philosophy only with learned scholars like Sanātana and Rūpa Gosvāmī, never with ordinary men. "Just chant Hare Kṛṣṇa," he said. "This should be appreciated."

Śrīla Prabhupāda installed the Deities of Rādhā-Kṛṣṇa and named the Nairobi temple Kirāta-śuddhi, "a place for purifying the aborigines." One day shortly after the Deity installation, however, Prabhupāda walked into the temple room and was shocked to find the Deities out of Their proper place in the center of the altar. Kṛṣṇa was standing to the far left beside the bottom step leading up to the altar, and Rādhārāṇī stood to the far right.

"Who has done this?" Prabhupāda called out loudly. Bhāgavata came running into the temple room. He also was astonished.

"Who has put Rādhā and Kṛṣṇa ten miles apart?" Prabhupāda demanded. "Don't you know these things? How many times do I have to teach you?"

Bhūta-bhāvana suddenly appeared, admitting that he was the culprit. "Why are They so far apart?" Prabhupāda asked.

"I don't know, Śrīla Prabhupāda," said Bhūta-bhāvana. "I guess I just forgot. I was being rushed to go to the festival."

"So," Prabhupāda demanded, "does that mean They should be put out in the street?" Bhūta-bhāvana froze, unable to reply. Prabhupāda relented. "Take Them and put Them together," he said. "They should not be moved more than three inches apart. Now do it nicely."

After a week Prabhupāda left Nairobi and returned to Bombay. He had gone there to get Brahmānanda Swami. And he had acccomplished his mission. "Unless you agreed to take charge," Prabhupāda said, "I could not go ahead and pay so much money. Now it is decided." He felt new hope.

Prabhupāda envisioned his Bombay project as extraordinary within ISKCON and even among all the temples of India. Many of the details of the project already existed within his mind, but he needed competent disciples to carry them out. He was still the lone leader of ISKCON, forging ahead to bring into reality new phases of the Kṛṣṇa consciousness movement. His disicples were behind him, but it was always he who led. Even when he wanted his disciples as leaders of various ISKCON projects, they sometimes could not handle the responsibility. Therefore Śrīla Prabhupāda had gone to Nairobi in the mood of the Bengali aphorism he sometimes quoted: "If you want to accomplish a thing, do it by your own hand." So by his own hand he had brought Brahmānanda Swami from Nairobi to Bombay. And simultaneously he had benefited the devotees and the general populace of Nairobi.

* * *

Bombay
February 8, 1972

Prabhupāda met with Mr. N. and reiterated that he wanted to move onto the land as soon as Mr. N. received the second fifty thousand rupees. Mr. N. stood firm on their agreement, and Prabhupāda put the matter into the hands of his lawyer, Mr. D., for legal processing.

Although Prabhupāda was making all the managerial decisions, he wanted the G.B.C. secretaries to take on the responsibility for these practical affairs. He thought it better to use his energy in writing and translating books. "If you G.B.C. do everything nicely," he told his secretary Śyāmasundara, "then my brain will not be taxed and I can utilize my time completely to produce further books. I can give you *Vedas, Upaniṣads, Purāṇas, Mahābhārata, Rāmāyaṇa*—so many. There are so many devotional works in our line by the Gosvāmīs. This administrative work is taking too much time. I could be discussing philosophy. My brain is being taxed day and night. Because of this I'm neglecting my real work."

Aside from directly managing the Indian projects, Prabhupāda was answering as many as a dozen letters daily from devotees around the world. "Why do they keep writing, asking so many questions?" he asked his secretary.

"The devotees prefer to ask you personally," Śyāmasundara said, "because their G.B.C. men don't always know the right answer."

"They know everything by now," Prabhupāda replied. "I have given you everything. If they don't know the answer, they can find it in my books. Now I am an old man. Let me settle down to philosophy. All day reading letters, doing business, all night signing letters—this is not right. I want to be free from these things. The G.B.C. can do everything now."

But it wasn't possible. As soon as Prabhupāda would sense that one of his devotees was being cheated, he would immediately become actively involved. And his disciples continued to write him regarding important business and managerial decisions. Nor would he discourage them. His desire for retirement and exclusive literary work remained, but it seemed to be only a wishful thought, a dream. If ISKCON were to develop, then there seemed little scope for his retirement.

After the meeting with Mr. N., Prabhupāda prepared to leave for South India for a five-day *paṇḍāl* program in Madras; also on his itinerary were visits to Calcutta, Māyāpur, and Vṛndāvana. As he prepared to leave Bombay he felt happy that ISKCON would soon occupy the new Juhu property, and he frequently spoke of his plans.

ISKCON would erect a fabulous temple and form a cooperative housing society of devotees of Kṛṣṇa—the first ISKCON city. Respectable men would purchase flats in ISKCON's highrise condominium. Devotees would have to become expert to develop and operate such a complex, and as they became successful, they would introduce the same pattern in other cities. Businessmen and professional workers could live as devotees in a co-op society, housing their families and sending their children to an ISKCON school.

Prabhupāda repeatedly talked of constructing an international hotel, somewhat like a Holiday Inn, suitable for foreigners and traveling businessmen, yet reserving a floor for ISKCON life members, who would receive free accommodations. The restaurant would be managed by expert *brāhmaṇa* cooks, who would prepare dozens of different preparations of sumptuous *prasādam.* The Deities Rādhā-Rāsavihārī would receive fifty-two offerings daily, and the *prasādam* would be distributed to residents and guests.

To start things in the right direction, Prabhupāda ordered the devotees to immediately arrange for a ten-day public festival on the new land. First Brahmānanda Swami should pay the agreed balance and move onto the land along with all the devotees and the Deities, Rādhā-Rāsavihārī. Then they should prepare a big *paṇḍāl* tent and arrange a full program as they had previously in Bombay, in Calcutta, and in Delhi. Prabhupāda wanted everything ready for his return in two weeks.

* * *

Although, as Prabhupāda would sometimes mention, in South India the original Vedic culture was most intact, he had not been there in several years. Most of the great *ācāryas*, Śaṅkara, Rāmānuja, and Madhva, had come from South India, and Lord Caitanya Mahāprabhu, during His own touring, had found South India especially favorable.

Just after the Hare Kṛṣṇa *paṇḍāl* festival in Delhi, on the eve of Prabhupāda's first tour of Vṛndāvana with his disciples, back in November of 1971, Acyutānanda Swami, Brahmānanda Swami, and Girirāja had volunteered to go to Madras to arrange a preaching program for Śrīla Prabhupāda. When Acyutānanda Swami had informed Prabhupāda of the plan, Prabhupāda had asked, "Oh, you are not going to Vṛndāvana with us?"

"ISKCON is Vṛndāvana," Acyutānanda Swami had replied.

"Yes," Prabhupāda had said, "my Guru Mahārāja used to think like that."

"But which do you want us to do?" Girirāja had asked. "What is the better service?"

"I want to put on a *paṇḍāl* in Madras," Prabhupāda had replied. "That would be more pleasing."

Madras
February 11, 1972

Prabhupāda, accompanied by twenty disciples, arrived in Madras and immediately took part in a parade through the streets. The parade, led by a decorated elephant and a marching band, followed by the devotees' *kīrtana*, featured Prabhupāda riding in an old, flower-covered American limousine.

Prabhupāda stayed as the guest of Mr. Balu, a Madrasi businessman. For three nights in the large hall packed with five thousand people, Prabhupāda lectured in English. One evening he told a story from the *Caitanya-caritāmṛta* of an illiterate South Indian *brāhmaṇa* whom Lord Caitanya Mahāprabhu recognized for his staunch devotion to his spiritual master and to the *Bhagavad-gītā*. The next morning and each subsequent morning *The Hindu*, one of Madras's two leading newspapers, printed a full summary of Prabhupāda's lecture. The other principal newspaper gave a more general account of A. C. Bhaktivedanta Swami's arrival and the parade with his Western followers.

The large three-day program was followed by a more select gathering, sponsored by Mr. K. Vira Swami, the chief justice of Madras. Attending the function were judges, lawyers, and other leading citizens of the city. Several thousand people gathered beneath the open pavilion as Prabhupāda spoke about Rūpa Gosvāmī and Sanātana Gosvāmī of Vṛndāvana, who had given up their important government positions to join the movement of Caitanya Mahāprabhu. Indirectly, Prabhupāda was requesting all the attending leaders of Madras to join the Kṛṣṇa consciousness movement.

Prabhupāda was aware that his audience, although respectful, was steeped in impersonalism—deep-seated conviction that impersonal Brahman was supreme and that all Hindu gods were equal manifestations of the One. And Prabhupāda ended his talk by imploring his audience to accept Kṛṣṇa as the Supreme Personality of Godhead. "Just repeat," he said, " 'Kṛṣṇa is the Supreme Personality of Godhead.' " His appeal was so urgent and humble that some members of the audience actually repeated aloud, "Kṛṣṇa is the Supreme Personality of Godhead." *The Hindu's* editor and publisher, Mr. Kasturi, was in attendance, and he printed a detailed summary of Prabhupāda's speech in the next day's paper.

In addition to the usual news coverage, Śrīla Prabhupāda held a press conference at a Madras hotel. Already happy with the press coverage, he appealed further to the roomful of reporters.

Girirāja: *Prabhupāda wasn't speaking to them as if they were newspaper reporters. Usually a newspaper reporter has a stereotyped idea of who he is, and you giving an interview, so you have your stereotyped idea of who you are. And you answer his questions, thinking of how it will be published. But I could see that Prabhupāda was speaking to these reporters as spirit souls, as individual persons who are meant to be devotees of Kṛṣṇa. Even though they were addressing him as newspaper reporters, he was answering them in a completely different way. He was encouraging them and saying, "This reporting that you have done is very nice. Kṛṣṇa will bless you. Please help spread this movement." They were asking questions, thinking of his answers in terms of something to publish in the newspapers. But Prabhupāda took it that they were spirit souls reaching out toward Kṛṣṇa consciousness, and he answered in that way.*

Within a few days of Prabhupāda's arrival, the whole city was feeling the presence of the Hare Kṛṣṇa movement. Prabhupāda scarcely slept, using the early-morning hours for translating, even after his late-night speaking engagements. He would go from place to place all day with great vitality, outdoing his young followers.

Prabhupāda's host, Mr. Balu, although a prominent businessman, was also well known as a religious man. He received Prabhupāda warmly and respectfully, according to proper Vedic etiquette. Prabhupāda noted that Mr. Balu had his own temple with beautiful Rādhā-Kṛṣṇa Deities and a large *tulasī* plant. When the devotees accompanying Śrīla Prabhupāda asked Mr. Balu why the Deities were often dressed in black, he replied that They were so effulgent that if he didn't dress Them in black he wouldn't be able to look on Them. He did not make prostrated obeisances to his Deity because he and his wife were Kṛṣṇa's father and mother, he said, and how can the father pay obeisances to his son?

Prabhupāda and his host related to each other graciously. But one night Mr. Balu and his wife came to Śrīla Prabhupāda and asked him to please speak about the *rāsa-līlā** of Rādhā and Kṛṣṇa. Prabhupāda replied that the *rāsa-līlā*, being the most exalted spiritual topic, was meant only for liberated souls. Only one completely free of material desires, Prabhupāda explained, was fit to hear the *rāsa-līlā.*

"No, Swamiji," Mr. Balu insisted. "My wife and I are very keen. You must recite *rāsa-līlā.*"

Again Prabhupāda described the exalted position of the *rāsa* dance, repeating that only when one is completely free of all material attachments to wife, family, home, and money could he become fit to hear of Kṛṣṇa's *rāsa* dance. Mr. Balu then folded his hands and politely repeated, "Swamiji, my wife and I plead with you. Please recite *rāsa-līlā.*"

Then Prabhupāda replied, "Well, you may be fit to hear *rāsa-līlā*, but I do not feel that I am qualified to speak it. So kindly ask someone else."

Prabhupāda met privately with various important citizens of Madras. If the leaders of society became Kṛṣṇa conscious, he would explain, then they, by their example, would create Kṛṣṇa consciousness in the general populace. Never compromising, never flattering his important visitors, he tried to impart Kṛṣṇa consciousness to whomever he met.

He met with the governor of Madras, K. K. Shah, a staunch Māyāvādī and follower of Śaṅkarācārya. Patiently Prabhupāda tried to teach him

* The most exalted and intimate of Lord Kṛṣṇa's pastimes, His dancing with the cowherd girls in Vṛndāvana.

Kṛṣṇa consciousness, but the governor would interrupt with his own philosophy. When Prabhupāda asked him to somehow help the Kṛṣṇa consciousness movement, the man replied that as governor there was nothing he could do, since everything was in the hands of the chief minister.

Residing in Madras was an elderly scholar and former leading politician who had written several books and translations of Vedic philosophy from the impersonalist point of view. Prabhupāda visited him, but the man was paralyzed and could only sit, trembling, without speaking. Prabhupāda spoke for some time about personalism in the *Gītā*. The old scholar sometimes responded with a glimmer in his eye, but he could only make incoherent sounds. Previously Prabhupāda had criticized this man's translation of the *Gītā*, which declares that although Kṛṣṇa says surrender unto Him, we don't actually have to surrender unto the person Kṛṣṇa but to the impersonal, eternal principle *within* Kṛṣṇa. The meeting seemed to have a strong effect on Śrīla Prabhupāda, and for days afterward he would sometimes soberly mention how the old Māyāvādī scholar was living almost like a vegetable.

Śrīla Prabhupāda also met with V. Raj Gopala Acarya (Rajaji), who had been India's first chief executive after independence. A friend of Mahatma Gandhi, Rajaji was high in the public sentiment as a religious politician. Although in his nineties, he was alert and very sympathetic to Prabhupāda's movement. Rajaji expressed only one doubt: Prabhupāda had created such a huge institution that now his disciples might identify with the institution rather than with Kṛṣṇa. If that were to happen, then by identifying with the institution they would again fall into the same type of materialism or false identification as before. Prabhupāda replied that because Kṛṣṇa is absolute, Kṛṣṇa and Kṛṣṇa's institution are non-different. To identify with Kṛṣṇa's institution was to identify with Kṛṣṇa directly. Rajaji was satisfied by Prabhupāda's answer, and after a pleasant conversation the two friends parted.

Prabhupāda received an invitation to Chief Justice Vira Swami's home. The two became friends, and the chief justice requested to join the Kṛṣṇa consciousness movement as soon as possible. He liked Prabhupāda's followers, especially three-year-old Sarasvatī, and gave her a six-inch silver *mūrti* of Kṛṣṇa playing the flute.

Another evening, Mr. Vira Swami came to see Prabhupāda, and Prabhupāda mentioned that he thought Sarasvatī too young to have such a valuable silver *mūrti* and that he had taken it from her and was going to give her another one. But while they were talking, Sarasvatī burst into the room and ran to her mother, crying, "Kṛṣṇa is gone!"

Śrīla Prabhupāda then called her forward and asked, "Sarasvatī, where is Kṛṣṇa?"

In anxiety, Sarasvatī replied, "I don't know. Someone took Him."

Prabhupāda repeated, "But where is Kṛṣṇa?"

Sarasvatī replied, "I don't know."

"Is He under the cushion?" Prabhupāda suggested. And Sarasvatī ran over to the cushion Prabhupāda pointed to. She picked it up, but Kṛṣṇa was not there.

"Is He on the shelf?" Prabhupāda asked. Sarasvatī ran to the shelf. Her eyes darted in all directions.

"Where is Kṛṣṇa?" Sarasvatī began appealing to the faces of the devotees, glancing at their hands, looking behind their backs, searching everywhere.

Prabhupāda, intently watching Sarasvatī, began reciting a verse about the six Gosvāmīs: *he rādhe vraja-devike ca lalite he nanda-suno kutaḥ.* "This is the mood of the Gosvāmīs," he said. "They never said, 'Now I have seen God. Now I am satisfied.' No, rather they were saying, 'Where is Rādhā? Where is Kṛṣṇa? Where are You all now? Are You on Govardhana, or are You under the trees on the bank of the Yamunā? Where are You?' In this way they expressed their moods of Kṛṣṇa consciousness."

Sarasvatī's anxiety had become heightened to the point of tears. One of the devotees then hinted, "Sarasvatī, where is Kṛṣṇa? *Who* has Kṛṣṇa?" Sarasvatī's eyes widened. She exclaimed, "*Prabhupāda* has Kṛṣṇa!" and she rushed up to Prabhupāda, convinced that he was holding Kṛṣṇa. And Prabhupāda reached behind his seat and pulled out a small Kṛṣṇa *mūrti* similar to the silver Kṛṣṇa he had taken from her.

"Here is Kṛṣṇa, Sarasvatī," Prabhupāda said. Sarasvatī was in ecstasy. All the devotees were struck by Prabhupāda's exchange of devotional feelings with even a small child; by his expertise he had created within her a mood of separation from Kṛṣṇa. Prabhupāda continued explaining to the chief justice about the mood of separation from Kṛṣṇa.

For centuries certain religious and social controversies had divided Madras, and Prabhupāda often addressed these issues. One conflict was between the *brāhmaṇas* and the non-*brāhmaṇas.* Because those born in *brāhmaṇa* families had traditionally monopolized the important governmental, social, and religious posts, the non-*brāhmaṇas* had developed a powerful political opposition, passing laws banning such things as religious pictures. In their mundane political conception of the sacred *Rāmāyaṇa*, they had even committed offenses to the Deities of Lord Rāma.

In talking with his disciples, Śrīla Prabhupāda said, "The chief justice is *brāhmaṇa*? I don't think so. He may be a *kṣatriya*. But you can tell him that we can solve the whole problem between the *brāhmaṇas* and the non-*brāhmaṇas*. We will give facility that anyone can become a *brāhmaṇa*. He simply has to follow our principles, and we will make him a *brāhmaṇa*." Prabhupāda said the *śāstra* states that in Kali-yuga the demons will take birth as *brāhmaṇas*, thus this deep controversy. The so-called *brāhmaṇas*, the leaders, were not satisfying the people. Prabhupāda said that anyone who followed the four regulative principles, chanted Hare Kṛṣṇa, and took Vaiṣṇava initiation could become a *brāhmaṇa*, and that would solve the whole problem.

They should begin, Prabhupāda said, by making Chief Justice Vira Swami a *brāhmaṇa*. Mr. Vira Swami admitted that he was already eager to take initiation from Śrīla Prabhupāda; his only difficulty was giving up tea-drinking. When Prabhupāda heard this, he said that even if the justice did drink a little tea, he would accept him—as an exceptional case.

Some of Madras's caste-conscious *brāhmaṇas* criticized Śrīla Prabhupāda's creating *brāhmaṇas* from low-born Westerners. During a gathering at the home of a Madrasi *brāhmaṇa*, one of the guests commented to Prabhupāda, "Swamiji, your disciples don't pronounce the Sanskrit very nicely. Even the Hare Kṛṣṇa *mantra* they sometimes do not say correctly."

"Yes," Prabhupāda replied, "that is why we have come here—to get your association so you can teach us."

Śrīla Prabhupāda encountered another long-standing South Indian feud—between the Śaivites (followers of Lord Śiva) and the Vaiṣṇavas (followers of Lord Viṣṇu). The Śaivites generally espoused an impersonalistic philosophy, declaring God to be the Impersonal One appearing in many forms, such as Śiva and Kṛṣṇa. But since all the forms were one ultimately, fighting as to which god was best was petty and childish. Prabhupāda's disciples found this philosophy difficult to deal with, and when Girirāja had argued with a wealthy Śaivite, Mr. Ramakrishna, they had separated with hurt feelings. But in meetings with other persons in

Madras, Girirāja was often reminded, "Have you met Mr. Ramakrishna? He is a very good man and a leader in religious functions." Girirāja became embarrassed and decided to make another attempt to win Mr. Ramakrishna's friendship.

They talked again, but remained unsatisfied. Girirāja then informed Prabhupāda and asked if he would meet Mr. Ramakrishna himself. Prabhupāda agreed.

When they met, Mr. Ramakrishna began by saying, "Swamiji, we have been having some discussion about devotion to Lord Kṛṣṇa and devotion to Lord Śiva. What do you say? Who is greater? Kṛṣṇa or Śiva?"

Prabhupāda replied that actually the word *bhakti,* or "devotion," could not properly be applied to the worship of Lord Śiva. *Bhakti,* he said, meant service without any material desire, whereas *pūjā* included service with the desire for some return. *Bhakti,* therefore, could only be applied to Kṛṣṇa.

"But isn't it possible," asked Mr. Ramakrishna, "for someone to be a *bhakta* of Lord Śiva and to worship Lord Śiva simply out of devotion, without desiring any material benefit?"

"It may be possible," Prabhupāda replied, "but generally not. Just like when a person enters a liquor shop, generally it's taken that he is going for drinking, although there may be some exception."

Prabhupāda gave the example of the *gopīs*' worship of the goddess Kātyāyanī; their worship had not been for material benefit but for devotion to Kṛṣṇa. Similarly, if one worshiped Lord Śiva with the aim of serving Lord Kṛṣṇa, that would be *bhakti.* But people generally approach Śiva for material benefit. Although Mr. Ramakrishna was usually prone to argue these points, Prabhupāda's answer satisfied him.

Śrīla Prabhupāda's most acute controversy in Madras was not with *smārta-brāhmaṇas,* Māyāvādīs, or Śaivites, but with some of his own Godbrothers. Although some of them acknowledged Śrīla Prabhupāda's incomparable preaching in the West on behalf of their spiritual master, Śrīla Bhaktisiddhānta Sarsasvatī, others were envious. One envious Godbrother wrote to Śrīla Prabhupāda in Madras.

> Reverend Swamiji,
>
> I listened to your discourse on Bhakti at Rajiswari Kalayana Mandapam on the 12th instant. I am filled with doubts on the following:

> Your disciples dance with Hare Krishna mantram, (I) are they really God-intoxicated as Lord Chaitanya (II) Have you Swamiji really got free of your ego? If so, why you said, "I challenge," and why are words like "I" and "my" always on your lips? (III) Why do you use a cushion unlike a real yogi—Did Lord Chaitanya use cushions? (IV) Why do you wear ring and a wrist gold watch? Are you not free from material attachment? (V) Did you visit Lord Chaitanya Krishna Temple at Gaudiya Math? If not, why not—The purest Vaishnava cult is indwelling there with pious Swamijis with Lord Krishna dwelling therein. Melodious sound from your throat is absent but a jarceing [sic] undivine comes out. Is there any divinity in your person? I doubt. One disgusted on hearing your speech.

Although Śrīla Prabhupāda was surprised and hurt by the extreme virulence of such a letter, he was accustomed to his Godbrothers' slights and insults. He forbade his disciples, however, to get involved in fights with his Godbrothers. Rather, they should simply avoid them. He said that persons who criticize the spreading of the Kṛṣṇa consciousness movement were useless and that he would push on: "The dogs may bark, but the caravan will pass."

In contrast to the venomous letter came a letter from Tridaṇḍī Svāmī B. V. Purī Mahārāja, another of Śrīla Prabhupāda's Godbrothers. Purī Mahārāja, as Prabhupāda called him, had a small *āśrama* in Visakhapatnam, on the Bay of Bengal between Madras and Calcutta. Hearing that Prabhupāda was going next to Calcutta, Purī Mahārāja invited him to visit.

> With innumerable Satsanga Dandabats at Thy lotus feet, I beg to acknowledge the kind letter. . . . The citizens of Visakhapatnam are very anxious to have the darshan of your holiness. . . . We are exceedingly glad and eager to hear Sankirtana and the divine message from your holy lips. I hope the Sankirtana movement at Madras is attracting thousands of citizens. Again, with dandabats to all the Vaishnavas, I remain dasanu B.V. Puri.

* * *

Visakhapatnam
February 17, 1972

A broad beach of white sparkling sands and the Bay of Bengal's warm, clear waters were special features of Śrīla Prabhupāda's visit to Visakhapatnam. Purī Mahārāja's small *āśrama*, where Śrīla Prabhupāda stayed, was only five minutes from the ocean, and every morning Prabhupāda and his entourage of about fifteen devotees would take long walks along the seashore.

Yamunā: *I don't think Prabhupāda ever excluded any of us from going with him to the beach. All the devotees knew at which time Śrīla Prabhupāda would be taking his walk, and we would come out from our different quarters and follow him to the seashore. The walks were brisk and refreshing and full of talk about Kṛṣṇa. Somehow or other, we were all able to hear Śrīla Prabhupāda speak.*

Guru dāsa: *I always went on every morning walk. But one time I was sitting in the temple, when suddenly I saw Prabhupāda and the devotees going toward the beach. I immediately ran out of the temple to join them, without even taking time to get my shoes. But there were barnacles and rocks leading down to the beach. When Prabhupāda saw me coming, lifting my feet up high, painfully hobbling down the rough road, he looked over and said, "Oh, your feet are hurting? Why aren't you wearing shoes?" And I said, "Prabhupāda, when I'm with you, I don't feel any pain." Prabhupāda stopped and said, "Then why don't you cut your throat?" Everyone laughed, and I laughed also. He said, "There is enough* tapasya. *Why create your own?"*

Gurukṛpā: *Prabhupāda would talk philosophy on and on. There were many things I couldn't understand. I would just listen anyway, although I couldn't remember anything. I would just hear and hear, but it hadn't registered yet. I used to walk behind him on the beach, and I figured that, "If I can't follow his teachings or example yet, at least let me step in his footsteps in the sand."*

Viśākhā: *Sometimes a dog would try to follow us or would bark at us. We were all surprised to see how Prabhupāda would flick his cane and the dog would run away. Once when we passed a cow on the road, Prabhupāda gave her ample room to pass, and he told us the story of how he had been gored by a cow shortly after he had taken* sannyāsa.

Tejās: *Once on a morning walk Prabhupāda was speaking about the dog. He gave a reference to a* śloka *by Cāṇakya Paṇḍita about the five good qualities of a dog—that he is very faithful and satisfied with anything. And soon Prabhupāda said we should be Kṛṣṇa's dog. He was also speaking about how our* pūjārīs *should never be paid. The teacher and the* pūjārī *should never receive a salary. They must work in pure devotion. The* kṣatriya *also. He said that was the mistake in government today, that the* kṣatriyas *are being paid. He discussed so many things, one after another.*

Nanda-kumāra: *Śrīla Prabhupāda would tell us to go bathe in the ocean. "Go to the beach," he would say. So one day I asked him, "Śrīla Prabhupāda, whenever I go down to the beach, the sun is warm on my body, the water feels so good, the sand—it seems like such a comfortable material situation. How should I understand your reason for asking us to go to the beach? I know the spiritual master never gives the disciple anything that will cause him to become materially attached but always gives him whatever he needs to remember Kṛṣṇa. But when I go to the beach, it seems I just enjoy my senses. How can I relate that to Kṛṣṇa? How can I understand that this instruction is for my spiritual benefit?"*

Prabhupāda said, "The sun is there—Kṛṣṇa is the light of the sun. The ocean is there—Kṛṣṇa is the taste of water. You are surrounded *by Kṛṣṇa. How can you forget Kṛṣṇa? He is all around you."*

Pāñcajanya: *I was a new devotee, and I asked Prabhupāda, "What about swimming, Śrīla Prabhupāda? Is that not* māyā?" *Prabhupāda said, "Lord Caitanya used to go swimming all the time. He used to play ball. So you can go and swim. Just make sure you remember Kṛṣṇa."*

Purī Mahārāja's *āśrama* was a simple single-story building of about eight rooms. When he offered Prabhupāda a room next to his own, Prabhupāda was pleased, accepting it as an expression of friendship. Prabhupāda relaxed with his Godbrothers, Purī Mahārāja and Ānanda Brahmacārī, speaking with them in Bengali. Purī Mahārāja said he appreciated Prabhupāda's work and his Western disciples.

Prabhupāda's disciples had already seen formal exchanges of obeisances between Prabhupāda and his Godbrothers, as when in Bombay they had seen Prabhupāda get off his *vyāsāsana* and offer *daṇḍavats* to his Godbrothers. But in Visakhapatnam they saw more intimate dealings. They saw for the first time Śrīla Prabhupāda living comfortably, at ease, in the same quarters as his Godbrothers. And they didn't feel themselves being treated condescendingly or superficially, or being regarded as oddities. Through Prabhupāda's guidance they began to learn more of the essential friendly and humble exchanges between Vaiṣṇavas.

Prabhupāda's Godbrother Ānanda was eager to cook and serve not only Śrīla Prabhupāda but all his disciples. Ānanda was elderly, and yet he took the position of always offering menial service. Although he spoke very little English, Prabhupāda's disciples could perceive the affection of Ānanda and Śrīla Prabhupāda for each other. Ānanda's communication with Prabhupāda's disciples was particularly through his cooking and serving of *prasādam.*

Each morning everyone would gather on the veranda outside Prabhupāda's quarters, the men sitting on one side, the ladies on the other. Down the center aisle Ānanda would walk briskly, distributing *prasādam,* while Prabhupāda sat at one end in a wooden chair, fingering his *japa* beads and observing the devotees take *prasādam.* Prabhupāda had supplied money to the *āśrama,* and Ānanda was regularly cooking sumptuous feasts: deep-fried chunks of potatoes in powdered spices, rice, yogurt, *dāl,* three different types of *sabjīs,* french fries, chutney, *malpurā, rājkeli, sandeśa, kṣīra*—and everything cooked to a nectarean standard of excellence.

Prabhupāda would sit at the head of the two rows of devotees and encourage them to take *prasādam:* "Give him more!" Prabhupāda would praise Ānanda's cooking, smiling with pleasure to see his disciples accept *prasādam.* The devotees would finish, having been induced to eat as much as they possibly could, and Śrīla Prabhupāda would say aloud the *prema-dhvani.* Then all the devotees would shout in response, "Jaya!"

After one such feast, Prabhupāda called the devotees into his room and remarked, "See how he is cooking. He cooks everything, he serves it, and then he doesn't eat until everyone is fully satisfied. This is Vaiṣṇava, how he should act. He is more satisfied to serve than to enjoy himself." The feasts continued twice a day, and in the evening many guests arrived to take *prasādam,* chant in the *kīrtanas,* and hear Śrīla Prabhupāda lecture.

One day Śrīla Prabhupāda took his disciples to see a famous temple of Lord Nṛsiṁha, Śrī Siṁhācalam, on top of a hill about five miles north of Visakhapatnam. Thousands of stone steps led up the hill to the temple, which was situated in a natural amphitheater on the side of the hill. Prabhupāda said the temple, which was now run by followers of the Rāmānuja sect, was particularly important because Lord Caitanya had visited there on His tour of South India.

Śrīla Prabhupāda chose to approach the temple by car, riding up the winding road past orchards of mango, jackfruits, and cashew, and fields of pineapple. On arriving at the temple, Śrīla Prabhupāda and his disciples met one of the temple *brāhmaṇas*, who showed them around the grounds. The temple buildings were of black granite, and carved into the rock were the forms and pastimes of Viṣṇu, especially in His incarnation of Lord Nṛsiṁha. As Prabhupāda moved from place to place, building to building, he sometimes rode up steep stairs on a palanquin carried by four men.

When Prabhupāda came upon an immense banyan tree at the lower end of the temple grounds, he said that the tree must be thousands of years old. As he stood beneath the tree, his servant, Nanda-kumāra, handed him a small *campaka* flower. Extending his thumb and forefinger from his bead bag, Prabhupāda held the *campaka* flower and looked fondly at it. "This flower," he said, "is the color of Lord Caitanya. And this flower is the most loved all over India. This flower is beautiful to look at and beautiful to smell." He carried the small saffron-gold flower between his fingers throughout the rest of the morning.

When Prabhupāda and his group entered the inner sanctum, where the Deity of Lord Nṛsiṁha resided, their guide explained that the *mūrti* dated back to the time of Prahlāda Mahārāja. An ancient king named Purūravā and his consort Urvaśī had once visited this hill, and at the request of Urvaśī, the *mūrti*, who appeared to her in a dream, had been excavated. The Lord had ordained that He should be worshiped in this place but that He would give *darśana* only one day a year, during the month of Vaiśākha. The rest of the year He would be entirely covered with ground sandalwood pulp mixed with camphor and other scents. Therefore, the Deity now appeared to be only a lump covered with a layer of sandalwood. Prabhupāda commented that the sandalwood was to keep the Deity "cool-headed."

Mādhavānanda: *When Prabhupāda was at the Nṛsiṁha temple in Visakhapatnam, it was the same as when he was in Vṛndāvana. When he got out of the car, he was very grave. We went into the temple, and there was a chamber. Then we went down. The walls were four feet thick, and it seemed like hundreds of feet of tunnels before we got into the inner sanctum. There was the Deity with just a mound of sandalwood paste on Him. As soon as we entered, Prabhupāda said, "Begin chanting the Nṛsiṁha* mantra.*" So we started singing* tava kara-kamala-vare nakham adbhuta-śṛṅgam. *And we circumambulated the Deity. Then we stood before the Deity, and Prabhupāda offered obeisances.*

Gurukṛpā: *When we came into the Deity room, Prabhupāda had us sing the Nṛsiṁha prayers. He always manifested such devotion. That was what separated him from us—not only his learning or his knowledge, but his devotion. In these places we would see him become very silent, very grave, and when he would speak, such peace would fill us from within. When he would speak, you could feel it. He was constantly convincing us of Kṛṣṇa consciousness. Not purposely, but he was just being himself. In these places it would come out.*

When Prabhupāda stood with us before the Deity, we couldn't even see. There was just a mound of sandalwood. There was one brāhmaṇa *with big earlobes, and he had a ring in his ear. We offered some money. But it was a very devotional time. Prabhupāda didn't say much, and the main reason was that these places are appreciated according to one's spiritual advancement. The details and facts and the history are not really that important. There is nothing really to say. Prabhupāda would just make sure we had the proper respect and didn't commit any offense.*

Prabhupāda would lecture in the evening, speaking sometimes at schools and social clubs in Visakhapatnam. During the program at the Ramakrishna Hall, where more than a thousand people attended, Śrīla Prabhupāda's dancing induced the entire audience to dance. The devotees danced in a ring around Śrīla Prabhupāda, and the *kīrtana* continued for an hour.

At another program a bearded American anthropologist rode up on a motorcycle to attend Prabhupāda's lecture and *kīrtana.* Afterward, the anthropologist told Śrīla Prabhupāda that he had come to India to study the primitive tribes. Prabhupāda told him it was simply a waste of time. "Why do you want to study the primitive people?" he asked. "Why don't you study the exalted people?" And Prabhupāda narrated a story:

One time a poor man roasted a cob of corn and then began picking off the kernels one at a time and eating them. In this way it took him many hours to finish. He did this, Prabhupāda said, because he had nothing else to do, just to pass the time of day. In the same way, the study of anthropology was simply a waste of time. Prabhupāda asked, "Why don't you study some person or group of persons from whom you can learn something?"

During the day Prabhupāda would sit outside his room and enjoy the atmosphere. He wore no shirt, and his healthy body shone with a golden luster as he sat drinking freshly pressed sugarcane juice. "This is just how it is in Vaikuṇṭha," he said. "There is always a very cool, pleasant breeze." He often walked about, chanting, talking about Kṛṣṇa, listening to the devotees' *kīrtanas*, and observing the activities of the temple.

Repeatedly Prabhupāda invited Purī Mahārāja to come and preach in the West. He requested him to at least come to Māyāpur for ISKCON's international gathering of devotees. Prabhupāda felt that Purī Mahārāja, on seeing all the Western disciples, might feel moved to join him and preach. Purī Mahārāja agreed to accompany Prabhupāda to Calcutta and Māyāpur, and the pleasant week in Visakhapatnam came to an end with Prabhupāda, his disciples, and Purī Mahārāja looking forward to traveling together to Calcutta.

Gurukṛpā: *Although we arrived at the train station early, the train was already at the platform. It was very hot, and five or six of us were having* kīrtana. *Then Śyāmasundara climbed up a coconut tree and got this fantastic coconut. He opened it and gave it to Prabhupāda, who proceeded to drink a lot. Then Prabhupāda gave it to Śyāmasundara, and Śyāmasundara drank. Then Prabhupāda said, "Give it to the* kīrtana *members." Each man in the* kīrtana *group was so thirsty that he wasn't even thinking of leaving any for the next man, but would just pass this coconut around. And the thing wouldn't empty. I tilted it up, and the coconut water was coming out, pouring on my shirt, and I was drinking and drinking. But still it wouldn't empty. We were amazed. Prabhupāda was smiling, and we were chanting. We all became cool and satisfied.*

Śyāmasundara: *Prabhupāda and I were in a first-class railway coach, a private compartment for two persons, clackity-clacking through the warm Indian night, somewhere between Visakhapatnam and Calcutta. Prabhupāda was talking and joking and playing tapes until around ten-thirty P.M., when he lay down to take rest. For a while I switched off the lights. At about midnight Prabhupāda sat upright and called my name. "Śyāmasundara, take dictation," he said. Then followed a train of thoughts so lucid and coherent that I could only conclude that while we think Śrīla Prabhupāda is sleeping he is usually not sleeping but is thinking, reflecting on ways to serve Kṛṣṇa more and more.*

CHAPTER THREE

Prabhupāda had postponed the Māyāpur cornerstone-laying ceremony until Gaura-pūrṇimā (the appearance day of Lord Caitanya), February 29, 1972. He had requested a big festival, with a *paṇḍāl* and free feasting for guests. His disciples from all over the world would attend.

> I want very much to hold this function this year with all of my students. . . . It is a very important day and it will be a great service to Srila Bhaktivinode Thakur and to His son Srila Bhaktisiddhanta Saraswati Thakur. So please arrange for this program.

In December, when the war had broken out between India and Pakistan over Bangladesh, near Māyāpur, the Indian government had forbidden foreigners to stay in the northern area of West Bengal. The devotees had vacated, returning a few weeks later when the war had ended. They had continued arranging for the festival, and a few days before Gaura-pūrṇimā Prabhupāda arrived to stay with them.

When Prabhupāda saw a banner on bamboo poles—"Welcome Śrīla Prabhupāda!"—he remarked, "I don't know if my Godbrothers will like this." He had already heard that some of his Godbrothers objected to his taking the same title as their spiritual master, Bhaktisiddhānta Sarasvatī Prabhupāda. He had not actually *taken* the name, but his disciples had *given* him the name a few years ago in America. In May 1968 while in Boston, Prabhupāda had been dictating a letter and had mentioned to his secretary that Swamiji was a third-class title for the spiritual master. "Then why do we call you Swamiji?" his secretary had asked.

"The spiritual master," Prabhupāda had replied, "is usually addressed by names like Gurudeva, Viṣṇupāda, or Prabhupāda."

"May we call you Prabhupāda?" his secretary had asked.

Prabhupāda had replied, "Yes," and his disciples had switched from "Swamiji" to "Prabhupāda." One of the devotees had inquired further from Prabhupāda about the meaning of the word and had published a statement in *Back to Godhead* magazine.

> Prabhupada
>
> The word Prabhupada is a term of the utmost reverence in Vedic religious circles, and it signifies a great saint even among saints. The word actually has two meanings: first, one at whose feet (pada) there are many Prabhus (a term meaning "master," which the disciples of a Guru use in addressing each other). The second meaning is one who is always found at the Lotus Feet of Krishna (the Supreme Master).
>
> In the line of disciplic succession through which Krishna Consciousness is conveyed to mankind, there have been a number of figures of such spiritual importance as to be called Prabhupada.
>
> Srila Rupa Goswami Prabhupada executed the will of his Master, Sri Chaitanya Mahaprabhu, and therefore he and his associate Goswamis are called Prabhupada. Srila Bhakti Siddhanta Saraswati Goswami Thakur executed the will of Srila Bhaktivinode Thakur, and therefore he is also addressed as Prabhupada. Our Spiritual Master, Om Vishnupad 108 Sri Srimad Bhaktivedanta Swami Maharaj has, in the same way, executed the will of Srila Bhakti Siddhanta Saraswati Goswami Prabhupada in carrying the message of love of Krishna to the Western world, and therefore we American and European humble servants of His Divine Grace, from all the different centers of the Sankirtan Movement have followed in the footsteps of Srila Rupa Goswami Prabhupada, and prefer to address His Grace our Spiritual Master as Prabhupada, and he has kindly said "Yes."

Everyone concerned had been happy about the title Prabhupāda, and no one had foreseen the envy the name would uncover. How could Prabhupāda compete for the honor due his own spiritual master? He was fixed as the humble servant of his spiritual master.

The members of ISKCON saw no harm in calling their spiritual master Prabhupāda. And there could be no stopping them—he was their Prabhupāda. They had even printed *A. C. Bhaktivedanta Swami Prabhupada* on their invitations for the Gaura-pūrṇimā festival. But Prabhupāda knew it would raise the eyebrows of certain of his more critical Godbrothers.

When inspecting the living accommodations for the devotees, Prabhupāda found spacious white canvas tents—one for the men and one for the women—with fluorescent lighting inside. A large *paṇḍāl* tent stood in the center of the other tents, and a small tent in the rear served as a kitchen. Immediately surrounding the small compound were rice fields. The ground, therefore, was slightly moist, and the wet fields bred large mosquitoes, which emerged at sunset. Conditions were primitive, but many of these devotees were the same disciples who had traveled with Prabhupāda for a year and a half in India, sometimes living in dirty *dharmaśālās* with bare rooms and sometimes living in cold tents in Allahabad. The devotees had not come to Māyāpur to be comfortable but to serve Prabhupāda. In future years, by the result of their efforts, many, many devotees would be able to gather comfortably in Māyāpur in the spacious buildings Prabhupāda was planning.

Well aware that Westerners were unaccustomed to the austerities of living in India, Prabhupāda wanted to provide facilities so his disciples could feel comfortable and be able to focus their stay in India on spiritual life, without distracting inconveniences. Therefore he was pushing them to help in various ways to establish a Māyāpur building with running water, electricity, and other conveniences.

Prabhupāda's dwelling was a simple thatched Bengali hut about twelve feet square, with a dirt floor. A thin partition divided the main room from the servants' quarters. In front was a small veranda, and in back a garden, where Prabhupāda could sit and take massage. Also in back were a hand pump for bathing and an outhouse. When the devotees apologized for offering Prabhupāda such a humble residence, he replied that he liked the natural simplicity. "Even if you build me the biggest palace," he said, "still I would prefer to live here."

While living so simply in Māyāpur, Prabhupāda spoke of his vision of a grand project yet to come. Although the Deities of Rādhā-Mādhava—whom he had worshiped at the 1971 Ardha-kumbha-melā in Allahabad—were installed in a tent, he spoke of a marble palace. He also spoke of first-class accommodations for guests and devotees, although as yet he had little to offer. Living simply and happily in his thatched hut, he gathered his disciples together and told them of his plans. At his request, devotees had built a small model of the proposed first major building, and there were also drawings of the proposed Temple of Human Understanding. He wanted to build a Māyāpur city, he said, with quarters for each of the four social classes of the *varṇāśrama* institution.

Tatpara: *When Prabhupāda would go to the Western countries, he would be interviewed by many great persons, but when he came to Māyāpur, he was talking so friendly, sometimes taking juice or giving instructions, and he lived simple, like a villager. The Western devotees think sometimes of Prabhupāda in one* līlā *only, like a great king. But when he comes to India, he is like another person. He was laughing and talking like a friend.*

Bhavānanda: *In his straw house Prabhupāda sat on a bamboo platform. There was a bed and some mats on the floor. That was all. He was happier there than anywhere. We put a fan in there too, and Prabhupāda liked it. He liked it because it was so simple. There was an outhouse, but he didn't mind it at all. He was relishing everything. At that time he made Jayapatāka and me codirectors of Māyāpur. He made four signers on the checking account for the building construction. In India, just to open up an account is very difficult. We were seeing that part of Prabhupāda, where he was very strict because he knows the difficulties you can run into. If you don't fill out the proper forms, the bank can even keep your money. Or you may want to close your account and they won't let you. Our mood was splayed out—we were babies. So Prabhupāda was training us in keeping accounts and management.*

Jananivāsa: *The first time Prabhupāda came to see the Deities, he said, "Who is dressing the Deities?" Someone said, "Jananivāsa." The Deities were just standing on a tile platform with no decoration. They were just standing there, but Prabhupāda looked on Them so lovingly. He used to come and take* darśana *every day. One time he came to the Deity room and I wasn't there. There were some Indian people taking* darśana, *and I had gone to get them a* Back to Godhead *magazine from a room about ten feet away. When I came back, Prabhupāda was there. He was also taking* darśana, *but he said, "You should always be standing here. People are coming, but no one is here." I said, "Śrīla Prabhupāda, I just went to get a* Back to Godhead. *It is only ten feet away." But he looked at me as if to say, "You are defending yourself again, making excuses." Then he told Bhavānanda, "This boy, Jananivāsa, should have some help. He can't do everything. He is an ordinary person."*

The five-day Gaura-pūrṇimā festival featured twenty-four-hour *kīrtana*, with groups of devotees chanting in two-hour shifts. Each morning the main body of devotees would form a *kīrtana* procession and go out visiting Navadvīpa's holy sights: the *nīm* tree under which Lord Caitanya was born, the house of Śrīnivāsa Ācārya, where Lord Caitanya and His associates had performed nocturnal *kīrtana*, the spot where the Kazi had tried to stop Lord Caitanya's *saṅkīrtana*, the residence of Bhaktivinoda

Ṭhākura. (Often Bhaktivinoda Ṭhākura had stood in front of this house, Prabhupāda told the devotees, and looked out across the Jalāṅgī toward where Śrīla Prabhupāda now had his land.)

Throughout the day and especially in the evenings, the devotees would gather on the stage of the orange-striped *paṇḍāl*, while Rādhā-Mādhava stood at stage center within a traditional Bengali *siṁhāsana* of carved banana stalks covered with colored foil and flower garlands. Prabhupāda would have his disciples do most of the public speaking, with Acyutānanda Swami, lecturing in Bengali, as the main speaker.

Hundreds of people came and went in a steady stream, and the devotees distributed Bengali, English, and Hindi *Back to Godhead* magazines. In the evenings they would present a slide show or a film. Prabhupāda was especially pleased to watch the *prasādam* distribution from his window, hundreds of villagers squatting in long rows, eating *kicharī* from round leaf plates. "Continue this forever," Prabhupāda told his disciples. "Always distribute *prasādam*."

Even without a building, Prabhupāda's preaching in Māyāpur was significant. While other nearby *maṭhas* were also observing Gaura-pūrṇimā—mostly by hosting Calcutta widows who paid a fee to live a few days in a temple and visit the holy places of Navadvīpa—Prabhupāda's *paṇḍāl* program was the most vigorous celebration and drew the most visitors. The birthplace of Lord Caitanya Mahāprabhu, Prabhupāda said, had no meaning without preaching. Except for this time of the year, very few people visited Māyāpur.

"Which is more important," Prabhupāda asked, "Lord Caitanya's birthplace or His activities? It is His activities, His *karma*. His activities are more important than His *janma*, or place of birth." The activities of Lord Caitanya were chanting Hare Kṛṣṇa and distributing love of God to all people, and this should be the activity of devotees in Māyāpur.

On Gaura-pūrṇimā day, ten of Prabhupāda's *sannyāsī* Godbrothers visited to participate along with Prabhupāda's disciples and hundreds of visitors in the dedication and cornerstone-laying ceremony. Prabhupāda was gracious and friendly toward his Godbrothers, and he was gratified that they could all sit together to dedicate the world headquarters of the International Society for Krishna Consciousness.

Sitting on a cushion next to the sacrificial arena, chanting on *japa* beads, Prabhupāda initiated six Bengali devotees and awarded the *sannyāsa* order to a young American disciple. Then Prabhupāda's Godbrothers spoke, each expressing appreciation of Prabhupāda's work in the West.

Finally they all gathered around the pit, five feet square and fifteen feet deep. Certain articles had been collected to be placed inside the pit in accordance with the scriptures: five kinds of flowers, five kinds of grains, five kinds of leaves, five kinds of metal, five kinds of nectar, five kinds of colors, five kinds of fruits, and five kinds of jewels. Prabhupāda's Godbrother Purī Mahārāja descended a ladder into the pit to put coconuts and banana leaves in a pot and to place this, along with flowers, onto the altar of bricks.

Next Prabhupāda entered the pit, carrying a box with a gold, ruby-eyed *mūrti* of Ānanta Śeṣa. Earlier that morning in his hut Prabhupāda had confidentially shown a few disciples the *mūrti.* "This is Lord Ānanta," he had said, "the serpent bed on which Lord Viṣṇu rests. He will hold the temple on His head." Prabhupāda now placed Ānanta Śeṣa on the altar of bricks and climbed back up the ladder. Then on Prabhupāda's blissful invitation, everyone began to toss in offerings of flowers and money, followed by handfuls of earth.

Although Prabhupāda's Godbrothers had praised his work on Gaura-pūrṇimā day, several of them returned a few days later to complain about his use of the title Prabhupāda. Prabhupāda asked his disciples to leave the room. When they were alone, one of the *sannyāsī* Godbrothers began challenging Prabhupāda in Bengali: "Why are you using *Prabhupāda*? You have no right. This is our Prabhupāda's title. You cannot take it."

"I did not take it," Prabhupāda replied. "They are calling me Prabhupāda. What can I do?" Although the *sannyāsī* Godbrother then began to criticize Prabhupāda for not joining their preaching and for awarding the sacred thread and *sannyāsa* order to Westerners, mainly the Godbrothers wanted an explanation for his use of the title Prabhupāda.

"Brahmānanda Mahārāja!" Prabhupāda called. "Bring me a copy of my letterhead." When Brahmānanda Swami returned with the stationery, Prabhupāda showed it to his Godbrothers. The letterhead read, "Tridandi Goswami A. C. Bhaktivedanta Swami." No "Prabhupāda." This proved that he himself did not use the title. This simple demonstration pacified his Godbrothers, and he then invited them to take *prasādam* with him, while his disciples served.

Later in his hut Prabhupāda talked with his disciples about envy. A devotee could judge his own advancement by how free he was from envy, he said. In the spiritual world envy was conspicuous by its absence. Although all the liberated associates of Kṛṣṇa were trying their best to serve Kṛṣṇa—in a kind of competition—everyone was pleased with one another. If Rādhārāṇī or a favorite *gopī* pleased Kṛṣṇa, the other *gopīs* did not think ill of her but thought, "Oh, how nicely she has served Kṛṣṇa. Let me try to offer some nice service to Kṛṣṇa so He will be even more pleased!" To be envious was materialistic.

Prabhupāda wished his Godbrothers had taken a different point of view. He wished they had not minded his being called Prabhupāda by his disciples. He was also sorry that some of his Godbrothers couldn't sincerely praise his work. If Bhaktisiddhānta Sarasvatī was working successfully through him, why should they be disturbed? Why not accept his work and be happy that the mission of Lord Caitanya Mahāprabhu was being spread effectively? They should see it as Bhaktisiddhānta Sarasvatī's work, the work of their own spiritual master. It was also *their* work, *their* responsibility, and they should recognize that through Bhaktivedanta Swami Mahārāja it was being wonderfully done. At the ceremony they had praised his work. So if they didn't mind praising him, then why not admit that for hundreds of Westerners whom he had saved from hell, he was Prabhupāda, that singular pure devotee whom they always thought of as seated at the lotus feet of Kṛṣṇa.

In terms of authorized books produced and distributed, numbers of devotees initiated and engaged in devotional service, and numbers of temples opened, no one could compare. Of course, in one sense all of Prabhupāda's Godbrothers were equally praiseworthy, as long as they followed the basic instructions of Bhaktisiddhānta Sarasvatī, chanted Hare Kṛṣṇa, and avoided sinful life. But if analysis or criticism was to be made with such scrutiny, then let the preaching records be scrutinized. Who, above all, was extending the mercy of Lord Nityānanda and making such tremendous gains on behalf of Bhaktisiddhānta Sarasvatī—gains that had previously seemed impossible? According to *Caitanya-caritāmṛta*, if a preacher could spread the chanting of Hare Kṛṣṇa, then he must be accepted as empowered by God.

Prabhupāda was certainly empowered, yet he conducted himself very humbly, with no assistance from others. He had repeatedly invited his Godbrothers to join him in the West and take their places beside him as preachers in the Kṛṣṇa consciousness movement. Why had they not come forward to assist him in their spiritual master's mission, instead of complaining about him, the one Godbrother who was carrying out Śrīla Bhaktisiddhānta Sarasvatī's mission?

It was not the place of Prabhupāda's disciples to criticize, however, and he had sternly warned them that they had no position to do so. They should treat his Godbrothers as disciples of Bhaktisiddhānta Sarasvatī and therefore as on the level of their own spiritual master. Nevertheless, Prabhupāda's disciples became sorry to see this lack of respect for their spiritual master. They could be humble and not protest, but how could they be affectionate toward persons who criticized their spiritual master and his Kṛṣṇa consciousness movement?

After the five-day festival, Prabhupāda left Māyāpur for Vṛndāvana, where he planned to hold another ground-breaking ceremony. The Māyāpur land was still completely undeveloped, and Prabhupāda urged his disciples in India to continue collecting the necessary funds.

> We are making a very gorgeous plan at Māyāpur, and if you all together can give shape to this plan it will be unique in the whole world. It will be a world center for teaching spiritual life. Students from all over the world will come and we shall revolutionize the atheistic and communistic tendencies of rascal philosophers. So we must be responsible for this great task. Not for a single moment shall we be without ISKCON thoughts. That is my request to you all.

* * *

February 1972

During Prabhupāda's absence from Vṛndāvana the devotees had been unable to persuade Mr. S. to grant legal permission for ISKCON to use the land. Prabhupāda had insistently directed one of his Indian-born disciples, Kṣīrodakaśāyī, to acquire from Mr. S. an actual deed. Kṣīrodakaśāyī had pleaded with Mr. S., and seeing Mr. S.'s indecision, he had spoken with Mrs. S. and then with the two of them together.

Mr. and Mrs. S. had agreed that since they could not decide, they would put the matter before Śrīmatī Rādhārāṇī Herself. Mrs. S. had asked Kṣīrodakaśāyī to take two slips of paper and to write *yes* on one and *no* on the other. These she had folded and placed before the family Deity of Rādhā-Kṛṣṇa. She had then asked Kṣīrodakaśāyī to pick one of the papers. Kṣīrodakaśāyī had done so, and in the presence of Mr. and Mrs. S. and Rādhā and Kṛṣṇa, he had opened the piece of paper on which was written the word yes.

When Prabhupāda had heard the news, he had been joyous.

> I am especially pleased upon you that you have secured the S. land for Krsna. Now let us cooperate to build up a wonderful center there in Vrndavana.

In March 1972 Prabhupāda returned to Vṛndāvana to sign the deed with Mr. S. and to perform the ground-breaking ceremony. With permission from the *gosvāmīs* at the Rādhā-Dāmodara temple, he arranged for quarters for his disciples so they would have a place to reside while the temple at Ramaṇa-reti was under construction.

Yamunā: *It just so happened that on the morning that the* gosvāmīs *were to sign an agreement with Prabhupāda for use of the rooms at Rādhā-Dāmodara, the electricity went out. Prabhupāda's secretary had only an electric typewriter, so I reminded Prabhupāda that I was trained in writing calligraphy. I had my writing pens with me, so immediately Prabhupāda drafted the writing that he wanted, and I took it into another room, sat down, and hand-lettered a contract with gold embossing on all the capitals. Within fifteen minutes we presented it to Śrīla Prabhupāda.*

Before the gosvāmīs, *Prabhupāda held up the document with pleasure and said, "Just see, my disciples are expert in everything." Now the devotees would be allowed to reside above his rooms at Rādhā-Dāmodara temple, and they would also have access to his rooms for cleaning. Prabhupāda felt it was a grand occasion that there was something in writing for the preservation of his rooms in the Rādhā-Dāmodara temple.*

To close the transaction for the land in Ramaṇa-reti, Prabhupāda and Mr. S. met at the Magistrate's Court in Mathurā. In the presence of lawyers they completed the formalities. Prabhupāda saw it as Kṛṣṇa's grace that he had acquired a good plot of land in Vṛndāvana, and writing to his G.B.C. secretaries in America, he asked them to send as many men as possible to help in the new project. He described his intentions "for raising up a very excellent center, to revive the spiritual life for Vrndavana on behalf of Rupa and Jiva Goswamis."

Prabhupāda told Kṣīrodakaśāyī, "I want on this occasion huge *prasādam* should be prepared, and every man in Vṛndāvana should be invited and take *prasādam.*" Two days later, with a hundred people attending, Prabhupāda held the cornerstone-laying ceremony at Ramaṇa-reti. Again he descended into the ceremonial pit and placed the Deity of Ānanta, on whose head the temple would rest.

But late that night the land was attacked. An elderly Indian widow, with local fame as a *sādhu*, became angry that Mr. S. had not given her the land, which she had several times requested. During the night she sent *guṇḍās* to dismantle the brick foundation of the ceremonial cornerstone and to desecrate the pit, which had just that day been filled with flowers and religious objects. The *guṇḍās* dug open the hole, threw garbage into it, and stole the "Posted" sign announcing the land's new ownership.

Prabhupāda was in his room at the Rādhā-Dāmodara temple when he heard what had happened. He became angry and told his disciples to show the deed to the police. That night several policemen guarded the land, and when the hired *guṇḍās* came again, the police accosted them and warned that if they caused any more trouble they would be arrested. And that was the end of that.

Prabhupāda had several times said that by becoming a devotee, one gains many enemies. The incident also served to confirm Prabhupāda's conviction that ISKCON's taking possession of the land should be followed as quickly as possible by construction of a temple. They should at least encircle the land with a fence, build small huts, and live on the land while preparing for temple construction.

Tejās: *"This will be the Kṛṣṇa-Balarāma temple," Prabhupāda said. We didn't really know what was going on. We all thought it was so far away. It was really the boondocks, Ramaṇa-reti. Nobody was out there. It was such an isolated place, and there were lots of dacoits living out there. We thought, "If we're going to have a temple out here, no one will ever come." But Prabhupāda said, "Wherever there is Kṛṣṇa, everyone will come."*

Prabhupāda's secretary, Śyāmasundara, wrote to a Godbrother about the newly acquired Vṛndāvana property.

> Earlier in the day, before breakfast, Prabhupada sewed up the 4,800 sq. yd. gift plot in Raman Reti where Krishna used to sport with Friends in the forest, about 10 minutes walk from Radha-Damodara. Prabhupada surveyed the land (with the rope from his mosquito-net), bargained-for, drew plans for, drew up the deed for, went to Mathura magistrate's court for and signed, sealed, and delivered in an instant.

> Prabhupada has asked me to request you that AT LEAST FIFTY (50) MEN FROM THE U.S. MUST COME TO INDIA IMMEDIATELY!!! At last we have got a solid programme in India: Huge projects at Mayapur, Vrindaban and Bombay. All the lands are acquired, arrangements made, and everything by Prabhupada. But only a few of us men are here to struggle with an immense task—the biggest by far within the Society, of developing these three places, and believe me these three projects are more dear to Prabhupada than any yet contemplated.

* * *

In the month while Prabhupāda was away from Bombay (he had left on February 10) the payment of fifty thousand rupees was duly made. Slowly at first, a few devotees moved to the Juhu land, living in a tent. At night the rats and mosquitoes would disturb the devotees' sleep. While attempting to clear the overgrown weeds, they came upon empty liquor bottles and overflowing sewage. Without Prabhupāda present, their resolution grew weak.

But then Brahmānanda Swami returned from Calcutta, where he had been with Śrīla Prabhupāda. Brahmānanda Swami was inspired, and he gave the Bombay devotees new impetus. They would have to clear the land and raise a *paṇḍāl* right away. Brahmānanda Swami had never put on a *paṇḍāl* program before, but he hired a contractor to build several *chātāi* (palm frond) houses for the devotees and a festival tent. Even before the construction could begin, however, the devotees would have to thoroughly clear the land.

Mr. Sethi, a neighbor and life member, hired a work crew to cut down the weeds and vegetation, and several life members and friends in Bombay also came forward to assist. Mr. N. offered to help by sending one of his assistants, Mr. Matar, to organize the hired laborers in clearing the fields. The devotees also worked in preparation for Prabhupāda's return.

Śrī Śrī Rādhā-Rāsavihārī arrived at Hare Krishna Land in a taxi, riding across the laps of several devotees. They had moved before, and this time Their residence was a tent. They had first come to be with the devotees of Bombay during the *paṇḍāl* program at Cross Maidan in downtown Bombay. On that occasion there had been a procession to Chowpatti Beach, and when the devotees had arrived, Rādhā-Rāsavihārī, beautifully dressed and decorated and installed in an ornate palanquin, had been awaiting them. Kṛṣṇa was white marble and held a silver flute; Rādhārāṇī's right hand, palm forward, extended a benediction. They were beautiful.

After Their first appearance at Chowpatti, Rādhā-Rāsavihārī had moved to the Akash Ganga Building, where gradually the devotees had established a decent standard of Deity worship. When Prabhupāda had left orders that Rādhā-Rāsavihārī should move to Juhu as soon as the down payment was made, some of the devotees had questioned him: Why should the Deity move before the facilities were proper? Shouldn't they wait until the temple was built?

"Once the Deity is installed on a piece of property," Prabhupāda had replied, "no one will remove Them."

More than anyone else, Prabhupāda was aware of the proper worship to be offered to Rādhā-Rāsavihārī, but his emphasis now was on securing the land. How else, he reasoned, could he eventually give Rādhā-Rāsavihārī a royal throne and temple unless They Themselves first established Their right of proprietorship by taking up residence at Hare Kṛṣṇa Land? The arrival of Rādhā-Rāsavihārī at Juhu also meant increased difficulties for the devotees, who now had to struggle to maintain the morning *pūjā* and cook six daily offerings in the meager kitchen. Even Rādhā-Rāsavihārī's tent was insubstantial and swayed in the wind.

Śrīla Prabhupāda, however, saw the move as a necessary, transcendental tactic. He felt certain that everyone involved—himself, the owners of the land, the Bombay municipality—would accept that the land belonged to Kṛṣṇa, since Kṛṣṇa was already residing there. And because he was asking Lord Kṛṣṇa Himself to accept these inconveniences, he prayed to the Deity, "My dear Sir, please remain here, and I shall build a beautiful temple for You."

By the time Prabhupāda returned to Bombay, Rādhā-Rāsavihārī were installed on the stage of the festival *paṇḍāl.* Attendance at the festival was not as great as it would have been in downtown Bombay—no more than five hundred people came a night—but Prabhupāda was satisfied. This festival was on their own property, and this was only the beginning.

Every evening Prabhupāda lectured at the *paṇḍāl* and attended the *kīrtana* and *ārati* before Rādhā-Rāsavihārī. Pañcadraviḍa Swami had collected donations of five tons of *dāl,* rice, and flour, and the devotees were regularly cooking enough *kicharī* to serve 125 people free *prasādam* daily. In the evening Prabhupāda himself would give out *hālavā* from the Deities' plate, and the crowd, including well-to-do businessmen and their wives, would press forward to receive the *prasādam*. Prabhupāda liked the festival so much that he told the devotees to arrange to keep the tent for a perpetual festival.

Prabhupāda lived on the land in a tent, just like the other devotees, until a Mr. Acharya, one of the more favorable tenants living in the back of the property, invited him to stay at his home.

Within a few days of his arrival at Juhu, Prabhupāda was ready to hold the ground-breaking and cornerstone-laying ceremony—another tactic for securing possession of the land. But it was more than a tactic, as he wanted a temple constructed as soon as possible. Rādhā-Rāsavihārī should not remain standing in a tent but should be protected by a silver and teakwood *siṁhāsana* on a marble altar. They should be surrounded by deities of the two *gopīs* Lalitā and Viśākhā, and Their temple should have marble domes more than a hundred feet high. Thousands should come daily for *darśana* and *prasādam*.

One morning, in the midst of the festival activities, the devotees of Hare Krishna Land joined Prabhupāda in a simple cornerstone-laying ceremony. They had dug a deep ceremonial pit and surrounded it with bricks. Prabhupāda descended and placed the Deity of Śeṣa. Then, sitting on a simple platform, Prabhupāda accompanied the *kīrtana* by playing a brass gong, while one by one the devotees came before him and threw dirt into the pit, filling it, while smoke rose from the sacrificial fire.

Prabhupāda was outraged that Brahmānanda Swami had agreed to pay the contractors forty thousand rupees for the *paṇḍāl* construction. It was the same old thing—the foolish Western disciples getting cheated. Prabhupāda refused to pay; four thousand rupees should be more than enough. When the contractors came to see him, he told them that he had little money and that they would have to be satisfied with four thousand rupees. They protested, but Prabhupāda became angry and insisted, "Accept it. You are making five hundred percent profit!"

"As soon as they see us," Prabhupāda said later, "they say, 'These Americans, they have got money!' Our work is going on in India, but as soon as money is being spent, fifty percent is being spoiled because you Americans are inexperienced. What can be done? The Indians want your money, and they cheat like anything."

During the *paṇḍāl* festival the tenement neighbors had become disturbed by *kīrtana*s over the loudspeaker. They were already disturbed that their landlord, Mr. N., was slow to repair the buildings and would sometimes let them go a full week without water before fixing the plumbing. Being suddenly forced to live with more than twenty American devotees only exacerbated their dissatisfaction. Some of the neighbors were converted Christians and unsympathetic to Vaiṣṇavism; they even feared their children might again be converted to Hinduism. Some tenants claimed the devotees were infringing on their privacy, some criticized the devotees for arguing among themselves, and others criticized that the unmarried men and women were living in close proximity—even though in separate quarters.

A few of the neighbors, however, could see that the Western Vaiṣṇavas were struggling to sincerely worship Rādhā and Kṛṣṇa. None of the tenants criticized Prabhupāda, however, so when he was present, he was able to pacify them and resolve any disagreements. But Prabhupāda knew that after he left, the situation could easily become volatile.

Prabhupāda was planning an extensive world tour, traveling eastward to Australia, Japan, Hawaii, the U.S., and perhaps Mexico and Europe. It might be as long as half a year before he would return to India, and he wanted things to progress smoothly in Bombay without him.

A few days before Prabhupāda's departure, Madhudviṣa Swami complained, "I'm not feeling very enthusiastic here. I think I need a change." Prabhupāda asked him where he wanted to go, and Madhudviṣa replied that he was thinking of Australia. Prabhupāda said, "Yes, I am going there. You also come." Brahmānanda Swami told Prabhupāda that the preaching was deteriorating in Nairobi in his absence, and Prabhupāda agreed that he should return to his duties there.

Again, Prabhupāda had to choose a new Bombay manager, and this time he chose Girirāja, a young *brahmacārī* and leading preacher in making ISKCON life members. Prabhupāda reasoned that since the essence of management was to collect donations and make life members, and since Girirāja was expert at that, then even though he was young and otherwise inexperienced, he had the most important qualifications. Prabhupāda had already found Girirāja to be simple and submissively dedicated to helping him develop Hare Krishna Land.

Girirāja: *Śrīla Prabhupāda said, "You will do, Girirāja?" So I said, "Yes, Śrīla Prabhupāda, whatever you say." I wasn't actually very happy about it, but I understood that one should be surrendered to the spiritual master and whatever he said, one should do. So I accepted. Prabhupāda said that good management meant that whatever needs doing, you do it—that's all. Later I went in to see Śrīla Prabhupāda, and he was sitting behind his desk. He said, "Now the full responsibility is on you." I winced when he said that, because I wasn't used to taking responsibility.*

During Prabhupāda's stay in Bombay, Hans Kielman, a young architect from Holland, had come to hear the lectures and had become interested in Kṛṣṇa consciousness. Prabhupāda convinced Hans to become a devotee and to help build the Hare Kṛṣṇa city in Bombay. Under Prabhupāda's direction, Hans at once began to make architectural drawings for the buildings.

Hans: *Prabhupāda said, "Now you listen carefully. Lord Kṛṣṇa has sent you here. You must design these temples for Him. You must do these very sincerely and not be afraid." I was completely surrendered. That moment was really ecstasy for me. He had a pile of photographs on his desk, and he gave them to me and said, "Look at this." I looked at the pictures, and they were photographs of the new Govindajī temple in Vṛndāvana. He said, "I want you to make a design like this." So I asked him, "How big, Śrīla Prabhupāda?" He gave me a piece of typing paper and said I should draw on this paper. Then he gave me the photographs and a pencil and a ruler. He took me to the next room and told me to sit down at the table. Pradyumna was there with all his Sanskrit books, Śyāmasundara was there typing the letters, and suddenly I was in between, making the drawings.*

Prabhupāda said Girirāja and the others would have to collect sixty-four lakhs of rupees for the construction. The devotees had no idea how they would raise even a fraction of that amount, but Prabhupāda gave them some ideas. He talked to them about enlisting the support of influential men by using the *bheṅt-nāma* system, whereby a person purchases the use of a guest room for life. And there were other ways.

But the immediate step was to get the land. They had possession of the land, but before building they should have the deed. Since Mr. N. was already overdue in delivering the deed, Prabhupāda told Girirāja to press him to comply with the written agreement and deliver the deed at once.

In Prabhupāda's last lecture in Bombay, he spoke about the six Gosvāmīs of Vṛndāvana and the bittersweet ecstasy of their hankering to be with Kṛṣṇa. Some of Prabhupāda's disciples took it that Prabhupāda was speaking about this because he was himself going to be leaving for a long time.

At the airport the next day there was a joyful farewell, as Prabhupāda waited for his flight to Australia. Sitting in the VIP lounge surrounded by devotees, Prabhupāda watched Madhudviṣa Swami lead an ecstatic *kīrtana*. "If you go on having *kīrtana*s like this," Prabhupāda told the devotees, "our Bombay project will be successful." When Prabhupāda saw Mrs. N. had come, he exclaimed, "Oh, Mrs. N., you are also here! You are becoming one of us."

* * *

Prabhupāda had the extraordinary ability to bring a spiritual vision into physical reality, to change a part of the material world into spiritual energy so that even a common man could perceive the spiritual reality. This was Prabhupāda's constant effort. Often a transcendentalist hesitates to deal with the material world, fearing he may become spiritually weakened. The Vedic injunctions, therefore, warn the transcendentalist to avoid associating with money and materialistic persons. But Prabhupāda, following the principles taught by Śrīla Rūpa Gosvāmī, saw that everything material had the potential of being used in the service of Kṛṣṇa and thus of regaining its spiritual nature. Following this principle, an expert devotee, although apparently acting within the material sphere, could remain always in touch with the spiritual energy. For such a devotee, nothing was material.

In the Vedic scriptures the great devotee Nārada Muni, because of his ability to convert materialistic men into devotees, is referred to as *cintāmaṇi,* touchstone. Just as *cintāmaṇi* is said to convert iron into gold, so Nārada could transform a beastlike hunter into a pure Vaiṣṇava. And as Nārada is glorified in the *Vedas* for accomplishing such feats in bygone ages, so Śrīla Prabhupāda is a similarly potent touchstone in the present age. Again and again he showed by his straightforward application of Kṛṣṇa consciousness that he could change a materialist into a completely renounced, active devotee of the Lord. And now, after recruiting a number of devotees from *māyā's* camp, he wanted to engage them in transforming as much as possible of the material world into living spirit. By his transcendental, visionary words, he was attempting to convert stone and human energy into glorious, spiritual temples.

While ambitious materialists sometimes criticize transcendentalists as unproductive, Prabhupāda, because of his constant activity, could never be so accused. Rather, people would criticize him as being a capitalist in the dress of a *sannyāsī*. But such criticism never deterred Prabhupāda; he was carrying out the desires of the previous *ācāryas*. He had written this conclusion in his *Śrīmad-Bhāgavatam* even before coming to America in 1965.

> Therefore, all the sages and devotees of the Lord have recommended that the subject matter of art, science, philosophy, physics, chemistry, psychology and all other branches of knowledge should be wholely and solely applied in the service of the Lord.

Prabhupāda wanted to convert significant portions of the material world into the spiritual world. In attempting to construct a spiritual city in Juhu, he realized he was launching a major attack against *māyā*. Within a few months so many complications and headaches had already disturbed his plans, and more would come; the battle was just beginning.

Sometimes Prabhupāda's disciples found the work to be draining and stressful; they would become bewildered. They had come to spiritual life for bliss, not for anxiety. Prabhupāda's presence and his constant encouragement helped them remain steadfast. He knew that once they tasted the nectar of selfless dedication to Kṛṣṇa, they would never accept anything lesser. He would encourage them, reminding them of the words of spiritual predecessors like Bhaktivinoda Ṭhākura, who had said, "Difficulties undertaken in the course of Your devotional service I will consider the greatest happiness."

CHAPTER FOUR

Prabhupāda traveled with three disciples: Śyāmasundara as his secretary, Pradyumna as his servant and Sanskrit editor, and Nanda-kumāra as his cook. The first stop was Singapore, where, without explanation, immigration authorities refused Prabhupāda entry into the country. Sympathetic Indians in Singapore had arranged for Prabhupāda to lecture and had even mailed hundreds of invitations, but Śrīla Prabhupāda, disappointed and feeling ill, had to continue the twelve-hour flight to Sydney.

April 1, 1972

Prabhupāda planned to stay a few days in Sydney before going on to Melbourne. Although the Kṛṣṇa consciousness movement was young in Australia, Prabhupāda saw positive signs: devotees to initiate, TV and radio appearances, and an interested crowd at his morning lectures in the temple.

This was only his second visit to Australia. On his first visit, almost a year ago, he had installed the Deities Rādhā-Gopīnātha and had prayed to Them, "Now I am leaving You in the hands of the *mlecchas*. I cannot take the responsibility. You please guide these boys and girls and give them the intelligence to worship You very nicely." Now, on returning and seeing the Deities beautifully dressed and well cared for, he felt happy. After five busy days of preaching he flew on to Melbourne.

Upananda: *In Melbourne Prabhupāda spoke at the Town Hall, and all the Melbourne hippies came. There was a man there called the Wizard. He used to be a professor at the university, but he resigned his post so he could carry out his shenanigans. He was very intellectual. He was dressed in a black cape and leotard, and he got up as soon as Śrīla Prabhupāda asked for questions. He had a group of his own followers. First he spoke very respectfully. "Excuse me, Your Divine Grace. I've been listening to your lecture, but I have one thing I would like to say in this regard. I believe that I am God. I am the center of the universe. And I will prove sometime next year that I am the center of the universe."*

Prabhupāda said, "That's all right. Everybody is thinking like that.

What makes you different?" Actually, the Wizard's whole game was that he wanted to be different—his dress, everything. So Prabhupāda exposed this, exposed him as just another materialistic fool. Everybody started laughing and clapping.

Auckland
April 14, 1972

The devotees had just opened a temple in New Zealand a few weeks before Prabhupāda's arrival. Prabhupāda stayed a couple of days and installed Rādhā-Kṛṣṇa Deities.

Bhūrijana: *Prabhupāda installed large marble Deities, but there was only one girl to take care of Them. Prabhupāda was insisting that the Deities should be installed anyway and that They should be taken care of properly. He demanded that They should have many sets of clothes immediately. So some devotees built a temporary wooden altar and put up a curtain for the Deities. The curtains fell down. Everything was going wrong. It was confusing, and everyone was upset.*

So Śrīla Prabhupāda just took over. He said, "Put this here. Put that back up there. Do this. Do that." He completely took command of the whole situation. The devotees put the curtains back, and Prabhupāda said, "Get rid of this vyāsāsana.*" And they took the* vyāsāsana *out, because it was so big and the room was so small that there was no room for the people. Prabhupāda just put a mat on the floor and sat down on that.*

Prabhupāda visited for one night in Hong Kong, where he lectured at a program arranged by Bhūrijana and his wife, Jagattāraṇī.

Bhūrijana: *We had taught the Indian children to sing the prayers to the spiritual master. So we had them sing for Prabhupāda. He looked at me, and he was really pleased. Then he said, "Your wife said there are no interested people, but you have so many students here." I said, "*You *have so many students, Prabhupāda."*

At the end of the lecture Prabhupāda asked if there were any questions, and a little Indian boy raised his hand and asked, "Who started the forest fire?" The boy was thinking of a forest fire mentioned in the Kṛṣṇa *book in Kṛṣṇa's pastime, but all he said was, "Who started the forest fire?" But Prabhupāda took the question in a different way—that this material world is like a blazing forest fire, just like the prayers to the spiritual master had described. So Prabhupāda said, "No one started the forest fire. It starts automatically—just like in the forest, by the rubbing of two bamboos a fire may start. But by chanting Hare Kṛṣṇa we can get out of this forest fire of material life.*''

In Japan the devotees lived in an old farmhouse in the hill country outside Tokyo. Śrīla Prabhupāda stayed in a nearby hotel, installed Rādhā-Kṛṣṇa Deities in the temple, and awarded *sannyāsa* to ISKCON Tokyo's leader, Sudāmā.

Prabhupāda said he knew "the pulse of his disciples.'' Thus he had recently sensed a tendency in his leading managers to be too absorbed in management and not enough in preaching. He had been telling his secretary that G.B.C. men should not simply sit behind their desks and try to centralize power but should become detached, take *sannyāsa*, and travel and preach. With this in mind he had awarded the *sannyāsa* order to two of his G.B.C. secretaries, Tamāla Kṛṣṇa and Sudāmā. Now he advised that they not give up their managerial burden but follow his example of preaching and managing their G.B.C. zones in a renounced spirit.

Śyāmasundara: *Prabhupāda's hotel room had rice paper walls and was very cold. It was like coming back into the northern climate, but without central heating. One day I came to Prabhupāda's room for* maṅgala-ārati, *and I had a blanket wrapped around me. I said, "Are you cold, Prabhupāda?'' I could see he didn't like the cold, but he wasn't going to let that stop him from serving Kṛṣṇa.*

Nanda-kumāra: *At the Sunday feast there were about thirty Japanese people, mostly young, and every single one brought Prabhupāda a flower, put it at his feet, and paid full* daṇḍavats. *They were so respectful. Prabhupāda said that it was a good sign that "these boys and girls are able to honor a saintly person.''*

Bhūrijana: *We had arranged a program in Kobe. Many Indians and Sindhis lived there. It was a long journey out of Tokyo. They put Prabhupāda on the third floor of the house, and there was no elevator. Prabhupāda just put his chin out and walked right up, even though it was a tremendous effort for him.*

The engagement was arranged in such a poor way that on the same speaking program with Prabhupāda was a Māyāvādī sannyāsī. *Prabhupāda wanted to speak first, so he spoke in English. There were quite a few Indians there—about a hundred. Prabhupāda explained very clearly and strongly that Kṛṣṇa is God.*

Then the other sannyāsī *began speaking in Hindi. Prabhupāda was just sitting there with his eyes closed, chanting* japa. *Suddenly he looked at us and said, "Start* kīrtana *immediately." So we got up in the middle of the* sannyāsī's *speaking and started* kīrtana. *Prabhupāda left quickly after the* kīrtana.

When we got back to the room with Prabhupāda, he explained what had happened. He said, "First he was preaching nicely. And then he started explaining pañcopāsana, *about the five different features of the Absolute. And then when he said that the Supreme is ultimately impersonal, I could not tolerate it." Prabhupāda said, "I am like a lion when I am out and a lamb when I am home."*

Prabhupāda had business in Tokyo with his printer, Dai Nippon. He was greatly pleased with the faith Dai Nippon Printing Company placed in him, giving him hundreds of thousands of dollars credit just on his word. One of the Dai Nippon executives even approached him submissively, inquiring about whether his son who had died a year and a half ago had gone to the Buddha.

A young Japanese executive, who translated the older man's questions and Prabhupāda's answers, explained to Prabhupāda, "Since then he has been very religious."

"He was the eldest son?" Prabhupāda asked.

"Twenty years. Youngest son."

The two executives spoke briefly.

"He is asking how he can be relieved from such sadness when his son has died."

"Oh, yes," Prabhupāda said. "The point is that the success of everything depends on how Kṛṣṇa is satisfied. That I have explained." He related the example of Sāndīpani Muni, the spiritual master of Kṛṣṇa and Balarāma. Sāndīpani Muni's son had died, and he requested his two students, "My dear boys, I lost my child very young. If You kindly bring him, then I will be very much pleased." So Kṛṣṇa went to the planet of Yamarāja and brought his son back.

"So you try to satisfy Kṛṣṇa, and you will be blessed. Your son will be blessed. You pray to Kṛṣṇa—wherever your son may be, he will be happy. You believe in reincarnation, next birth?"

The young man spoke to the elder executive in Japanese. The older man nodded.

Prabhupāda continued, "Yes. So your son, he must have taken a body somewhere. So if you pray to Kṛṣṇa, your son will be happy. He will benefit."

When Prabhupāda's G.B.C. secretary for the western United States, Karandhara, arrived in Tokyo to assist in dealing with the Dai Nippon Printing Company, Prabhupāda talked with him about his new project in Bombay. He also wrote two letters to Girirāja, urging him to begin constructing the Bombay buildings as soon as possible. He wanted Girirāja to model the temple after Jaipur's famous Govindajī temple and erect beside it a modern high-rise hotel. "And then you shall have the perfect Juhu plan." Prabhupāda said Hans (now Surabhi) should finish the drawings and get the city council's approval by June so that they could begin the foundation before the monsoon. "I do not think that it is possible," Prabhupāda wrote, "but if you can try for it that will be nice."

Hawaii
May 6, 1972

During Prabhupāda's week-long stay in Honolulu, he installed the five Deities of the Pañca-tattva: Lord Caitanya, Lord Nityānanda, Śrī Advaita, Śrī Gadādhara, and Śrī Śrīvāsa. He also lectured on *yoga* at a local *yoga*-meditation center. During his morning walks on the beach, he spoke about the fallacies of Darwinism. Waikiki Beach, he commented, was not as beautiful as Juhu.

Nanda-kumāra: *At that time all the devotees in Hawaii were wearing sleeveless T-shirts and bright colors, and they had really big* śikhās *hanging down very long. Prabhupāda said, "Gaudiya Vaiṣṇava* śikhā *is an inch and a half across—no bigger. Bigger* śikhās *means another* sampradāya. *And they have to be knotted." So I told everyone that, and they came back all bright and shiny with saffron shirts and proper* śikhās.

Govinda dāsī: *Prabhupāda stayed at a big house on the Makapu side of Oahu, right on the ocean—a very pleasant place. In the morning Prabhupāda would walk on the beach, and when he would return from his walk, he would sit down on a wooden bench on a little rock patio. We would all sit around, and he would give a little morning lecture. Later he would walk around and around in his room, chanting.*

One evening I went in while he was chanting, and he said, "Sixteen rounds finished today?" and I said, "Yes, Śrīla Prabhupāda, I am on my sixteenth round now." He said, "That is good."

Prabhupāda was also thinking a lot about his Bombay center, and he asked me to do an architectural rendering of his idea for the Bombay buildings. Fortunately, an architect friend drew it up very nicely, and Prabhupāda was pleased with it.

Prabhupāda had received a letter from a French disciple, Mandakinī-devī dāsī, who was going to join a Russian boy in the Soviet Union. She was going there to marry him and assist him in propagating Kṛṣṇa consciousness. When Prabhupāda read this letter, he smiled in ecstasy. The thought of the Kṛṣṇa consciousness movement increasing in Russia gave him great joy.

Then he turned to Govinda dāsī and said, "Preach while you are young. When you are old, retire to Vṛndāvana and chant Hare Kṛṣṇa. Therefore, these centers in India are being built. But you cannot retire unless you have preached sufficiently. The mind will agitate. If you have preached, you can retire and chant Hare Kṛṣṇa—so preach as much as possible."

Although sometimes Prabhupāda could spend only a day or even only a moment with an individual devotee, that brief association would leave a permanent inspiration. The devotees would realize that although Prabhupāda had touched them and given them guidance in a way that made these the most important moments in their lives, Prabhupāda was also beyond the moment and the place that he shared with them and was contemplating deeper issues and praying to Kṛṣṇa with an intensity that they could not yet understand.

Prabhupāda received a letter in Hawaii from Girirāja that made him doubt his Bombay manager's abilities to deal with the clever Mr. N. Girirāja had reported matter-of-factly that he had just paid 7,500 rupees to Mr. N., and Prabhupāda wrote back, "On what account is that paid?" Girirāja had intended it to be an installment toward the agreed two lakhs per year that they were supposed to pay Mr. N.—*after* they had received the deed. But why should they be unnecessarily paying Mr. N., since they still had no deed? Prabhupāda began to worry about his Hare Krishna Land.

Time and time again his thinking turned to Bombay, Vṛndāvana, and Māyāpur, but he did not talk much about the problems. Rather, the devotees and nondevotees in each place he visited got the full blessings of his attention. While lecturing on *Śrīmad-Bhāgavatam*, he was in full concentration, and when he spoke privately, cultivating a guest or guiding an individual disciple, he fully gave himself. That he took responsibility for many persons and worldwide matters and did it all so graciously, always appearing before his devotees each morning on a walk or in the temple as fresh as a morning-blooming lotus flower, was the expert nature of his devotional service to Kṛṣṇa. He was open and simple, with a motive so pure that anyone could see it, and yet he was also grave beyond anyone's vision. He served Kṛṣṇa simply in each time and place, whether riding the hotel elevator with his two disciples in Hong Kong, or curiously noting the details of Japanese culture, or walking on the beach beneath a Hawaiian sky.

* * *

Los Angeles
May 18, 1972

Word had spread that Śrīla Prabhupāda wanted G.B.C. secretaries to get out from behind their desks and preach, and four American G.B.C. men, eager to become *sannyāsīs*, were waiting when Śrīla Prabhupāda arrived in Los Angeles.

Satsvarūpa: *Prabhupāda said that because we were taking* sannyāsa *in the prime of youth, we had ample opportunity to do much more than he. He said he had taken* sannyāsa *at the fag end of life but that "a little is better than nothing." Everyone laughed at the thought that we could do more than Prabhupāda. One by one we went to the* vyāsāsana, *and Prabhupāda gave us our* tridaṇḍas *and said, "Now preach, preach, preach."*

Immediately afterward, Prabhupāda had us up in his room. We asked him if there were any special instructions. He said there were two restrictions in sannyāsa *life. One was that when meeting a rich man and seeing his opulent wealth we must not think, "Oh, I have given up everything, but I wish I could enjoy these things." And the other restriction was that when we see a beautiful woman we must not think, "I had a beautiful wife, and now this beautiful woman is here. I could enjoy her." In other words, do not have any regrets about having taken* sannyāsa.

Jagadīśa: *Prabhupāda had all the G.B.C. men come to Los Angeles, where some of them took* sannyāsa, *and we discussed reapportioning preaching zones. We had one special meeting with Prabhupāda. All the*

G.B.C. men were sitting there in the room, and Prabhupāda looked us all over. He said, "Are you all convinced?" We just sat there. Nobody said anything for about two minutes. It was one of the heaviest moments of my life—Prabhupāda challenging us: "Are you convinced? Are you sincere?"

As Prabhupāda spoke, his G.B.C. disciples listened intently. "As far as I am concerned," he said, "I am convinced. Therefore I am pushing on. It is a fact. I am pushing on because it is fact, not fiction. That much I am personally convinced. Whenever someone says, 'You believe,' I say, 'No, I do not *believe.* It is *fact.*' So you must spread your conviction by your literature, arguments, preaching, facing opposing elements. But are you convinced? If you are not convinced, then it is not good for me. The first thing is enthusiasm. Don't be dead. You have to work more than me. Anyone who has life, he can preach.

"So the local president and treasurer of the temple will manage. The G.B.C. can supervise that things are going on. But the first management is that each and every member is chanting sixteen rounds and following the regulations. Otherwise, that is our spiritual strength.

"Now it is in your hands. That was my plan—to give it to the Americans. But you have to be spiritually strong. If superficially you want to be managers, it won't be good. And simply touring is not required. By traveling you have to do something substantial to increase the society. At the time of Lenin, he had just a few men, and he took over the entire country. It is up to you to spread God consciousness. Don't be stagnant. Go and preach. Your duty is to inform them, 'My dear American brothers, you have so much wealth and pleasure. Use it for Kṛṣṇa. If not, it will be degradation.' "

Śrīla Prabhupāda met with many U.S. ISKCON leaders in Los Angeles and saw the wide array of Kṛṣṇa conscious activities in his Western world headquarters. He heard a new recording of Kṛṣṇa *bhajanas*, performed with guitars and other Western instruments, produced at the devotees' own Golden Avatar studio, and he approved it, saying, "This is better than George Harrison." He visited the art studio, where the devotees were painting illustrations for his books, and he made suggestions.

Anaṅga-mañjarī: *Prabhupāda was going around looking at all the different temple offices. In one office Karandhara was showing Prabhupāda a new computer. "Prabhupāda," he said, "all we have to do is type the words Rūpa Gosvāmī, and then it will automatically write everything you have ever said or written about Rūpa Gosvāmī." Prabhupāda had been looking at the computer without showing much interest. But when Karandhara said the name Rūpa Gosvāmī, Prabhupāda raised his eyebrows and said, "Oh? Yes, everything can be used in Kṛṣṇa's service."*

Then we walked out of that office and went to the telex machine. Prabhupāda sat before it in the chair, and everyone stood around him while Karandhara explained what the machine did. "It can write a message all the way to New York, and they can send a message back immediately, Śrīla Prabhupāda." So Karandhara typed on the telex machine, "Hare Kṛṣṇa. All glories to Śrīla Prabhupāda. Please respond."

There was no answer, so he typed it out again, and again there was no answer. So he typed it out again, and this time he typed out, "All glories to Śrīla Prabhupāda. Śrīla Prabhupāda is sitting right next to the telex machine. Please respond."

All of a sudden the machine started typing out a reply, and Prabhupāda was sitting there watching it. The type read, "Dear Śrīla Prabhupāda, please accept our most humble obeisances at your lotus feet. We will be very eager to see Your Divine Grace in three days in New York." Śrīla Prabhupāda spoke out, "Jaya! Haribol!" The message from New York was signed by many devotees, and Prabhupāda just smiled and said, "This is very nice."

At this time, distribution of Prabhupāda's books by his disciples was taking on a new dimension in America, and Prabhupāda heard the latest reports. From the beginning of his preaching in the West he had stressed printing and distributing his books as the most important method of preaching Kṛṣṇa consciousness. He said his spiritual master had told him to print and distribute books and that he was following "blindly." Bhaktisiddhānta Sarasvatī had been pleased if a disciple distributed even only a few copies of his magazine.

In the beginning years of ISKCON Śrīla Prabhupāda had also been pleased when his disciples had distributed a few hundred copies of *Back to Godhead* each month. Gradually his will for increasing the distribution of transcendental literature had manifested through certain devotees. In Los Angeles in 1968, Tamāla Kṛṣṇa had daily taken a large *kīrtana* party downtown. The party, in addition to chanting and dancing, had circulated among the crowd and distributed *Back to Godhead* magazines, as many as a hundred in a single day. When Prabhupāda had heard these reports, he had felt encouraged and had asked for the devotees to increase.

Prabhupāda saw book distribution not only as the best method of preaching but also as a fair means of income. In India the *brahmacārīs* in the traditional *gurukula* system would beg from door to door, but in the West such a practice would not be respected. "But every gentleman will give a quarter for *Back to Godhead,*" Prabhupāda had said.

Even as Prabhupāda turned more toward India and his projects there, he continued to encourage his disciples, especially in the West, to distribute his books: "Please increase your program of distribution to the public as well as trying to place our books and magazines in the libraries. I am simply interested in the book distribution."

To the devotees in New York he had written in 1971,

> I'm especially pleased to hear that your distribution of books and magazines has increased. Go on in this way, increasing more and more. Each time someone reads some solid information about Krishna his life becomes changed in some way. These literatures are the solid ground upon which our preaching stands, so I want that they should be available to everyone, as many as possible. So please try for this.

To the devotees in Australia he wrote,

> The best news is that you are increasing nicely the distribution of my books and literature. This is the best activity, to distribute solid information about Krishna. Our preaching stands solid on these books. No other movement has such vast background of authority.

And to the devotees of Africa Prabhupāda wrote,

> Distribution of books and magazines is our most important activity. Without books, our preaching has no solid basis. Especially the Africans want our books.

Śrīla Prabhupāda said that if there were ample books, then everything else in ISKCON would succeed.

> Practically, our Society is built on books. One book is not very impressive. Still, a blind uncle is better than no uncle at all, so it is very nice that one book has appeared, and that BTG is appearing at least several issues in other languages. But now try to produce at least four or five new books per year in several languages, plus regularly BTG every month . . . apply yourself fully to this very great responsibility of producing numerous books in foreign languages.

Back in 1968, when ten thousand copies of *Teachings of Lord Caitanya* had arrived at the temple in New York, Brahmānanda Swami had wondered how they would ever distribute so many hardbound books on the lofty philosophy of Lord Caitanya. But in 1970, with the publication of another book, *Kṛṣṇa, the Supreme Personality of Godhead,* some of the devotees in San Francisco had begun to go door to door, person to person, and sell the books. And not only one or two books, but twenty, thirty, even forty a day. The enthusiasm had spread as devotees in other temples had begun to sell increasing numbers of Śrīla Prabhupāda's books. Next, the young men had begun traveling in vans, going out all day, day after day, to discover the greatest ecstasy of distributing Prabhupāda's books.

Then a competition had started. Keśava's boasts that the devotees in San Francisco were the best had drawn challenges from the devotees in Los Angeles, New York, Denver, and Dallas. A "*saṅkīrtana* fever" had begun. And at the center was Śrīla Prabhupāda, assuring that unquestionably book distribution had the topmost priority of all his missionary activities.

Prabhupāda also stressed that all the devotees should regularly study his books. The books were not only for the public; the devotees must *read* them and *know* them. Or else how could they preach? In the Los Angeles temple room Prabhupāda would have the devotees take part in pronouncing and chanting responsively the daily Sanskrit verse from *Śrīmad-Bhāgavatam.* Then individual devotees would take turns chanting the verse alone, while the other devotees would again respond collectively.

Hṛdayānanda Goswami: *When Prabhupāda came to Los Angeles in 1972, he started the* Bhāgavatam *class where everyone chanted the Sanskrit. One effect was that devotees became more grave, a little more civilized. Just at that time things were a little wild in America. The* saṅkīrtana *parties were doing so many wild things, staying out all hours of the night, sleeping anywhere, eating anything. Previously the temples had been a little sedate, and actually, even a little dry, because the devotees weren't giving out many books. And then, when the* saṅkīrtana *got a little heavy, it was almost like a rodeo consciousness, this wild* saṅkīrtana*—like bronco busting. But Prabhupāda came and introduced the chanting of Sanskrit* mantras *word for word, and the devotees submitted to a more grave and formal program.*

On the first of June Śrīla Prabhupāda left Los Angeles for Mexico City. He said he would return in a few weeks.

* * *

Prabhupāda conducted an intensive three-day lecture campaign in Mexico City, speaking at the National University of Mexico, the Masonic Lodge, and the Theosophical Society, and appearing on a television show with some thirty million viewers. He also held initiations at the temple on two consecutive days. Mexico was similar to India, he said, with pious people and a tropical climate. Even when he walked early in the morning in Chapultepec Park, many people followed him back to the temple. They recognized him as a saint and wanted his benediction.

Cit-sukhānanda: *On Sunday afternoon there were more than five hundred people in the temple room. After the lecture Śrīla Prabhupāda went back to his room alone, and there was a big* kīrtana *with five to six hundred people chanting, "Jaya Prabhupāda! Jaya Prabhupāda! Jaya Prabhupāda! Prabhupāda! Prabhupāda! Prabhupāda!" They became very, very ecstatic, and it seemed like the temple walls were going to come down. I was in Śrīla Prabhupāda's room, and he said, "What is this?* Kīrtana? *They are making so much noise."*

I said, "They are chanting your name." And I went down to see what was going on. And all the people were waiting to come into Prabhupāda's room. It was like they wanted to charge up to Prabhupāda's room to be able to see him. They kept yelling his name, "Prabhupāda! Prabhupāda!" So I came up to Śrīla Prabhupāda. "Prabhupāda, they want to see you." And Śrīla Prabhupāda said, "Well, let them come."

So I immediately arranged that people could come in. He had two doors in his room, and they were coming in through one door on the left side and leaving through the door on the right. One by one, in a line, they just filtered through like a great parade, coming and offering different words to Śrīla Prabhupāda. Most of the people were saying in Spanish, "Your Divine Grace, Your Holiness, please bless me. Give me your benediction." Everyone was praying for his benediction. And as the people would come in, they would bow down. Everyone was extremely submissive, and there were many people with tears in their eyes to see the great saint Śrīla Prabhupāda. And they said to Śrīla Prabhupāda, "Please give me your blessings."

Prabhupāda asked me, "What are they saying?" And I said, "Give me one blessing, one benediction."

So he had his hand in his bead bag, and with his finger outside his bead bag he would point to them and say, "Hare Kṛṣṇa." And they were all very happy.

Prabhupāda also traveled to Cuernavaca, where he lectured out-of-doors at the city plaza before a crowd of thousands. The audience sat patiently and heard his words translated into Spanish.

Cit-sukhānanda: *Just then we had turned out our first book,* La Conciencia de Kṛṣṇa Es el Sistema Mas Elevado de Yoga [Kṛṣṇa Consciousness, the Topmost Yoga System], *and Śrīla Prabhupāda, during his lecture at the plaza at Cuernavaca, saw Haihaya dāsa arrive with newly printed copies of this red book,* La Conciencia de Kṛṣṇa Es el Sistema Mas Elevado de Yoga. *Śrīla Prabhupāda looked at him and was very happy to see his book printed. He stopped his lecture and said, "Now you can all take one of these books and read them." And the people actually came up to Śrīla Prabhupāda to get the books. We only brought about fifty copies, but all fifty copies Śrīla Prabhupāda sold personally. The people took the liberty to ask Śrīla Prabhupāda for an autographed book, and he autographed almost all fifty copies.*

After the plaza lecture there was a hotel lecture, and then Śrīla Prabhupāda was supposed to go to a devotee's home in Cuernavaca to take prasādam *and rest. But Śrīla Prabhupāda decided he wanted to return to the temple in Mexico City. He got back around eight P.M., so from eight in the morning until eight that night he had not taken a bite of food, only a little water. We offered him fruit and things, but he didn't want anything.*

When he returned to his room, his eyes were shining and his smile was broad, and he said, "This is the way to be happy. Work all day for Kṛṣṇa." All he wanted was a cup of hot milk with purīs *and a cup of sugar. He pressed the* purīs *into the sugar, and he drank the milk with great joy and happiness. He said, "This is our life, to serve Kṛṣṇa. Work all day for Kṛṣṇa and take a little* prasādam *at night."*

* * *

On returning to Los Angeles, Prabhupāda was again the center of the burgeoning Kṛṣṇa conscious activities there. But again his thoughts turned to Bombay, and he telegrammed Girirāja, instructing him to settle the conveyance immediately.

Girirāja, after receiving Prabhupāda's cable, went to Mr. N., only to learn of a further complication. After Prabhupāda had signed the sales agreement, the Indian government had passed a law obliging Mr. N. to pay a five-lakh gains tax upon executing the conveyance. Mr. N. didn't have five lakhs at present and told Girirāja that ISKCON should pay it, and he would apply it toward the mortgage. But Bombay ISKCON didn't have five lakhs either, so Mr. N. suggested Girirāja take a bank loan or secure funds from ISKCON temples in the U.S. He promised that in the meantime he would not sell the land to anyone else.

Girirāja tried to get a loan from the bank, but he had no security or credit. He turned to some of the life members for help, to see if they could act as guarantors for a loan. But although sympathetic, they could not help him raise the money.

Girirāja also began to doubt Mr. N.'s word. Although naive about legal matters, Girirāja was becoming suspicious of Mr. N.'s character and of his dealings. Talking with life members, Girirāja learned that actually Mr. N. was notorious for illegal business tactics. When previously Mr. N. had signed an agreement with C. Company for the very same land he was now selling to Prabhupāda, the sales agreement had eventually been canceled because C. Company had not gotten permission from the municipality for subdividing plots of land—and one of the conditions of Mr. N.'s sale of the land had been that C. Company get government permission to use the land. According to some of the businessmen with whom Girirāja spoke, Mr. N., through his political connections, had influenced the government against the C. Company.

Mr. N. had *seemed* very helpful, giving the devotees a good price for the land, and even providing workers for clearing it. And Mrs. N. had often attended Prabhupāda's classes. But there also seemed to be many contradictions in Mr. N.'s behavior.

Hearing of these problems by mail, Prabhupāda considered them manageable. If a government tax had been imposed, then the devotees should deal with that and also continue trying for a loan. Certainly Mr. N. was tricky, but Prabhupāda felt ISKCON's position was strong. Girirāja should persist, without becoming confused by Mr. N. Prabhupāda advised Girirāja to approach Mrs. Sumati Morarji and other supporters for financial help.

> It is a unique temple in the world and if you show your wonderful abilities as American and European boys and girls to manage everything superbly, she will not hesitate to entrust you in every way. Therefore, there must always be good will and cooperation amongst

> yourselves for this huge task ahead. I always think of our Juhu place, and I want that it shall be the model for all the world to emulate and respect as the perfect example of a Krishna Conscious community.

Portland, Oregon
June 8, 1972

From Los Angeles Prabhupāda went briefly to Portland, where fifty of his disciples from San Francisco, Seattle, and Vancouver, as well as Portland, had congregated to meet him. From Portland he rode by car to Eugene, where he lectured at a large hall before an audience of mostly hippies.

Every temple in the U.S. wanted Śrīla Prabhupāda, and although Prabhupāda could not visit them all, he remained open to brief visits and public lectures in faraway places. He would sometimes confide to his traveling secretary that his disciples should do this preaching; but then another lecture opportunity would arise, promoted by an enthusiastic group of devotees, and Prabhupāda would surprise everyone by agreeing to go.

After returning to Los Angeles for four days, Prabhupāda then flew to New York for a week and then on to London for two weeks. In London George Harrison and Ravi Shankar visited him several times at the Bury Place temple. When George asked if he should shave his head and try to live like the other devotees, Prabhupāda replied that he should continue to be a singer. "If you tell people to chant Hare Kṛṣṇa," Prabhupāda reminded George, "they will do it."

July 20

From England Prabhupāda went to Paris, where he lectured and performed an outdoor initiation ceremony at the Luxembourg Gardens. Hundreds of people, most of them student radicals from the nearby university, gathered to watch. Śrīla Prabhupāda began his talk, saying, "You French people have a history of being revolutionary, because you are looking for a better way of life." When the words were translated into French, the students cheered and applauded. Śrīla Prabhupāda continued, "Therefore, you should inquire into this Kṛṣṇa consciousness. It is a revolutionary movement for reviving our original God consciousness."

About thirty devotees from Germany had come to Paris, and most of them, along with many devotees from England, Amsterdam, and Paris, received initiation that day at Luxembourg Gardens. In Paris Prabhupāda also attended a successful four-day indoor festival, where he was pleased to lecture and lead *kīrtanas* each night.

July 26

In Amsterdam Prabhupāda installed deities of Lord Jagannātha, Lord Balarāma, and Subhadrā and lectured at Vondelpark before thousands of hippies. One day at Vondelpark a devotee was addressing the crowd when Prabhupāda suddenly told his disciples to stop. "These people are useless," he said. "Just hold *kīrtana*."

Later he wrote to a disciple in the West,

> We are observing here in Europe many, many hippies have become so disgusted with material life, but they are also now so much degraded that they will not hear our philosophy, simply mocking. So our devotees may become very much learned to remove their doubts and become very much fixed up in Krishna consciousness. But so far preaching to the general public, especially the hippie class, it is better not to preach very much philosophy, just somehow or other get them to chant Hare Krishna mantra, and if some of them are curious to learn something, they may purchase one of our books. Only if they chant with us, that will help them.

July 29

At Edinburgh Prabhupāda was greeted by almost a dozen reporters from various newspapers in Scotland.

Kiśora: *Edinburgh is a stuffy, puffed-up, tradition-steeped place, but Prabhupāda was very cordial and humble with the reporters. He was giving them so much credit about how nice the country was and how nice Edinburgh was—what nice buildings we have here—and he was saying, "You have two colleges here?" "Yes, yes, we have two." Very proud they were. "So you have many students here?" "Yes, yes." "It's a very affluent city, Edinburgh?" "Yes, oh, yes, very rich and opulent." And then Prabhupāda said, "So you have so many students, and you have so many nice big, big buildings. You have so much facility for enjoyment." And they were agreeing: "Yes, yes, we have all this." And Prabhupāda just looked at them straight and said, "Then* why *are your universities producing hippies?"*

They looked at one another, and no one could answer. And Prabhupāda began to explain how society cannot bring happiness or contentment simply with buildings. "Stones and windows," he said. "Where is the happiness there?"

In Glasgow Prabhupāda lectured at Woodside Hall before an audience of almost one thousand.

Kiśora: *Prabhupāda was sitting onstage on his* vyāsāsana. *The crowd was very large, and even the balcony was overflowing. When Prabhupāda arrived, the students greeted him like a pop star. They were cheering and whistling. Prabhupāda immediately began lecturing very heavily on the basic science of* Bhagavad-gītā*—how Arjuna became a successful devotee by killing all his friends and relatives. At the end of the lecture, I was a little apprehensive as to whether the people would accept that heavy lecture or not. But they cheered and applauded.*

When it came to question-and-answer time, one man came all the way down the aisle from the back of the hall and stood at the foot of the stage and looked up at Prabhupāda. For several moments he spoke, on and on and on, talking very proudly—"I am this. I am that"—and then concluding, "I am God." That was the conclusion of his little monologue. The whole crowd was hushed, and I thought, "What's going to happen now?" Prabhupāda simply looked down and let the silence continue for a few moments more. Then Prabhupāda spoke. "So, you are God—you have nothing more to say? You are not God—you are dog." And immediately the crowd stood up and applauded and cheered. The man just looked at Prabhupāda, and a smile came on his face. With just those few words he had been defeated. He simply walked all the way back again to the back of the hall and was finished. It was ecstatic, because the crowd was participating in the whole thing. They all realized that God is not cheap.

Then we had kīrtana, *and everyone in the audience was dancing. At that time they had gotten a bit lax at the door, and the local street urchins from this low-class area of Glasgow came into the hall, and they all began dancing and singing. Some of them tried to get up on the stage. Prabhupāda was also chanting, and so these kids were all trying to get around him and get on the stage to chant. The devotees started to push these dirty little children off the stage, but Śrīla Prabhupāda said, "Don't do that. These children are all devotees. Let them chant."*

When Prabhupāda finally got up to leave again, he reminded me of some big celebrity. He was smiling and waving and walking off the stage, and the audience were all shouting, "No, no, no!" They began chanting, "More, more, more, more!"

August 1

When Prabhupāda returned to London and heard that Sumati Morarji was arriving there, he went with a group of his disciples to meet her at the airport. He talked with her about his plans for Hare Krishna Land at Juhu and of his desire to form a board of trustees consisting of ISKCON's Bombay life members. Sumati Morarji agreed to be president of the board, which would meet regularly and give advice for managing ISKCON's Bombay project. Each trustee would also contribute a large sum of money toward developing a particular area of the project. Prabhupāda asked Mrs. Morarji to donate for the temple. He would request Mr. Khandelwal to donate for the library and Mr. N. for the two other wings.

That Mr. N. had not yet produced the deed, however, continued to weigh heavily on Prabhupāda's mind, and he questioned Mr. N.'s intentions and Girirāja's competence. If the only obstacle was the five-lakh tax, then Prabhupāda had already instructed Girirāja to approach ISKCON's wealthy friends and secure a loan. What was the difficulty? But Girirāja's communications sounded as if such a solution was "impossible." On August 27 Prabhupāda telegrammed Girirāja: "HAS CONVEYANCE DEED BEEN SIGNED IF NOT FINISH IMMEDIATELY AND WIRE DETAILS."

Again Girirāja went to Mr. N., although anticipating Mr. N.'s reply. This time, however, Mr. N. added yet another complication, reminding Girirāja that ISKCON had not yet obtained permission from the charity commissioner. ISKCON was a public charitable trust and so required permission from the charity commissioner before acquiring property. Mr. N. put the burden back onto ISKCON.

At the charity commissioner's office, Girirāja learned that he should have applied for permission six months prior to signing the agreement for the land. To Girirāja and the other devotees in Bombay, the affair had become a huge Gordian knot.

* * *

New Vrindaban, West Virginia
August 30, 1972

Only two days remained until the Janmāṣṭamī celebration, and more than three hundred disciples had gathered to be with Śrīla Prabhupāda. Janmāṣṭamī, Kṛṣṇa's appearance day, is always followed immediately by Śrīla Prabhupāda's appearance day, and this year, with so many devotees gathered in a holy place with Prabhupāda, the occasion promised to be especially auspicious.

Prabhupāda had agreed to lecture every evening in an outdoor pavilion, constructed for the occasion atop one of New Vrindaban's many hills. The lecture series was titled "Bhāgavata Dharma Discourses," and through these meetings Prabhupāda set an example for his disciples that they hold similar festivals in other parts of the country. Through *bhāgavata-dharma* discourses and book distribution, the Kṛṣṇa consciousness movement would increase its purifying influence throughout the world.

Prabhupāda lived during these days in a small wood-frame house in the New Vrindaban woods. He regularly received visitors and lectured in the evening. Each evening, before his lecture at the pavilion, the devotees would hold a *kīrtana* and carry Prabhupāda up the long, steep hill on a palanquin; and afterward, as they carried him back down, he would be surrounded by chanting disciples bearing lanterns and torches.

Sureśvara: *The path from the pavilion wound down and around on its way to the temple. I got there at dusk and beheld Śrīla Prabhupāda floating jubilantly in his palanquin atop a sea of devotees. There were hundreds of devotees, with tumultuous* kīrtana *and roaring, plus dust was being kicked up everywhere from all the people. It looked spectacular, like a panoramic scene from one of those epic movies,* The Ten Commandments *or* Exodus, *only much more, because it was transcendental. I just fell down in the dust as Prabhupāda's palanquin came gliding past. It was very wild, but devotional.*

Baṭu Gopāla: *It was a small palanquin carried by four men. There were some ropes for Prabhupāda to hold on to, and it wasn't a very comfortable ride for him. But it was an amazing scene. Devotees with torches—electric torches and fire torches, and lanterns—and Prabhupāda coming down in his palanquin, down the trail. Hundreds of devotees were surrounding him.* Kīrtana *was roaring. I kept trying to get up close to Prabhupāda and get a glance.*

Jāhnava-devī dāsī: *We were running down the steep hill in the dark amid the loud chanting of a river of devotees. And our feet seemed to never touch the ground. About halfway down, I caught up to the palanquin. But then I realized that being close to Śrīla Prabhupāda meant far more than physical proximity and that I needed to become much more serious about Kṛṣṇa consciousness in order to feel less distant from him.*

On Janmāṣṭamī night Prabhupāda went to the temple and listened to readings from *Kṛṣṇa, the Supreme Personality of Godhead* about Lord Kṛṣṇa's birth. Around two A.M. he noticed many devotees were nodding. "You are getting tired," he said, smiling, and he ended the program.

Even in the midst of such a large festival, Prabhupāda was again plunged into the struggle over the Bombay land. A letter arrived from Girirāja explaining his failure to secure the five-lakhs loan owed the government and the government's refusal to grant permission. He also mentioned his suspicion that Mr. N. was influencing the charity commissioner's decision.

Prabhupāda had a copy of the purchase agreement with him, and he studied it carefully. Again he concluded that his position was strong, since he was occupying the land according to the terms of the agreement. He had paid two lakhs as promised, but Mr. N. had not turned over the deed. Now more money was being demanded, and Prabhupāda had said Girirāja should pay this money and get the deed. As for the permission from the government charity commissioner, there was no mention of it in the agreement. Although Mr. N.'s tactics were apparently bewildering Girirāja, Prabhupāda saw them as only empty bluffs. He telegrammed Girirāja, "TAKE BANK MORTGAGE PAY OFF N." Before receiving any reply from Girirāja, Prabhupāda sent another telegram: "WHY DO YOU SAY CONVEYANCE IMPOSSIBLE EVERYTHING CLEAR IN AGREEMENT OF PURCHASE CONVEYANCE TO BE EXECUTED IMMEDIATELY ACCORDING TO TERMS OF AGREEMENT OF PURCHASE."

On Śrīla Prabhupāda's appearance-day morning, he went up the hill to the pavilion to speak. It was a beautiful late summer's day, and he sat on the stage on a red *vyāsāsana* beside the Deities of Rādhā-Dāmodara and Lord Jagannātha. In addition to hundreds of his disciples, hundreds of guests were also present, the entire audience numbering about one thousand. The festival was a newsworthy turnout of the Hare Kṛṣṇa movement, and reporters from *The New York Times* and other newspapers were on hand, along with television film crews.

Prabhupāda spoke, explaining how, although an observer might misunderstand the devotees' worship of their spiritual master, no one should think that the spiritual master was presenting himself as God. Prabhupāda compared the spiritual master to a tax collector. As the tax collector collects money only on behalf of the king, so the spiritual master receives honor, but on behalf of Lord Kṛṣṇa. Everyone should serve and bow down to the Supreme Lord, and the spiritual master comes and "collects" obeisances and worship on behalf of God, who accepts any sincere worship of the spiritual master as an offering to Himself.

Prabhupāda ended his lecture, and a great feast climaxed the day and a half of fasting. Prabhupāda then returned to the back yard of his little house, where he talked with some of the devotees.

Hṛdayānanda Goswami: *Prabhupāda was taking his massage, sitting on a straw mat outside his cabin. Suddenly, two little kittens appeared by his mat. And they were rolling around, tumbling. They were wrestling, tumbling, rolling around and around. Immediately I thought, "Oh! They are contaminated. I have to get them away." The cats actually tumbled right onto Prabhupāda's mat. They rolled in a little furry ball right over to Prabhupāda's feet. Prabhupāda began tickling them under their chins. He was laughing, rubbing under their chins. Then he turned to me, sort of in a very jolly mood, and said, "Just see, even here there is love."*

Śrutakīrti: *I was in charge of the kitchen, so I was too busy to see Prabhupāda at all. He was there for a week, and practically the whole time I didn't get to see him. I was so upset. I was doing all this service, and I had no opportunity to see Prabhupāda—always cooking until midnight. I felt so bad.*

So the day before Prabhupāda left, Kīrtanānanda Mahārāja came up to me and said, "So you are going to be Prabhupāda's servant." I said, "Oh, no! This is wonderful! No, this is terrible!" I was so worried. Then he said, "You'll be leaving tomorrow morning to go to Pittsburgh." I thought, "Wow, that was quick! I didn't know anything about it."

The following morning Kīrtanānanda Mahārāja brought me over to the farmhouse Prabhupāda was staying at. He took me into Prabhupāda's room and said, "This is Śrutakīrti. He is going to be your servant." Prabhupāda looked, and I paid my obeisances. Kīrtanānanda Mahārāja said, "He cooks very well, Prabhupāda." And Prabhupāda said, "That's very good." "But he hasn't massaged," Mahārāja said. I had never done it before in my life. And then Prabhupāda said, "'That's all right. Anybody can massage. It is very easy."

Satya-nārāyaṇa: *I was with a group of devotees. We would travel around the country in an old bus, preaching. On the bus we had Deities, a kitchen, and a shower. Prabhupāda was outside of his cabin when we drove up in the bus. When he came on, we received him just as in a regular temple, and we gave him* caraṇāmṛta. *He looked at everything and said that there should be hundreds of buses like this. It wasn't such a big event for him, but he really liked it.*

Satsvarūpa dāsa Goswami: *I saw different leading devotees go down to that house to see Śrīla Prabhupāda on important business. I had no important business that hadn't been answered by him in letters, but I began to feel anxious that I was not going to him while others were. Finally, one day my anxiety grew so great that I decided I would go and see His Divine Grace.*

When I arrived at the door of the house, Prabhupāda's servant gladly let me in, and in a moment I was seated before Śrīla Prabhupāda. He was seated to take his massage. I expressed to Śrīla Prabhupāda that I had no very urgent questions to ask him in particular, but that I had become anxious to see him, and so I had come. Prabhupāda replied that I should know better than to come to him out of such anxiety. He said he had already answered everything in his books. Actually, this was very inspiring. On the one hand, he was telling me that as an older devotee I should be assured that by studying his books everything was there. Not that out of anxiety I should feel a lacking and on an impulse have to personally see my guru.

But now, since I was in his presence, Śrīla Prabhupāda asked me, "What are *you doing?" When Śrīla Prabhupāda said that, I got the strong impression that he was regarding me in the proper place, as a tiny fool. Here I had just been initiated* sannyāsa, *and I was coming before Prabhupāda with my assistant and asking for his attention. Now that I had asked for his attention, he gave me a surveillance-glance, and by his question he seemed to imply that I was doing nothing or very, very little to spread Kṛṣṇa consciousness. That was how I interpreted his question, "What* are *you doing?"*

I replied that I was, according to the instruction that I had received from him in a letter, going from temple to temple in my zone and implementing his desire that the students there study the Śrīmad-Bhāgavatam *in the morning class. I had previously felt very confident that I was exactly following direct orders I had been given in a letter from him. But to my surprise, in that room in New Vrindaban, he began to tell me that visiting temples was not the most important thing. He said that he was pleased with the program of Viṣṇujana Mahārāja, who was traveling on a bus. He said I should do like that.*

I immediately replied, "Then your instruction that I should go to the different temples is not very important? I should take a bus?" And Śrīla Prabhupāda became annoyed and said, "It is not that because one thing is more important the other thing is less important. Everything is important. Not that just because I say this is important, to travel in a bus, now you say traveling to the temples is not important. Kṛṣṇa's head is important, and Kṛṣṇa's foot is important. Everything about Him is important."

While Prabhupāda participated fully, both formally and informally, at New Vrindaban, he still carried a special burden of concern for Bombay. Although he had appointed G.B.C. secretaries to oversee the Kṛṣṇa consciousness movement in various parts of the world, he was the real G.B.C. secretary of India. Wherever he traveled, therefore, he remained partial to those projects.

He was setting the perfect example of a G.B.C. secretary. While conscientiously tending to practical affairs, he remained always transcendental—fully dependent on Kṛṣṇa and always preaching. After drafting a telegram to Girirāja or hearing of difficulties in Bombay, he would immediately return to his peaceful routine and active preaching. He would take his late-morning massage, bathe, put on *tilaka* methodically and delicately, say his Gāyatrī *mantra* with silent composure, take his *prasādam*, rest for an hour, and in the evening, after a full day's activities, go into the temple room of whatever temple he happened to be in, sit on the *vyāsāsana* and chant *Jaya Rādhā-Mādhava,* and speak pure Kṛṣṇa consciousness.

September 8

After New Vrindaban Prabhupāda went to Pittsburgh, where he attended a successful engagement at a large hall, the Syria Mosque. He also met with a Catholic bishop, whom he asked, "Why do the Christians kill cows in slaughterhouses and thus break the commandment 'Thou shalt not kill'?" Prabhupāda had often asked this question of Christian priests and was always unsatisfied with the answer. This was no exception.

In an informal gathering in his room, Prabhupāda stressed outgoing preaching programs, and he advised his newly initiated *sannyāsīs* present to follow the example of their Godbrother Viṣṇujana Swami: to travel in a bus from town to town and hold festivals and distribute books and magazines.

* * *

September 9

The devotees in Dallas had purchased a large church facility and were forming the first ISKCON children's school, known as Gurukula. Prabhupāda, while traveling in India during 1971 and 1972, had sent a series of letters to the Dallas teachers, explaining the basic direction he wanted them to take for beginning a Kṛṣṇa conscious primary school.

> We will teach the basic requirements of reading and writing but also give them real spiritual knowledge how to live perfectly. What other school of learning offers such a wonderful educational opportunity?. . . Last night the topic of my lecture at our Delhi pandal was the necessity for teaching Krishna Consciousness in all our schools and colleges. This is a revolutionary thought. But we have seen that the practical outcome of so much godless education in technology and science is that they are producing only hippies, one after another. What is the use of their skyscraper buildings if their sons will not maintain them? The old system of *gurukul* should be revived as the perfect example of a system designed to produce great men, sober and responsible leaders, who know what is the real welfare of the citizens. Just as in former days, all big, big personalities were trained in this way. Now you have got the responsibility to inject this idea in your country. Please do it with a cool head, and very soon we shall see the practical benefit for your countrymen.

These letters had assured the Dallas devotees that they were doing the most important work for the pleasure of Śrīla Prabhupāda. The school had gained support from other ISKCON members, and many parents had sent their children. By the time of Śrīla Prabhupāda's visit, about fifty students were enrolled.

Prabhupāda said Dallas's weather reminded him of Calcutta, even though he felt uncomfortably hot. Disdaining the use of air conditioning, he shed his *kurtā* and sat on the lawn with his inexperienced but eager group of teachers. The best system of education, he said, was as he had known as a child: one teacher in a room with up to fifty students of various ages and aptitudes. One at a time the students would come to the teacher's desk, receive guidance and a further assignment, and then return to work.

The *gurukula* teachers were particularly concerned and puzzled about how to discipline children without being punitive, and Prabhupāda unhesitatingly solved all their puzzles. He said the students should both fear and love their teachers. The teacher, by stern countenance, may threaten an unruly child and make him submit, but the teacher should not hit the child.

The next day Śrīla Prabhupāda went into a classroom and sat on a cushion before the class. Holding a blackboard pointer in each hand, he joked that one stick could be used for hitting the students' heads and the other for hitting their hands. The children and teachers became delighted to see Prabhupāda's playful mood. And when he asked if anyone wanted to get hit, both teachers and students moved forward, holding their hands out for a merciful slap from Śrīla Prabhupāda.

To demonstrate how to teach, Prabhupāda called for a volunteer. Dvārakādhīśa came forward. Prabhupāda, placing his venerable hand over the boy's, guided him repeatedly in forming the first letter of the Sanskrit alphabet.

News of Bombay followed Prabhupāda to Dallas. A devotee who had recently come to the West from Bombay informed Prabhupāda of Girirāja's recent talk of resigning as president of the center. Depressed by his ineffectiveness in dealing with Mr. N., the lawyers, and the government, and harassed by bickering and uncooperative devotees, he was considering himself unworthy to keep the charge.

Now Girirāja's anxiety became Prabhupāda's as again he concerned himself with all the affairs of his Juhu project. There seemed to be no one he could discuss this with, since the devotees in America knew almost nothing of matters in Bombay.

The night was too hot for sleeping, and Prabhupāda could not concentrate on translating *Śrīmad-Bhāgavatam*. So he stayed up late, talking with his secretary about Bombay. Surmising the mind and mood of

Mr. N. and expressing his concern for his Hare Krishna Land and his wonder at the devotees' hesitation and disheartenment, he turned the argument this way and that, considering it in different lights, until in the early morning he finally put it aside. Afterward, he composed another telegram: "SETTLE LAND IMMEDIATELY AT BEST PRICE POSSIBLE N. PROMISED TO PAY IT IF HE WONT WE CAN PAY SUGGEST 15000 DONT CHANGE PRESIDENCY UNTIL I COME."

Large marble Deities of Rādhā and Kṛṣṇa arrived in Dallas by trailer from New York. Prabhupāda had specifically selected these Deities for Dallas Gurukula while in India and ordered Them to be shipped to the United States. The Kṛṣṇa Deity was magnificent. He was tall, bigger than most ISKCON Deities, and His limbs and head were strikingly large. According to one story, the Deity was several hundred years old and therefore carved according to an ancient tradition. Even though the devotees in Dallas were unprepared to install Rādhā-Kṛṣṇa Deities, Prabhupāda told them to get ready in two days for the installation, which he would personally perform.

Jāhnava-devī dāsī, however, unauthorizedly removed the original paint from the Deities and began to repaint Them. When Prabhupāda heard this, he became furious. He called the Dallas president, Satsvarūpa dāsa Goswami, to his room and demanded an explanation. Satsvarūpa said that he was a fool but that Jāhnava had also acted without his permission.

Prabhupāda then called for Jāhnava and yelled at her furiously. She began to cry. "Why have you done this?" Śrīla Prabhupāda demanded.

"Nonsense," was her choked reply.

"Nonsense," Śrīla Prabhupāda affirmed, "*suicidal* nonsense! You are a nonsense, and you will always remain a nonsense. So, what are you going to do about this?"

"Well, Śrīla Prabhupāda," Jāhnava replied weakly, "I called up Baradrāja in Los Angeles, and he said if I use a certain kind of paint . . . "

"Baradrāja!" Prabhupāda yelled. "Who is this Baradrāja! I am your spiritual master, and I am sitting before you. Why do you not ask me?" Disgusted, he then turned to the others in the room. "So, what is to be done about this?" One of the ladies said that with a quick-drying paint, they could repaint the Deities just as before in time for the installation. "Yes," Śrīla Prabhupāda said, "Do it immediately."

Jāhnava stayed up all night, carefully repainting the Deities as before.

Early the next morning, which was to be the morning of the Deity installation, Kṛṣṇa looked very beautiful, although His body was tacky in spots from the fresh paint.

During that morning's walk around White Rock Lake, while talking philosophically about various topics, Prabhupāda turned casually to Satsvarūpa Mahārāja and asked about the preparations for the installation. When Satsvarūpa said he was uncertain whether Kṛṣṇa's paint would be dry enough, Prabhupāda suddenly stopped. If the Deities weren't ready, he said, there was no use in his staying any longer in Dallas. Turning to his secretary, he told him to change their flight reservations as soon as possible. Satsvarūpa begged forgiveness and said that maybe everything could still be done on schedule. Prabhupāda's angry mood changed, and he continued walking, talking about other matters.

Later in his room, Prabhupāda talked alone to Satsvarūpa, continuing on the point of his morning lecture about materialistic life. In a casual way, as most people would talk about ordinary things, Prabhupāda spoke of the foolishness of the conditioned souls. "They think that just by having a big family and being absorbed in mundane activities they do not have to concern themselves with death or with the next life." As Prabhupāda spoke, he shook his head in disbelief, considering the incredulous position of the materialist.

All of Prabhupāda's disciples noted the same amazing thing about him: wherever he went, his consciousness was always in transcendence. Whether staying up late worrying and talking about Bombay, or criticizing devotees for repainting the Deity, his mind was ever moving from one Kṛṣṇa conscious consideration to another. The devotees with him would sometimes observe his awesome Kṛṣṇa consciousness from a respectful distance. At other times they might, in the name of service, speak up and become more personally involved. Or they might find themselves thrust under the direct scrutiny of his demanding attention. No one could presume or accurately predict in what way Prabhupāda would act in his constant, grave service to his spiritual master.

While sitting with Satsvarūpa Mahārāja, Prabhupāda began humming and singing a Sanskrit phrase from the morning's *Bhāgavatam* class, *gṛheṣu gṛha-medhinām* . . . Then he asked, "So, how is the Deity?" Satsvarūpa said he thought He was dry.

Prabhupāda stood and walked into the room where Jāhnava was examining the repainted Deity. Calmly he stood before Rādhā and Kṛṣṇa, singing to himself. "Yes," he said, "now it's all right."

Later that morning in the temple room, Prabhupāda sat on his *vyāsāsana* and installed Rādhā and Kṛṣṇa, reciting the prayers from the *Brahma-saṁhitā.* He then offered the first *ārati* to the Deities, who had been hastily dressed and placed on an almost bare altar. Prabhupāda seemed pleased, however, and later went up to his room and wrote on a piece of paper, "Radha Kalachandji, the Deity of Dallas, September 12, 1972—A. C. Bhaktivedanta Swami." *Kālacandajī,* he said, meant "black moon."

* * *

Prabhupāda was preparing to return soon to India via a western route, and he paid another visit to his Western world headquarters in Los Angeles. On the very day he arrived, however, he wrote more directions to the devotees in Bombay, reassuring them the Juhu land was not just a trouble spot but a special place where a great plan would be carried out. It was worth fighting for.

> . . . now I am anxious to hear if the conveyance deed has been signed and what are the contents. Kindly send me the copy duly signed as quickly as possible. This will give me great relief. As soon as the conveyance has been signed you may begin the building work immediately. I am coming to India soon, at least by October, and I want to see that the building projects in Bombay, Mayapur and Vrndavana are going on nicely. This Bombay project is one of our most important projects in the whole world and I am looking to you and the others there in Bombay to see that it is done very magnificently.

Prabhupāda's secretary had recently shown him a new advertisement booklet printed by Air India in which the art theme was exclusively dedicated to Kṛṣṇa in Vṛndāvana. Prabhupāda was encouraged to see that Air India was enticing tourists to come to India to experience Kṛṣṇa culture. This confirmed his idea that in the future Hare Krishna Land and his other Indian projects would be important showpieces for tourists wanting to experience real Vedic culture.

Mail from Bombay always received first priority, and every morning Prabhupāda would ask for news from Bombay, giving any letter from Girirāja immediate attention. Early in October he received a long letter from Girirāja.

> We just cannot control the material nature, and although everything is going on slow, Mrs. Morarjee, Mr. Munim, the bank, and Mr. N.

> all feel that they are proceeding as quickly as possible. And they do not respond very favorably to being overreminded by me of the urgency of the matter and of Your anxiety that it be finished.

Nothing new had developed; the deed still had not been signed.

Although Girirāja said he now had no intentions of resigning his post, Prabhupāda, after studying the letter, concluded that other senior devotees in India should also help. He therefore wrote to Tamāla Kṛṣṇa Goswami and Bhavānanda, both in Vṛndāvana, asking them to go immediately to Bombay and try to expedite the conveyance.

Prabhupāda was asking Tamāla Kṛṣṇa Goswami to revive his active status as a manager in India.

> ... Girirāja is finding difficulty, from his letter I can understand. So I think you have to revive your position as GBC again and look after all the business of India affairs nicely.

Prabhupāda also wrote Girirāja, informing him that other devotees were coming to help and reminding him to also work with the board of trustees.

> I cannot tax my brain so much from such distant places as to what to do if there is any difficulty, therefore I am relying completely on you, my trusted senior disciples, to finish up these things nicely.

Prabhupāda repeatedly instructed the managers in Bombay not to deviate from the terms of the purchase agreement. He was willing, as a matter of concession, to pay the five lakhs, to be deducted from the total price. But no more changes. The devotees should press Mr. N. to the original agreement.

Prabhupāda was worried that he had not heard from his lawyer, Mr. D. Two weeks before, he had telegrammed both Mr. N. and Mr. D., asking for reports on the delays, but he had received no replies from either of them. He had since written to another lawyer, a friend in Bombay, asking about the delay, and in Los Angeles he received the reply: Mr. D. was no longer his attorney. A couple of days after receiving this shocking news, Prabhupāda received a formal letter from the office of Mr. D, informing him of the same.

Of all the recent news from Bombay, this was the most disturbing. Prabhupāda began to see how Mr. N. had been devising a devious plot from the beginning. It was not just a matter of slowness or bureaucratic delay; Mr. D. had been in league with Mr. N. They were cheaters. So now it was going to be a real fight. ISKCON would have to go to court and file criminal charges against Mr. N. There was no avoiding the fight, but Prabhupāda still felt that his position was legally very strong.

Before leaving Los Angeles, Prabhupāda thought of a further tactic. He wrote to Girirāja that he should put a notice in the newspapers advising the public that ISKCON had signed an agreement for purchasing Mr. N.'s land at Juhu. He then traveled to Berkeley.

October 6

During his brief visit to Berkeley, Prabhupāda met with a group of professors from the University of California and also installed Rādhā-Kṛṣṇa Deities in the Berkeley temple. But still he was meditating on Bombay. He wrote to Tamāla Kṛṣṇa Goswami,

> The Bombay dealing has been muddled by the tactics of Mr. N. and Mr. D. Girirāja is in trouble. He is a child in these worldly dealings, so immediately go to help him. . . . But you must be careful to pay the money in the court (registrar's office) and not in the hand of Mr. N. or his solicitor. . . . Settle up the things properly, otherwise let us go to the court for specific action, either civic or criminal against the tactics of Mr. N.

Prabhupāda decided to send Karandhara, whom he considered expert, to help in Bombay. He also wanted to send Śyāmasundara, but Śyāmasundara had gone to London regarding a large country estate George Harrison was donating. Prabhupāda notified Śyāmasundara, however, that once the London transaction was completed, he should go to Bombay. Prabhupāda was ready for the fight. He would not be cheated.

During his return trip to India, Prabhupāda again visited Hawaii. Then on October 11 he went for the first time to Manila, where a small number of disciples had arranged preaching programs for him, both in the temple and at the Hotel Intercontinental.

In Manila Prabhupāda carefully considered his position regarding the Juhu property and concluded that he would come out victorious. He listed the points of his argument in a letter to Girirāja.

> 1. We have fulfilled all the conditions as purchaser.

2. Mr. N. has purposefully delayed with a motive to cheat us as he had done with some others in this connection.
3. But this time he cannot cheat us because we are in possession of the land and our deity Radha-Krishna is installed there.
4. Therefore we must immediately go to the court for enforcing him to execute the conveyance immediately.
5. Even if the court case goes on for a long time, still our business there cannot be stopped.
6. Without going to the court, we cannot make any compromise with him.
7. But I think we can arrange the full amount of 14 lacs to get out this rascal out of the scene.
8. But we cannot do it without going to the court otherwise we shall become a party for breaking the purchase agreement. Therefore we have to go to the court before making any compromise.

CHAPTER FIVE

Vṛndāvana
October 17, 1972

Prabhupāda had come to Vṛndāvana to observe the Kārttika season (from October 16 to November 14). He planned to lecture daily at the *samādhi* of Rūpa Gosvāmī in the courtyard of the Rādhā-Dāmodara temple, speaking from *The Nectar of Devotion*, his own translation of Rūpa Gosvāmī's book, *Bhakti-rasāmṛta-sindhu.* On his Western tour he had invited devotees to join him for Kārttika in Vṛndāvana, and now a few dozen devotees from America, Europe, India, and other parts of the world had gathered to be with him.

He was concerned with developing his Vṛndāvana project, so rather than immediately rushing to Bombay, he had come here first, sending some of his leading disciples to tackle the problems in Bombay. Now, like a general engaged on a different front, he awaited word from his lieutenants in Bombay. He moved into his two small rooms at the Rādhā-Dāmodara temple, while his disciples stayed nearby in the former palace of the Mahārāja of Bharatpur, an old building near the Yamunā.

Although Prabhupāda was introducing his disciples to Vṛndāvana, he was also introducing the residents of Vṛndāvana to his disciples. Already his group was encountering some of the same attitudes Bhaktisiddhānta Sarasvatī and his party of pilgrims had met in 1932: the people's refusal to accept lowborn persons as Vaiṣṇavas. Prabhupāda trusted, however, that if his disciples could construct a wonderful temple for Kṛṣṇa and Balarāma, the hearts of the Vṛndāvana residents would change, and they would accept his disciples. He tolerated the roughness and slowness of his disciples, and when Vṛndāvana residents came to see him, he humbly requested they also overlook his disciples' faults and recognize them as genuine devotees of Kṛṣṇa; after all, they had given up sinful life and were regularly chanting the holy names of God.

Prabhupāda lectured both morning and evening. Sitting on a simple *āsana* about two feet high, a bare bulb suspended over his head, Prabhupāda would address his disciples and the few interested guests who sat before him.

Some of the devotees had speculated that since they were now in Vṛndāvana, Prabhupāda would probably talk on highly elevated spiritual topics, such as Kṛṣṇa's *rasa* with the *gopīs*. But it was not so. Rather, one of his disciples would read from *The Nectar of Devotion*, and Prabhupāda would interject extensive philosophical comments on attaining pure love of Kṛṣṇa through the successive stages of *bhakti-yoga*.

While Prabhupāda's talks were especially for his disciples, he also stressed that the *brāhmaṇas* of India accept the Western Vaiṣṇavas. And he cited dozens of scriptural references to prove his point that birth status, being a material designation, did not apply in spiritual life. Stressing preaching as the essence of Kṛṣṇa consciousness, he urged the disciples present to continue propagating the Kṛṣṇa consciousness movement.

Prabhupāda's disciples were thrilled by these talks and by Prabhupāda's personal dealings with them in the intimate atmosphere of his rooms at the Rādhā-Dāmodara temple, which he referred to as his "eternal residence," the place where he had actually begun his plans for the Kṛṣṇa consciousness movement. His disciples could hear him rise early and begin translating *Śrīmad-Bhāgavatam* and dictating his purports. At *ārati* time, he would open the shutters of his room and behold the Deities. At other times the devotees might see him walking on the terrace chanting *japa*. And they found him always available to answer their questions and help them with their personal problems.

*   *   *

Tamāla Kṛṣṇa Goswami, Śyāmasundara, and Karandhara arrived in Bombay. Things had worsened, Girirāja informed them. When Mr. N. had seen the notice in the newspaper publicly advising that ISKCON had entered into an agreement for the Juhu property, he had become furious. Girirāja had gone to him with folded hands and bowed down before him, but Mr. N. would not be appeased. He had gone back on all his promises and had canceled the sales agreement, on the plea that the devotees had not obtained the deed within a six-month period. The two-lakh down payment, he had claimed, was now his, and the devotees should vacate the land immediately.

Mr. N. had shut off the water supply to Hare Krishna Land. Several days later, a hoodlum had shown up at the entrance to the property, brandishing a machete whenever devotees passed by. A friend of Mr. N. had printed a handbill ascribing scandalous behavior to the American Hare Kṛṣṇa devotees and was having it distributed at the nearby Ville Parle train station. Although a few devotees had left and others wanted to, about thirty devotees still remained in Bombay.

The first thing to do, Karandhara said, was to find a new lawyer, and he went to Bombay's most prominent solicitors and hired a specialist in land transactions and conveyances. Next, the leading devotees and their solicitor met with Mr. N. in his office. Mr. N. was stubborn and uncooperative, and the ISKCON lawyer was threatening. A court battle seemed inevitable.

Tamāla Kṛṣṇa Goswami, Karandhara, Bhavānanda, and Śyāmasundara talked together, and the more they talked, the more they began to see the entire Juhu scheme as impossible. Even without Mr. N.'s treachery, just to live on the land was very difficult. The devotees and the Deities had such poor living facilities that the roof leaked and the cement floor was crumbling. Rats, flies, cockroaches, village dogs, and mosquitoes infested the place—with even an occasional poisonous snake. Devotees were always contracting tropical diseases, especially malaria and hepatitis.

So although ISKCON's new lawyer was prepared to take the case to court, the devotees were hesitant. Mr. N. had said that they—not he—were criminals, because they had not gotten permission from the charity commissioner; they were on his land illegally. He said he would sue for damages. He even seemed to be on the verge of some violent action. Considering all angles, the leaders whom Prabhupāda had entrusted to solve the Juhu entanglement decided that ISKCON should relinquish the land. Drafting a joint letter to Śrīla Prabhupāda, they had Śyāmasundara hand-deliver it to him in Vṛndāvana.

Sitting in his room at the Rādhā-Dāmodara temple, Śrīla Prabhupāda read the letter from Bombay and then set it aside. He walked out into the open courtyard. In the last light of day many birds were chirping, and the devotees sat on the ground on a dhurrie, waiting. Prabhupāda sat on the simple raised seat and began singing *Jaya Rādhā-Mādhava.*

He had Pradyumna read, stopping him to explain a point whenever he felt inclined. He spoke of the special benefits of residing in Vṛndāvana, but warned that one should not come to the *dhāma* to do business or to commit any offenses. If, however, a Vṛndāvana resident did commit an offense, he could still receive the special benefits—provided he remained "sticking to the dust of Vṛndāvana."

Night fell, and in the dark courtyard Prabhupāda continued lecturing beneath the dim electric bulbs. Visiting pilgrims came and went, watching "the Swamiji" lecturing in English to his Western disciples.

After the question-and-answer period, Prabhupāda walked back to his room, exchanging words along the way with Gaurachand Goswami, the temple proprietor. Some devotees lingered in Prabhupāda's room, and many Indians peered through the barred windows, although they had never cared to look years ago, before the room's permanent resident, Bhaktivedanta Swami, had gone to America.

When Prabhupāda was finally alone, he began to think of Bombay. Although hundreds of miles away, the occurrences there were beating on his heart here in Vṛndāvana. He took out his copy of the agreement he had signed with Mr. N. Then he called his secretary and began dictating a letter to his leaders in Bombay.

He began his letter like a lawyer, answering logically, point by point. One reason his disciples had given for wanting to give up the land was that the charity commissioner had refused them permission. In that case, Prabhupāda reasoned, they should try to get back the money and give up the land. But it appeared that the charity commissioner's permission was *delayed*, not denied—a small matter. Although Mr. N. had mentioned a six-month time limit for obtaining the charity commissioner's approval, Prabhupāda pointed out that the original agreement mentioned no such time limit.

Another reason Prabhupāda's men had given for wanting to relinquish the land was that, according to Mr. N., they had failed to obtain the conveyance within six months, as per the original sales agreement. Prabhupāda replied that, according to the clause in question, "it is *our* option to rescind the contract within six months, not the vendor's." But the real point was that Mr. N. had accepted checks worth one lakh rupees as down payment within the six-month period, and therefore the sales agreement was completed.

> . . . we consider that he has completed the conveyance and we do not want to rescind but we shall close the deal immediately, finished, that's all. He's trying to avoid this issue by tricks, and he has dominated you and you are little afraid of him, and he has fooled you to think

> he is in superior legal position so that you will give him some money. But this is cheating. We shall not give him any more money. Don't pay him any more. First of all bring a criminal case against him. . . . So why you should be disappointed and afraid of him? Our position is very, very strong.

If Mr. N. was threatening violence, that also was not grounds for quitting the land. The devotees were on the land legally and should seek police protection.

> Therefore I say that you boys cannot deal very well in these matters, because you are too timid. Now whatever you like you may do. Immediately criminal case should be taken, that you are not doing because he is bluffing you. He says big words and makes threats and you believe him foolishly and do like he says. That I shall not do.

Prabhupāda's conclusive advice was that the devotees go to the magistrate and tell him, "We gave Mr. N. money, and now he is threatening violence to drive us away." They should not be afraid.

Prabhupāda had not come to Vṛndāvana only to lecture; he wanted to begin construction on his new property. And the news from Bombay didn't distract him from his purpose. Every day he would have the devotees hold a *saṅkīrtana* procession from the Rādhā-Dāmodara temple to the property at Ramaṇa-reti. He would also go out occasionally to see the site, still nothing more than grass huts, a wire fence, and a small stock of building materials. Subala, the disciple in charge of construction, was slow and reluctant, and Prabhupāda sent for Tamāla Kṛṣṇa Goswami to come from Bombay and take charge.

Early one morning Subala left the land at Ramaṇa-reti, where he had been staying, and approached Śrīla Prabhupāda on the roof of the Rādhā-Dāmodara temple. "Prabhupāda," he said, "I am having so much difficulty. I don't have time to read, I can't chant my rounds properly, I can't think of Kṛṣṇa. I'm always thinking of how this contractor is cheating us, or I'm thinking of signing checks for labor and materials. It's just too much. All these things on my mind are stopping me from thinking of Kṛṣṇa."

"Do you think Arjuna was simply meditating on Kṛṣṇa on the battlefield of Kurukṣetra?" Prabhupāda replied. "Do you think Arjuna was sitting in yogic trance, while on the battlefield Kṛṣṇa worked? No, he was fighting. He was killing for Kṛṣṇa. He was thinking of all the soldiers he had to kill for Kṛṣṇa.

"Thinking of the checkbook, thinking of the men, thinking of the contractors—this is also like Arjuna's thinking. This is Kṛṣṇa's service. You should not worry about thinking of Kṛṣṇa directly. Arjuna wasn't sitting before Kṛṣṇa in a trance, meditating on His form. He was engaged in Kṛṣṇa's service. Similarly this is Kṛṣṇa's service, and you should engage. Your life is full of Kṛṣṇa's service, and that is very good."

Subala was still unsatisfied. He complained to Prabhupāda that the other devotees wouldn't cooperate with him. He wanted to go into seclusion in Vṛndāvana for the rest of his life and chant, instead of becoming a full-time preacher in ISKCON.

Śrīla Prabhupāda asked, "What do you mean, no one will listen to you? You think that means they are defective? No, *you* are defective." Prabhupāda raised his voice. "If you are preaching and no one will listen, don't think you should go away in disgust and save yourself by chanting. No, that is not our line. We must qualify ourselves so they will listen. Do you know the story of Mr. Beecham?"

Subala shook his head.

"No one would buy his medicine," Prabhupāda continued, "so he became anxious. Still he tried, and one day a man approached him in his shop and asked if he had any Beecham's Powder, and in excitement that someone had asked for his medicine, he died. Similarly, better we spend our whole life and die just to make one person Kṛṣṇa conscious. That is our line, to become so absorbed in preaching Kṛṣṇa, whether in Vṛndāvana or anywhere. We must save all these *asuras* from destroying the world."

In stressing active service and practical results, Śrīla Prabhupāda was exactly following the teaching and example of his spiritual master. According to Bhaktisiddhānta Sarasvatī, to chant in a secluded place and not preach was "a cheating process." Devotional service meant practical work for Kṛṣṇa. The simple, positive way to control the senses was to engage them fully in the service of Kṛṣṇa. Active service was the topmost *yoga*, Prabhupāda told Subala, a fact that he had repeatedly explained in his books. In the recently published Second Canto of *Śrīmad-Bhāgavatam*, he had written,

> Here it is clearly mentioned that the inhabitants of Vṛndāvana were extensively busy in the hard labor of their day's work, and due to the

> day's hard labor they were engaged in sound sleep at night. So practically they had very little time to devote to meditation or to the other paraphernalia of spiritual activities. But factually they were engaged in the highest spiritual activities only. Everything done by them was spiritualized because everything was dovetailed in their relationship with Lord Śrī Kṛṣṇa. The central point of activities was Kṛṣṇa, and as such the so-called activities in the material world were saturated with spiritual potency. That is the advantage of the way of *bhakti-yoga*. One should discharge one's duty on Lord Kṛṣṇa's behalf, and all one's actions will be saturated with Kṛṣṇa thought, the highest pattern of trance in spiritual realization.

As far as possible, Prabhupāda engaged each disciple in a certain service according to the particular disciple's psychophysical nature. But everyone had to take up some kind of work for Kṛṣṇa. Since Prabhupāda desired to build a temple in Vṛndāvana, then whoever would help him do it, whether they were trained or not, or whether it was their tendency or not—whoever offered him assistance—would become very dear to him and to Lord Kṛṣṇa.

When a householder couple, Guru dāsa and Yamunā, agreed to remain in Vṛndāvana to help Prabhupāda build the temple, Prabhupāda welcomed it and shared with them the intention of his plan.

> If you can construct a nice temple in Vrndavana for me in this way, I shall be eternally grateful. Because we are a worldwide movement of Krishna, and if we do not have a nice place at Vrndavana, then what will be the use? Vrndavana is Krishna's land, and in the future many of our disciples will go there just to see, along with many tourists and other friends, so therefore we must have sufficient place for them. . . . I know that you are not trained up for being construction manager, neither that job must be very tasteful to you, but because you are sincere devotee of Krishna, He is giving you all strength and intelligence how to do it. That is what we want; that is advancement in Krishna consciousness.

By the time Prabhupāda and most of his disciples left Vṛndāvana at the end of Kārttika, relations between his disciples and the residents of Vṛndāvana had improved. The people of Vṛndāvana were impressed by the devotees' daily *saṅkīrtana* procession to Ramaṇa-reti, and they were impressed by Prabhupāda. Although Prabhupāda felt that much time had been wasted—it had been a year since Mr. S. had offered them the land—he was now hopeful.

ISKCON projects were developing all over the world, and all were struggling. The devotees' only means of income was from the sale of books and, to some degree, from their Spiritual Sky incense business. As yet Prabhupāda had no architectural plan for his Vṛndāvana project, but he determined to gather from his Book Fund and from devotees enough money for materials and labor. One day he went to the building site and asked a devotee to mix a little cement, and with his own hand, he laid down the first concrete for the foundation.

* * *

Hyderabad
November 11, 1972

Prabhupāda had come to Hyderabad for a *paṇḍāl* program. Big crowds attended his lectures, and wherever he went, even while getting into and out of his car, people surrounded him to touch his lotus feet. Although Hyderabad had been suffering from drought, a few days after Prabhupāda's arrival rains came. One newspaper suggested that the *harināma-kīrtana* Śrīla Prabhupāda and his devotees performed so enthusiastically must have ended the drought. Prabhupāda agreed.

Śrīla Prabhupāda met with Mr. N., who was visiting Hyderabad from Bombay. Śyāmasundara still had a cordial relationship with Mr. N., because Mr. N. had been fond of his three-year-old daughter, Sarasvatī. So he went to Mr. N. and convinced him to speak to Prabhupāda. Mr. N. agreed, but being suspicious that Prabhupāda might try to use mystic power to persuade him to do something against his will, he brought a *guru* with him, thinking the *guru* would counteract Prabhupāda's spiritual power.

Mr. N., his *guru*, and Śyāmasundara all came to the home of Panilal Prithi, where Prabhupāda was staying. Prabhupāda met informally with his guests, conversing with them over *prasādam*, until he yawned, and Mr. N.'s *guru* said, "Oh, Swami, you must be very tired. We should not disturb you now. You should rest, and we may talk later."

"Oh, yes," Prabhupāda replied, "I am very tired."

So Mr. N. and his *guru* excused themselves and retired to the adjoining room.

After a few minutes Prabhupāda called Tamāla Kṛṣṇa Goswami into his room. "When someone asks you if *you* are tired," Prabhupāda said, "it means *he* is tired. If you go into the other room, you will see that they are sleeping.'' He instructed Tamāla Kṛṣṇa to carefully awaken Mr. N. without disturbing his *guru* and bring him in.

Tiptoeing into the room, Tamāla Kṛṣṇa found both Mr. N. and his *guru* asleep on the beds. He went over to Mr. N., touched his arm, and said quietly, ''Mr. N., Mr. N., wake up. Prabhupāda would like to speak with you. Come quickly.'' Mr. N., being roused from his slumber, obediently walked into Prabhupāda's room, forgetting his *guru* friend.

For two hours Prabhupāda talked with Mr. N., and by the end of the discussion they had worked out a new sales agreement. Tamāla Kṛṣṇa and Śyāmasundara, working in a separate room, drafted and typed the documents, while Prabhupāda and Mr. N. settled the final legal points. Then Mr. N. signed the agreement, while his *guru* friend continued sleeping soundly.

Later that day Tamāla Kṛṣṇa confided to Śrīla Prabhupāda, ''I am so disturbed by these dealings that I can't chant my rounds properly.'

''That is natural,'' Prabhupāda replied. ''Sometimes when I am disturbed, I also.''

''But I can see that I am making spiritual advancement, even so,'' Tamāla Kṛṣṇa admitted.

Prabhupāda nodded.

''I used to think how to avoid difficult situations,'' Tamāla Kṛṣṇa said. ''But now I think I should not run away from them.''

''Yes,'' said Prabhupāda, ''we should welcome these. They give us an opportunity to advance more.''

Śyāmasundara and Tamāla Kṛṣṇa Goswami flew back to Bombay with Mr. N. that afternoon. According to the new terms, ISKCON would pay Mr. N. the five lakhs of rupees for the government tax, and in return Mr. N. would execute the deed. But there was also a new time limit—three weeks—and the devotees would have to work fast. Prabhupāda himself would soon come to Bombay to settle the matter once and for all.

* * *

Bombay
November 25, 1972

Although Prabhupāda had come to Bombay with hopes of finishing the land transaction, Mr. N. was still delaying, despite the new agreement. Obviously his stalling was simply part of his plan to cheat ISKCON. Śrīla Prabhupāda waited many days in Bombay, finally departing for a *paṇḍāl* program in Ahmedabad. He left behind instructions for his disciples to get the deed on the new terms or else to take back the original two lakhs of rupees paid as the down payment.

While Śrīla Prabhupāda was away, however, Śyāmasundara, Tamāla Kṛṣṇa Goswami, and the others began talking about how even if they could one day get the deed to the Juhu property, to develop Hare Krishna Land the way Prabhupāda had envisioned would be practically impossible. Śyāmasundara argued that even if they got the land, how could they really expect to build a big temple and hotel out here in the jungle? It just wouldn't work. Meanwhile, from Ahmedabad Prabhupāda continued to wage his Bombay campaign, and he requested Mr. N. and Mr. D. to come to Ahmedabad to try and make a settlement. They declined.

In Bombay the devotees learned that if they wanted to get back their down payment as well as the money they had deposited toward the five-lakh gains tax, then they would have to cancel the new agreement. They were confused, and their time was running out.

One morning one of Prabhupāda's disciples, Viśākhā-devī dāsī, arrived in Ahmedabad from Bombay. Prabhupāda called for her and told her to return to Bombay immediately with a message. Out of concern that his leaders in Bombay not make a wrong decision and decide to relinquish the land, he told her to tell them that they should not under any circumstances cancel the agreement with Mr. N. "Actually," he said, "this is not a woman's job, but everyone else here is either engaged in the *paṇḍāl* or has not been with us long enough to do this task."

Viśākhā took the next train out of Ahmedabad and arrived in Bombay the following morning. But what Prabhupāda had foreseen had already happened: the devotees had canceled the sales agreement. They were convinced that to get the land would be a mistake, and their lawyers had agreed, pointing out that if the devotees wanted to retrieve their money, they should cancel the agreement immediately. When the devotees heard Prabhupāda's message from Ahmedabad, confusion reigned. They now had no legal standing, no claim to the land. And they had failed to carry out Prabhupāda's desire! Girirāja phoned Prabhupāda in Ahmedabad to tell him what had happened.

"Bhaktivedanta Swami here," Prabhupāda said as he took the telephone. Girirāja was saying that a devotee had come from Ahmedabad with a message. "Yes, yes," Prabhupāda said, "what is the point?" Finally Girirāja blurted out that they had canceled the sales agreement. Prabhupāda was silent. Then in a voice that expressed both anger and resignation, he said, "Then everything is finished."

"I shall be the last man to give up the Hare Krishna Land to the rogue Mr. N.," Prabhupāda wrote to a life member just before leaving Ahmedabad for Bombay. Prabhupāda was now immediately planning how to rectify his disciples' mistake. No money had yet been transferred, so perhaps it was not too late.

Mr. N. could not possibly understand why Prabhupāda was so determined in his fight to keep the Juhu land. Not that Prabhupāda had kept his motives hidden, but only a devotee can understand the mind or actions of another devotee. Mr. N. was dealing with Prabhupāda just as he had dealt with C. Company. He had cheated them, and now he would cheat ISKCON. He could only surmise that Prabhupāda and his disciples were driven by the same motive as he himself, the only motive he could understand: material possessiveness.

Actually, even Prabhupāda's disciples were having difficulty understanding Prabhupāda's unbreakable determination. Prabhupāda's main motive was to preach Kṛṣṇa consciousness in Bombay. Śrīla Prabhupāda said, "My Guru Mahārāja ordered me to preach Kṛṣṇa consciousness in the West, and I have done that. Now I want to preach in India." Bombay was the most important city in India—the gateway. And within Bombay, Kṛṣṇa had somehow led Prabhupāda to this land, where he had begun preaching and had brought the Deities of Rādhā and Kṛṣṇa. In Prabhupāda's eyes, the land was suitable for the large, gorgeous temple and international hotel he had planned.

Bombay was an important city and required grand temple worship, large festivals, mass *prasādam* distribution, and a variety of Vedic cultural programs. The Juhu land seemed ideal for a school, a theater, a library, apartments—a Hare Kṛṣṇa city. So how could Prabhupāda retreat from this rogue who was trying to cheat him? There would always be persons opposed to Kṛṣṇa consciousness, Prabhupāda said, but that did not mean the devotees should give in. A preacher had to be tolerant, and sometimes, when all else failed and Kṛṣṇa's interest was at stake, he had to fight.

Another reason Prabhupāda refused to give up this particular plot of land was that he had promised the Deities, Rādhā-Rāsavihārī. He had invited Kṛṣṇa here and prayed, "Dear Sir, please stay here, and I will build You a beautiful temple." When Prabhupāda had been touring and a devotee from Bombay had written him that the Deities were being neglected, Prabhupāda had written back insisting that these "abominable activities" be rectified. The Deity of Kṛṣṇa was not a stone statue but was actually Kṛṣṇa, eager to reciprocate with His sincere devotee.

So if using the land for missionary work was the obvious or external reason for Prabhupāda's determination to keep his Hare Krishna Land, then the internal reason was his personal commitment to Their Lordships Śrī Śrī Rādhā-Rāsavihārī. Certainly Mr. N. and his associates could never understand this. Even Prabhupāda's own disciples could not realize it fully. Prabhupāda had brought Rādhā and Kṛṣṇa into very poor conditions, but with the promise of something wonderful to come. At his request Rādhā and Kṛṣṇa had come, and They were standing patiently, giving eternal benediction to Their worshipers, while Prabhupāda struggled to fulfill his promise.

Five hundred years ago each of the six Gosvāmīs of Vṛndāvana had had his own Deity, for whom he had built a beautiful temple. But Prabhupāda was empowered to install and maintain many Deities. In his Western world headquarters were the opulent Rukmiṇī-Dvārakādhīśa, in New York Rādhā-Govinda, in Dallas big Rādhā-Kālacandajī, on a traveling bus in America with Kīrtanānanda Swami and Viṣṇujana Swami were Rādhā-Dāmodara, in London Rādhā-Londonīśvara, in Māyāpur Rādhā-Mādhava, and in Australia Rādhā-Gopīnātha. All were Prabhupāda's worshipable Deities, *arcā-vigraha* incarnations of Rādhā and Kṛṣṇa appearing at the request of Their pure devotee for the benefit of neophyte devotees in various places around the world.

To establish many Deities was one of Śrīla Prabhupāda's prime contributions as a world preacher. And when he would visit each temple, he would always stand reverently before the Deities, taking Their blessings, and then he would offer prostrated obeisances. "Be humble," he would instruct the devotees. "Always remember you are dealing with Kṛṣṇa." And sometimes he would be unable to suppress his ecstatic symptoms of love for the Deities. Through his representatives, his many disciples, he worshiped all these Deities, but in the case of Rādhā-Rāsavihārī his involvement was more direct. Having taken India as his own managerial duty, he considered caring for this Deity his specific responsibility.

Prabhupāda's fighting spirit to keep the land was so keen that he sometimes appeared to be fighting for fighting's sake. He sometimes even compared Mr. N. to the demon Kaṁsa in *Śrīmad-Bhāgavatam*, who had repeatedly tried to kill Kṛṣṇa. Just as Kaṁsa had employed many minor demons in his attempts to kill Kṛṣṇa, so Mr. N. had employed demoniac agents like lawyers, friends, and hoodlums. Kṛṣṇa's killing of demons like Kaṁsa was His pastime, or *līlā*—He enjoyed it. And Prabhupāda, as the servant of Kṛṣṇa, was fully absorbed in this fighting. He was vigilant, militant. When Mr. N. bluffed or frightened the devotees, causing them to back down, Prabhupāda held his ground. He took naturally to the fight; Kṛṣṇa and Kṛṣṇa's mission were being challenged.

Never before had Prabhupāda been so threatened or met such active enemies. In New Delhi, when he had been selling his *Back to Godhead* magazines, he had often met with brusque words, and in America people had ignored and occasionally heckled him. But no one had seriously attempted to stop his preaching. Here, however, was a demon working actively to cheat him, to destroy his preaching, to disperse his disciples, and to displace his Deity. He was forced to fight, and his disciples, if they were to understand his mood, would also have to fight.

Prabhupāda was acting as the protector and the parent of the Deities and of ISKCON Bombay. As he had described in *The Nectar of Devotion*, many great devotees have an eternal relationship with Kṛṣṇa as His protector. When as a child Kṛṣṇa had fought the serpent Kāliya, Kṛṣṇa's mother and father had been plunged into transcendental anxiety. They had seen their child entangled in the coils of the serpent and, fearing for Kṛṣṇa's life, had wanted to protect Him. The eternal mother and father of Kṛṣṇa always worry that Kṛṣṇa may meet with harm, and when danger appears to come, their natural anxiety increases many times. In this way they show the most intense love for Kṛṣṇa. Śrīla Prabhupāda's mood was to protect Rādhā-Rāsavihārī and also his Kṛṣṇa consciousness movement. Although he knew that Kṛṣṇa was the supreme protector and that nobody could oppose His will, out of a protective desire to spread Kṛṣṇa's glories he feared that the demon Mr. N. might harm Kṛṣṇa.

Prabhupāda's feelings of anxiety and protectiveness extended to his disciples also. Although out of duty he often criticized and corrected them privately, before others he usually defended and praised them. When Dr. Patel, a Bombay physician, had criticized the way the devotees were living, not protecting themselves from mosquitoes, Prabhupāda had said that because his devotees were liberated and did not identify with their bodies, such things did not trouble them.

Prabhupāda saw his disciples as children, with little worldly experience;

they did not know how to deal with rogues and could be easily tricked. But if the son was gullible, the father would have to be shrewd and strong to protect his family. As protector of the devotees and of Kṛṣṇa's mission, Prabhupāda wanted to establish good housing so that his disciples could serve Kṛṣṇa in comfort—even elegance. Prabhupāda's spiritual master, Bhaktisiddhānta Sarasvatī, had taught the same thing when he said that preachers of Kṛṣṇa consciousness should have the best of everything, because they were doing the best service to Kṛṣṇa. Prabhupāda was therefore determined to establish his Hare Kṛṣṇa city in Bombay. He did not take the attitude of a naked mendicant, who cares for nothing of this material world. He felt responsible for his thousands of disciples, and therefore he took on so many anxieties.

Mr. N. could not know what motives were driving Śrīla Prabhupāda. Nor could he imagine the full ramifications of opposing Kṛṣṇa and Kṛṣṇa's pure devotee, even though the danger of such a position had been explained in India's most famous classics, *Bhagavad-gītā, Śrīmad-Bhāgavatam*, and *Rāmāyaṇa.* Prabhupāda was fighting on the side of Kṛṣṇa; therefore, Mr. N. was opposing the Supreme Personality of Godhead.

By Prabhupāda's disciples' cancellation of the agreement, ISKCON's legal position had been weakened. But Prabhupāda had faith that if the devotees just maintained possession of the land, their position would remain strong. At the same time, he urged the devotees to preach more. They should not think that without a temple they could not preach, so he arranged for another big Bombay *paṇḍāl* festival downtown, which proved to be a great success, with twenty thousand attending nightly.

Important guests like Mr. R. K. Ganatra, the mayor of Bombay, made introductory speeches, and the devotees also took an active part, organizing, advertising, cooking and distributing *prasādam*, distributing Śrīla Prabhupāda's books, and preaching at a question-and-answer booth. The *paṇḍāl* festival served to lift the devotees out of the doldrums of their protracted legal fight and the austerity of their living at Juhu.

During the last week of January 1973, Prabhupāda met with Mr. N. at the residence of Mr. Mahadevia. Although Prabhupāda's lawyers had filed a criminal case against Mr. N., Prabhupāda wanted to attempt an out-of-court settlement. He had always been gracious and charming with Mr. N., and Mr. N. had always appeared responsive and polite. But this time was different. Gone were the smiles and friendly words. The two were remaining barely civil to each other. After a few minutes, Prabhupāda asked his disciples to leave the room.

Speaking in Hindi, Mr. N. began accusing Prabhupāda and the devotees of being connected with the CIA. "I will come on Monday," said Mr. N. tersely, "with a check for two lakhs to pay back your down payment."

"All right," Prabhupāda replied. "If you don't want to part with your land, then we will leave. But think before you do this."

Mr. N. continued his accusations. "You people are calling yourselves the owners of the land, but you are just a big disturbance to the whole area, getting up at four and all this . . ."

"We do not claim to be the owner," Prabhupāda replied. "Kṛṣṇa is the real owner. I am not the real owner. Kṛṣṇa is already there on His land. Why are you bothering us so much? Simply take the money and give us the land. Or, if you want us to vacate, then prepare the check." Prabhupāda had been speaking with restraint, but now his tone became angry. "Bring out your check, and we will vacate tomorrow morning. No, we will vacate tonight! Give us our money back. Have you the money?"

Mr. N. shouted, "I will remove the Deities myself! I will break the temple and remove the Deities!" Mr. N. then stormed out of the room.

That week Mr. N. was hospitalized after a severe heart attack. Two weeks later he died. When Prabhupāda heard of Mr. N.'s death, he was at first silent. Then he quoted a verse Prahlāda Mahārāja had spoken following the death of his demoniac father, Hiraṇyakaśipu: *modati sādhur api vṛścika-sarpa-hatyā.* "Even a saint is pleased when a snake or scorpion is killed."

Mrs. N., although not as legally astute as her late husband, carried on the fight, and her lawyers, eager to collect their fees, pursued even more intently than she the litigation to drive out ISKCON. In April 1973, at ISKCON's instigation, ISKCON's case came before the High Court. There were tactical delays, however, and month after month passed with no decision.

Prabhupāda did not commit himself to construction on the land, because he had no deed and no assurance of one. He toured the West, returned to India, but still nothing had happened to resolve the matter. Life in ISKCON Bombay was peaceful, but progress remained stunted, the outcome uncertain.

Then one day, without warning, Mrs. N. launched a violent attack. On the morning of June 1, while the devotees were attending their routine duties, a truck drove onto the Juhu property. A demolition squad had come to dismantle the temple. Somehow Mrs. N. had convinced an official in the city government to authorize demolition of the temple, a modest structure of brick and steel-reinforced concrete. When Girirāja attempted to show the officer in charge a letter establishing ISKCON's rights, the man ignored the letter and signaled for the demolition to begin. Soon more trucks arrived, until nearly one hundred demolitionists, working with blowtorches and sledgehammers, swarmed over the property.

The demolitionists mounted ladders and began breaking the roof of the temple hall with sledgehammers. Others used torches to cut through the steel supports. The plan of the demolition squad was to knock out the steel supports of the *kīrtana* hall and proceed methodically toward the Deity house, wherein Rādhā-Rāsavihārī stood. The devotees tried to stop the demolition, but policemen soon appeared on the scene and, working in pairs, would grab the dissenters by the legs and arms and carry them away. Police dragged the women away by the hair, while tenants on the land looked on. Some were glad to see the demolition, although others were sympathetic. Out of fear of the police, however, no one moved to help the devotees.

One devotee, Maniṣvi, ran to a telephone and called Mr. Mahadevia, who, along with his friend Mr. Vinoda Gupta, rushed to Hare Krishna Land, to find the police dragging off the last protesting devotee by the hair. She had been trying to close the doors to the altar to protect the Deities when three policemen had wrestled her away. Mr. Mahadevia rushed to the house of a sympathetic tenant, Mr. Acarya, and phoned his brother Chandra Mahadevia, a wealthy businessman and friend of Bal Thakura, the leader of one of the most influential political parties in Bombay.

Mr. Chandra Mahadevia informed Bal Thakura of the emergency: at the instigation of a Hindu and under the order of a Hindu municipal officer, a Hindu temple of Lord Viṣṇu was being demolished. Mr. Thakura in turn informed the municipal commissioner, who denied knowing of any order to demolish the temple and who in turn phoned the local ward office that had sent out the demolition squad. The ward office sent a man to stop the demolition. The officer arrived around two P.M., just as the demolition squad had cut through the last pillars and were dismantling the roof above the Deities. The order to stop the demolition was given to the ward officer in charge, who then stopped the demolition squad.

Prabhupāda was in Calcutta at the time of the attack, and when the devotees reached him by phone, he told them to organize the local ISKCON sympathizers and life members and protest the attack by mass publicity. They should also expose the persons responsible. This would be very effective against Mrs. N. and her party.

Prabhupāda mentioned various life members he thought would help. Mr. Sada Jiwatlal, the head of the Hindu Viswa Parishad, should help with publicity, since his organization was a defender of Hindu *dharma* and was meant for handling such cases as this. Mr. Sethi should help in preventing further violence. This episode, Prabhupāda said, had been part of Kṛṣṇa's plan; the devotees should not be afraid.

The next morning a photo of the demolished temple appeared on the front page of the *Free Press Journal* with the headline, "UNAUTHORIZED TEMPLE DEMOLISHED BY MUNICIPAL AUTHORITIES."

Devotees began counteracting the bad publicity. Mr. Sada Jiwatlal turned his downtown office into an ISKCON office, and he and the devotees began the campaign. Despite the unfavorable propaganda, many Indians were shocked at the violence, and the municipal corporation unanimously condemned those officials responsible for the attack on a Hindu temple. Devotees, working from six A.M. to nine P.M. at Sada Jiwatlal's office, phoned the newspapers, wrote letters and circulars, and contacted possible sympathizers.

Mr. Vinoda Gupta, a member of the Jan-Sangh political party, which favored maintaining India's Hindu culture, joined with Kartikeya Mahadevia and others to form a "Save the Temple" committee. Mr. Gupta published his own leaflet declaring ISKCON to be a bona fide Hindu organization. As Girirāja met with and elicited the support of government officials, many of Bombay's leading citizens, appreciating the authenticity of the Hare Kṛṣṇa movement, began to show sympathy and offer assistance.

Thus the plan of Mrs. N. and her lawyers backfired. Although they had been thinking they were dealing with only a mere handful of young foreigners, they soon found themselves facing many of Bombay's most influential citizens.

Śrīla Prabhupāda predicted that the results would be positive. A few days after the incident he wrote,

> The demolition of our temple by the municipality has strengthened our position. The municipality standing committee has condemned the hasty action of the municipality, and has agreed to reconstruct

> the shed at their cost. Not only that, the temporary construction shall continue to stay until the court decision is there as to who is the proprietor of the land. Under the circumstances we should immediately reconstruct the Deity shed. Barbed wire fencing should be immediately done to cover the naked land. And if possible, immediately in front of the Deity shed, a temporary pandal should be constructed, with our materials. If it is so done, then I can go to Bombay and begin Bhagawat Parayana, to continue until the court decision is there. This is my desire.

Prabhupāda also asked Girirāja to give full coverage of the temple demolition in his *Hare Krishna Monthly* journal to life members. Prabhupāda himself wrote an article for the *Monthly* describing his movement and the events leading to the attack on the temple. He condemned the Bombay municipality for having the "audacity to smash our temple, against the law and principle of religious faith." A clique in Bombay, he said, had conspired to drive the devotees from their land without returning their money, and he asked for sympathizers and life members of the Kṛṣṇa consciousness movement to come forward and help him at this difficult hour.

Only about a dozen ISKCON life members responded to Śrīla Prabhupāda's call. There were hundreds of life members in Bombay, each of whom had donated 1,111 rupees and were receiving Prabhupāda's books. But when it came to a personal commitment in a time of controversy, only a few were willing to help. Those who did help, however, were able to assist in ways that the innocent, naive, and uninfluential disciples of Prabhupāda could not.

The devotees began to see the entire course of events as Kṛṣṇa's mercy, since many life members were now rendering valuable service to Prabhupāda and Lord Kṛṣṇa. In the past Prabhupāda had stayed in the homes of many life members, preaching to them and their families, convincing them of his sincerity and of the noble aims of his movement. These friends and members—like Bhagubai Patel, Beharilal Khandelwala, Brijratan Mohatta, Dr. C. Bali, and others—were acting not simply out of Hindu sentiment but out of deep respect and affection for Prabhupāda.

Girirāja, working with Sada Jiwatlal, tried to convince the municipal council to authorize the rebuilding of the temple structure. While doing so, however, he discovered that Mrs. N. had that very day (a Friday) filed for a court injunction preventing ISKCON from rebuilding. Justice Nain told Girirāja that he did not want to grant Mrs. N.'s request and that he would hear the devotees' case on the following Monday. This meant that the devotees had from Saturday morning to Monday morning, two days, to rebuild the temple.

The devotees reasoned that, although they had no actual permission to rebuild the temple, there was as yet no law to stop them. If Justice Nain ruled against them, then to rebuild would be very difficult. They decided, therefore, to use the weekend to rebuild. Mr. Lal, a former contractor, helped arrange materials: bricks, mortar, asbestos sheets. Mr. Sethi offered a crew of laborers. At eight P.M. on Friday the masons began their work, continuing throughout the night despite the rain. And on Monday morning, when the judge learned of the new temple, he declared, "What is built is built. No one can destroy the temple."

When Prabhupāda heard the news, he considered it a complete victory. The temple had been rebuilt, and public opinion was swinging strongly in ISKCON's favor.

CHAPTER SIX

Māyāpur
June 1, 1973

Although the Māyāpur building was not yet completed, Prabhupāda had come there to reside. He took two adjoining rooms, one as his study and one as his bedroom, on the second floor. Meanwhile, construction work continued in the temple room and in other parts of the building. On Prabhupāda's first day there, a storm struck, with massive black clouds and high winds. The storm was brief, however, and damage was minimal.

> I have just now come to Mayapur and am very hopeful to regain my strength and health on account of being in this transcendental atmosphere. Every moment we are passing here in great delight.

In the evening the temple *pūjārī*, Jananivāsa, would come to Prabhupāda's room with a clay pot of red coals and frankincense and fan the frankincense until the room was filled with smoke. This was to drive out insects, but Prabhupāda also considered it purifying.

Although he was sometimes disturbed by the workers' hammering, he found the atmosphere otherwise peaceful. Only a few devotees were staying there, and Prabhupāda gave his attention to translating or to speaking with guests and to the devotees in charge of developing his Māyāpur center. He would express his desires especially to Bhavānanda Mahārāja and Jayapatāka Mahārāja, and worked his will through them.

The devotees living in the building with Prabhupāda considered themselves menial servants in Prabhupāda's personal house. Of course, all the buildings in ISKCON belonged to Prabhupāda, yet in Māyāpur that sense was intensified. Generally the devotees in each particular center would raise money to support their center, but Prabhupāda personally took charge of getting funds for Māyāpur. He had begun a Māyāpur-Vṛndāvana Trust Fund of donations from his disciples and interest from bonds and security deposits. If money was misspent, energy misused, or the building damaged in any way, Prabhupāda would become very concerned. Now that he was personally on the scene, he often walked about, giving detailed instructions and demanding that discrepancies be corrected. The pink and reddish building was like a huge transcendental ship, and Śrīla Prabhupāda, as captain, would walk the wide verandas, giving strict orders to all mates for keeping everything shipshape.

One day Prabhupāda was walking on the veranda near his room. The other rooms were locked, and as Prabhupāda walked alone, he would open the window shutters and look in. Suddenly he turned to Śatadhanya, who waited on call nearby. "The fan is going on inside, and this room is empty and locked," Prabhupāda said. "Who has done this?" Śatadhanya didn't know. "Whoever has done this," Prabhupāda said, "is a rascal! He should know he is a rascal!" For two days after, Prabhupāda continued to refer to the incident with disgust.

One day, after a huge wind and rain storm, water covered the twelve-foot-wide marble veranda outside Prabhupāda's room. Bhavānanda Goswami, taking a large squeegee a devotee had made, began cleaning the marble floor, and Śrīla Prabhupāda came to his door to watch. "This is the way to clean marble," Prabhupāda said. "Don't polish it with wax, but just keep plenty of fresh water and every day in the morning wipe it off. In this way the marble will become naturally polished and will shine like glass."

Prabhupāda felt affection and deep gratitude for those devotees dedicating their lives to the Māyāpur project. One night he called Bhavānanda to his room and began asking him about the devotees. Suddenly Prabhupāda began crying. "I know it is difficult for all you Western boys and girls," he said. "You are so dedicated, serving here in my mission. I know you cannot even get *prasādam*. When I think that you cannot even get milk and that you have given up your opulent life to come here and you do not complain, I am very much indebted to all of you."

Bhavānanda: *The marble workers lived in some* chāṭāi *houses right near the construction site. There was a hand pump just outside the building, and that's where we took our bath and where the workers got the water for the cement. Some distance off were two toilets—one for the men, one for the women. It was just two holes in the ground, and each hole surrounded by a* chāṭāi *wall. The storms and the rain would come, and we would have to sludge through the mud in the fields to go to the toilets. There were snakes all over the place. It was wild! It was a construction site. No one lives on a construction site, but we did. Śrīla*

Prabhupāda made us move in there. It was good for us. No bathrooms, nothing—just open floors with concrete.

Although the devotees endured the austerities of living at the Māyāpur center construction site, they sometimes felt it was too difficult. But Śrīla Prabhupāda never considered it difficult, and he would encourage the devotees: "Māyāpur is so wonderful. You can live on the air and water alone."

Bhavānanda: *We were able to face up to so many difficulties because we just took it as our order from Śrīla Prabhupāda. There was no conception of ever leaving. What else would I do? This was my order: "Take Māyāpur. I am giving you Māyāpur. Take it, develop it, and enjoy it." There was no question in our minds of going somewhere else.*

The surrounding grounds were rice fields, and to get to the temple building from the entrance of the property—a distance of more than two hundred yards—devotees would have to walk on paths made by ridges of earth that separated one rice field from another. The kitchen, which was made of tarpaulin and bamboo, was located near the entrance to the property.

The devotees had to live without electricity much of the time, since the power supply was often cut off. They would use kerosene lamps at night, and Prabhupāda said the lamps should be taken apart every day, the wicks trimmed, and the glass washed. "In the future," he said, "you should grow castor plants and crush the seeds and take the oil for burning."

Prabhupāda told the devotees how to build simple dwellings. He also wanted them to build a wall with a gate along the front of the property. They should build small rooms—hutments, he called them—against the wall. Devotees could stay in these simple cottages. They should plant coconut and banana trees.

Raising the money, buying the land, arranging for workers and materials—it had been an arduous struggle, replete with bureaucratic delays, forms, fees, supply shortages, and the like. Prabhupāda would not tolerate any carelessness or waste. The building, which was turning out to be so artistic, substantial, and useful, was actually a gift from Lord Kṛṣṇa. So to live here in Kṛṣṇa's building was to reciprocate lovingly with the Lord. The devotees should think of serving Kṛṣṇa, not of becoming comfortable and forgetting the purpose of both the building and of life.

The slamming of doors, although seemingly a minor fault, greatly disturbed Śrīla Prabhupāda. It symptomized carelessness and misuse, and Prabhupāda said the sound cracked his heart. One time Prabhupāda came out of his room and called out, "Who is that slamming the doors? No one knows from where this building has come. You take it for granted, that it is here. But no one cares."

More often, however, Śrīla Prabhupāda displayed a roselike softness, an intimate, informal, and affectionate nature. The holy *dhāma* of Māyāpur was the spiritual world, Goloka Vṛndāvana; so the devotees there were living with Prabhupāda in the spiritual world. More than most any other place in the world, the devotees living in Māyāpur knew they could walk into Prabhupāda's room and see him. He sometimes even walked into their rooms. While they were working, reading, or talking, he might suddenly walk in and speak with them, asking how they felt and how they were adjusting to living in India. "It is difficult living here?" he would ask. "I think India is too hot. What do you think?"

Even with the building incomplete, many guests were coming, especially to talk with Prabhupāda, who patiently spent many hours each day speaking about Kṛṣṇa consciousness with guests who came to inquire about his movement or who came only to talk about themselves and their own philosophy. Sometimes he would remark that an individual had wasted his time, but he never stopped anyone from seeing him. One wealthy Hindu man, Mr. Brijratan Mohatta, and his wife, a daughter of multimillionaire R. D. Birla, visited Prabhupāda from Calcutta. Śrīla Prabhupāda took care in properly hosting his guests, and he personally reviewed the menu and briefed his disciples on serving Mr. Mohatta and his wife. Offering *prasādam* was an important part of the Vaiṣṇava's etiquette, and Śrīla Prabhupāda always stressed that the devotees immediately offer *prasādam* to visitors.

"You should always be able to offer water, hot *purīs* and eggplant *bhājī* (fried eggplant), and sweets," Prabhupāda said. Even when guests appeared shy, Prabhupāda would insist they take a full meal. Mrs. Mohatta, even though a member of one of the wealthiest families in India, was satisfied with the simple hospitality Śrīla Prabhupāda and his disciples offered. The room she and her husband stayed in was unfinished—the slate floors hadn't been polished, and construction work was going on all around—and the devotees could only offer them a mattress on the floor with a pillow; yet they appeared to be quite satisfied and appreciative.

Bhavānanda: *Śrīla Prabhupāda introduced us to many of the details of Indian culture at Māyāpur. He had us put down mattresses covered with sheets in his room. In 1970, in Los Angeles, he had asked me to sew sheets together to make a covering for the rug in his room. And then he had gotten down on his hands and knees right next to me, and we had smoothed out the wrinkles in the sheet.*

So he had us do that same thing in Māyāpur, where we put mattresses from one end of the room to the other with bolster pillows against the wall. "Now you have white sheet covers," he said, "and you change these every day." When Bengali gentlemen visited Śrīla Prabhupāda in his room, they would sit on these mattresses around the edge of the room, their backs against the bolster pillows.

It was very aristocratic. The whole mood was that he was the mahant, *the master of the house, the* ācārya, *but also the aristocratic Bengali gentlemen saw that he was reestablishing the old aristocratic mood from the early 1900s or 1920s. It was from Prabhupāda's old days with the Mullik family, and it was rapidly dwindling. At that time you couldn't find a semblance of the old culture anywhere, because all those families had become degraded, and their wealth gone.*

When the evening's multitudes of varieties of insects gathered around Prabhupāda's light, he would sometimes comment on how they were such wonderful creations of God. "This little insect," he said one evening, "is both pilot and flying machine in one. Here there are hundreds of insects flying together, and yet there are no collisions. That is God's arrangement. They never crash, because the Supersoul is present—one in every heart. Let the material scientists manufacture such a wonderful machine with a built-in pilot that will not crash. When one man flies and then there are two planes, they have to be very careful."

While a few devotees sat on the sheet-covered mattresses in his room, Prabhupāda sat on his slightly raised *āsana,* leaning back against a white bolster pillow. Both spiritual master and disciple enjoyed bliss in speaking and hearing Kṛṣṇa consciousness. The devotees wanted to hear Prabhupāda's words and follow his will, and he wanted to instruct them.

"But these insects," Prabhupāda continued, "are not perfect. They are flying to the light. That also means they are attracted to death. So they are just like the materialists. The materialists are building skyscrapers, yet they don't know what will happen at death. Henry Ford and other big capitalists had to die. But so many others are trying to become just like them. They do not know it means their death also. They are like these small insects. In the morning we simply find heaps of them, all dead."

Often while Prabhupāda was talking in his room the lights would suddenly go out, and devotees would bring in kerosene lamps. And each night, while Prabhupāda was speaking, the *pūjārī* would come, filling the room with frankincense smoke. Ghee lamps faintly illuminated the large teakwood bas-relief carving of Rādhā and Kṛṣṇa on the wall opposite Prabhupāda's desk.

During this summer visit, Prabhupāda further revealed his vision for ISKCON's Māyāpur development. The devotees were already aware that the plan was vast and would cost millions of dollars. They now had one building, but this was only the beginning. In the total plan, this building was almost insignificant. Prabhupāda spoke about a colossal temple, its great dome rising above a transcendental city. This Mayapur Chandrodaya Mandir would house the greatest planetarium in the world, depicting the universe as it is described in the Vedic literature.

To execute such a project, Prabhupāda wanted to train his disciples in the Vedic arts, now dying in Bengal. Bhaktisiddhānta Sarasvatī had been greatly interested in using dioramas to depict the *līlā* of Kṛṣṇa and Lord Caitanya, and now Prabhupāda wanted his own disciples to learn the art by studying under local Māyāpur artists.

In June Baradrāja, Ādideva, Mūrti, and Īśāna arrived to begin learning the art of doll-making. Prabhupāda also wanted a disciple to learn to make *mṛdaṅgas*, and a potter began coming every day to teach Īśāna how to mold and fire the clay shells. The devotees converted Prabhupāda's original straw cottage into a workshop, and Prabhupāda began inviting other disciples to come to Māyāpur.

> Mayapur is already wonderful, being the transcendental birthplace of Lord Krishna. By utilizing Western talents to develop this place, certainly it will become unique in the world.

The Māyāpur city, Prabhupāda said, would be the fulfillment of the desires of the previous *ācāryas*. The city would grow to a population of fifty thousand and would become the spiritual capital of the world. With its gigantic temple in the center and separate quarters for *brāhmaṇas, kṣatriyas, vaiśyas,* and *śūdras*, the city would be a model for all other cities. The day would come when the world's cities would be ruined, and humanity would take refuge in cities modeled after Māyāpur. The development of Māyāpur would mark the beginning of a Kṛṣṇa conscious world. Thus the influence of Śrī Caitanya Mahāprabhu would increase, and His prediction would manifest: "In every town and village My name will be chanted."

Prabhupāda said that Māyāpur should eventually become more easily accessible—by bridge from Navadvīpa, by motor launch up the Ganges from Calcutta, and from all parts by air. In Bengal millions were by birth followers of Lord Caitanya, and they would recognize and take up Kṛṣṇa consciousness as the pure form of their own culture. There is a saying: What Bengal does, the rest of India follows. So if Bengal became reformed and purified by the Kṛṣṇa conscious example of American Vaiṣṇavas, then all India would follow. And when all India became Kṛṣṇa conscious, the whole world would follow. "I have given you the kingdom of God," Prabhupāda said to his Māyāpur managers. "Now take it, develop it, and enjoy it."

Throughout the month of June Prabhupāda continued to live happily and peacefully in the not-yet-completed building of the Mayapur Chandrodaya Mandir. Although he had been ill with a cough since Los Angeles—a cough he had been unable to cure while traveling in the West—on coming to Māyāpur his health had recovered.

> In Mayapur I am much improved from how I was in Los Angeles. The great advantage here is that there is always open air and a good breeze which is naturally very good for any breathing difficulties. . . . Certainly Mayapur is by far a better place than Los Angeles because you can enjoy the free air here. The climate is not too hot, but a little moist with humidity but on the whole it is very pleasing. Our building is most superexcellently situated, and it is the experience of many respectable outsiders that while the outer atmosphere is unbearably hot, in our building it is pleasing.

Prabhupāda praised the constant pleasurable breezes that passed through the building—he called them "Vaikuṇṭha breezes." Sometimes, however, a violent storm would suddenly appear. Although severe, these storms were also beautiful, with continuous lightning like neon lights filling the sky. One day a storm arose, and the winds began to howl through the building. Noticing that Prabhupāda's doors and windows were open, Śatadhanya rushed into the room and began frantically closing them. But Prabhupāda, seated at his desk, said, "Stop, leave all the windows open."

"Prabhupāda," Śatadhanya protested, "the storm is here."

"Just leave them open," Prabhupāda said, as the wind rushed through his room at more than fifty miles an hour. Prabhupāda smiled. "There is no place in the world like this!" he said, his saffron robes billowing.

Prabhupāda stood on the roof of his Māyāpur building, looking over to the birthplace of Caitanya Mahāprabhu less than a mile away. "Actually," he said to Bhavānanda Mahārāja, "their claim to the birthplace of Caitanya Mahāprabhu is not very important. Is Kṛṣṇa famous for having been born in Mathurā? No. He is famous for His activities. Similarly, Caitanya Mahāprabhu is not famous for having been born in Māyāpur. He is famous for His activities, for His *saṅkīrtana* preaching. This Mayapur Chandrodaya Mandir is the preaching of Caitanya Mahāprabhu. Therefore I want a place that is so attractive because of the activities of Caitanya Mahāprabhu that everyone will come here!"

* * *

While in Calcutta, before coming to Māyāpur, Prabhupāda had called several senior disciples into his room. "I have had many requests," he had said to them, "to translate *Caitanya-bhāgavata.* But I am going to translate the entire *Caitanya-caritāmṛta.* Is that all right?"

"Oh, yes, Prabhupāda," Bhavānanda Goswami had replied, "that's wonderful."

Decades ago Prabhupāda had written essays based on the *Caitanya-caritāmṛta*, and over the years he had translated some of the verses and written purports to them. Then in America in 1968 he had completed *Teachings of Lord Caitanya,* a summary study based on certain important passages of *Caitanya-caritāmṛta.* During his stay in Māyāpur, however, he began anew a translation and commentary of Kṛṣṇadāsa Kavirāja's *Caitanya-caritāmṛta*, beginning with the Seventh Chapter. As he progressed, he found a wonderful momentum and said he would publish a volume, starting with Chapter Seven, for Lord Caitanya's appearance day in March. Deciding to complete the entire *Caitanya-caritāmṛta*, he suspended his work on *Śrīmad-Bhāgavatam*.

In one of the first verses of the Seventh Chapter, Kṛṣṇadāsa Kavirāja states, "Let me offer my obeisances to Lord Śrī Kṛṣṇa, who has manifested Himself in five, as a devotee, expansion of a devotee, incarnation of a devotee, pure devotee, and devotional energy." Prabhupāda wrote that the only way for people to be elevated in love of Kṛṣṇa in the age of Kali is by the mercy of the Pañca-tattva, or Lord Caitanya in His form of five personalities. One should offer obeisances to Srī Caitanya Mahāprabhu by chanting the Pañca-tattva *mantra, śrī-kṛṣṇa-caitanya prabhu-nityānanda śrī-advaita gadādhara śrīvāsādi-gaura-bhakta-vṛnda.* This *mantra* should be recited before one chants the *mahā-mantra*, Hare Kṛṣṇa, Hare Kṛṣṇa, Kṛṣṇa Kṛṣṇa, Hare Hare/ Hare Rāma, Hare Rāma, Rāma Rāma, Hare Hare. "There are ten offenses in the chanting of the Hare Kṛṣṇa *mahā-mantra*," Prabhupāda wrote, "but these are not considered in the chanting of the Pañca-tattva *mahā-mantra*. . . . One must first take shelter of Śrī Caitanya Mahāprabhu, learn the Pañca-tattva *mahā-mantra*, and then chant the Hare Kṛṣṇa *mahā-mantra*."

Verse after verse of the Seventh Chapter confirmed the essential principles of Śrīla Prabhupāda's mission and attested that he was teaching exactly after the method advised by Lord Caitanya Mahāprabhu.

> The characteristics of Kṛṣṇa are understood to be a storehouse of transcendental love. Although that storehouse of love certainly came with Kṛṣṇa when He was present, it was sealed. But when Śrī Caitanya Mahāprabhu came with His other associates, the Pañca-tattva, they broke the seal and plundered the storehouse to taste transcendental love of Kṛṣṇa. The more they tasted it, the more their thirst for it grew.
>
> Śrī Pañca-tattva themselves danced again and again and thus made it easier to drink nectarean love of Godhead. They danced, cried, laughed and chanted like madmen, and in this way they distributed love of Godhead.

In commenting on these verses Prabhupāda wrote,

> The present Kṛṣṇa consciousness movement follows the same principle, and therefore simply by chanting and dancing we have received good responses all over the world. It is to be understood, however,

> that this chanting and dancing do not belong to this material world. They are actually transcendental activities, for the more one engages in chanting and dancing, the more he can taste the nectar of transcendental love of Godhead.

By the phrase "Kṛṣṇa consciousness movement," Prabhupāda spoke not only of his own disciples and his Kṛṣṇa consciousness society but also of the movement inaugurated by Lord Caitanya. Just as the original Personality of Godhead and the Deity of Kṛṣṇa in the temple were the same, so the movement of Lord Caitanya Mahāprabhu and Prabhupāda's Kṛṣṇa consciousness movement were identical.

> In distributing love of Godhead, Caitanya Mahāprabhu and His associates did not consider who was a fit candidate and who was not, nor where such distribution should or should not take place. They made no conditions. Wherever they got the opportunity the members of the Pañca-tattva distributed love of Godhead.

For Śrīla Prabhupāda, this verse directly confirmed the instruction he had received from his spiritual master, Bhaktisiddhānta Sarasvatī, that people of all births could become Vaiṣṇavas, *brāhmaṇas,* and *sannyāsīs.* Here was direct evidence from the scripture, yet Prabhupāda, like his own spiritual master, had often received criticism from the caste-conscious *brāhmaṇas* of India. With the proof in hand, Prabhupāda now challenged his envious critics.

> There are some rascals who dare to speak against the mission of Lord Caitanya by criticizing the Kṛṣṇa consciousness movement for accepting Europeans and Americans as *brāhmaṇas* and offering them *sannyāsa.* But here is an authoritative statement that in distributing love of Godhead one should not consider whether the recipients are Europeans, Americans, Hindus, Muslims, etc. The Kṛṣṇa consciousness movement should be spread wherever possible, and one should accept those who thus become Vaiṣṇavas as being greater than *brāhmaṇas,* Hindus or Indians. Śrī Caitanya Mahāprabhu desired that His name be spread in each and every town and village on the surface of the globe. Therefore, when the cult of Caitanya Mahāprabhu is spread all over the world, should those who embrace it not be accepted as Vaiṣṇavas, *brāhmaṇas* and *sannyāsīs*? These foolish arguments are

> sometimes raised by envious rascals, but Kṛṣṇa conscious devotees do not care about them. We strictly follow the principles set down by the Pañca-tattva.

Another criticism Śrīla Prabhupāda encountered was that his emphasis on proselytizing was actually alien to Indian spirituality. Even Prabhupāda's Godbrothers had occasionally made such remarks. More often, however, this sentiment came from the impersonalists, who argued that people should be left to conceive of religion in their own ways; religion, being an internal, spiritual affair, should not be propagated by zealous evangelism. Preaching and conversion, they said, were for the Christians, not for followers of Indian religion. In the Seventh Chapter of *Caitanya-caritāmṛta's Ādi-līlā,* however, Śrī Kṛṣṇa Caitanya, the Supreme Personality of Godhead, reveals His heart and emotion as the ideal preacher.

> Although the members of the Pañca-tattva plundered the storehouse of love of Godhead and ate and distributed the contents, there was no scarcity, for this wonderful storehouse is so complete that as the love is distributed, the supply increases hundreds of times.
>
> The flood of love of Godhead swelled in all directions, and thus young men, old men, women and children were all immersed in that inundation.
>
> The Kṛṣṇa consciousness movement will inundate the entire world and drown everyone, whether one be a gentleman, a rogue or even lame, invalid or blind.
>
> When the first five members of the Pañca-tattva saw the entire world drowned in love of Godhead and the seed of material enjoyment in the living entities completely destroyed, they all became exceedingly happy.
>
> The more the five members of the Pañca-tattva caused the rains of love of Godhead to fall, the more the inundation increased and spread all over the world.

This was Śrīla Prabhupāda's spirit in training young men and women in the International Society for Krishna Consciousness, and he was offering these words of Lord Caitanya to strengthen all the Lord's devotees. The members of the Kṛṣṇa consciousness movement should be confident that by preaching purely they would meet with success. Prabhupāda was confident. Here were the words of *śāstra,* words spoken by the Supreme

Personality of Godhead. And Prabhupāda's personal experience confirmed the same. Thus he could write,

> Our Kṛṣṇa consciousness movement was started singlehandedly, and no one provided for our livelihood, but at present we are spending hundreds and thousands of dollars all over the world and the movement is increasing more and more. Although jealous persons may be envious, if we stick to our principles and follow the footsteps of the Pañca-tattva, this movement will go on unchecked by imitation swamis, *sannyāsīs*, religionists, philosophers or scientists, for it is transcendental to all material considerations. Therefore, those who propagate the Kṛṣṇa consciousness movement should not be afraid of such rascals and fools.

The verses of the Seventh Chapter described a worldwide inundation of Kṛṣṇa consciousness. Thus the objections that Europeans and Americans could not become *brāhmaṇas* or *sannyāsīs* would be swept away as Lord Caitanya's mercy flooded the entire world. Nothing could check it.

The words of Kṛṣṇadāsa Kavirāja intensified Prabhupāda's desire to base his worldwide movement in the land where Lord Caitanya appeared and began His *saṅkīrtana* movement. The Pañca-tattva had begun in Navadvīpa, and from here the waves of love of Godhead were swelling outward.

> In Śrīdhama Māyāpur, there is sometimes a great flood after the rainy season. This is an indication that from the birthplace of Lord Caitanya the inundation of love of Godhead should spread all over the world, for this will help everyone, including old men, young men, women and children. The Kṛṣṇa consciousness movement of Śrī Caitanya Mahāprabhu is so powerful that it can inundate the entire world and interest all classes of men in the subject of love of Godhead.

In this Seventh Chapter of the *Ādi-līlā*, Prabhupāda found many other evidences authorizing ISKCON under the principles of Lord Caitanya's teachings and activities. Kṛṣṇadāsa Kavirāja says that Lord Caitanya's taking *sannyāsa* was a trick for delivering certain classes of society who would otherwise not have shown Him respect. Prabhupāda, in his commentary, explained that he also had devised schemes for offering the benefits of Kṛṣṇa consciousness to as wide a spectrum of society as possible, and he cited his acceptance of women into the Kṛṣṇa consciousness movement. "Therefore it is a principle," he wrote, "that a preacher must strictly follow the rules and regulations laid down in the *śāstra*, yet at the same time devise a means by which the preaching work to reclaim the fallen may go on with full force."

* * *

June 27, 1973

From Māyāpur Śrīla Prabhupāda went to Calcutta. He wrote to Tamāla Kṛṣṇa Goswami,

> . . . There is a suggestion by Shyamsundar that I may go to London for meeting very important men there in the new house given us by George. . . . But I want to make some definite settlement of Bombay affairs before I return to Europe or America. If there is a suitable place for me to stay for a few days in Bombay I can go there immediately and from there I may go to London.

While considering his itinerary, Prabhupāda passed some days in the Calcutta temple on Albert Road. He was very free about allowing people to see him, and his room was often filled with local Bengalis as well as his own disciples, seated on the white sheet before him. In the evenings he would go, even when it meant riding for miles through congested parts of the city, to spend an hour in someone's home, preaching Kṛṣṇa consciousness.

Śrīla Prabhupāda's sister, Bhavatāriṇī (known as Piśimā to Prabhupāda's disciples), would also visit the Calcutta temple to see her beloved brother and, as usual, to cook for him. One day, however, a few hours after eating her *kachaurīs*, Prabhupāda felt sharp pains in his stomach. He closed his doors and went to bed. His followers became very concerned. When his servant, Śrutakīrti, came into the room, he found him tossing.

"Śrīla Prabhupāda, what's wrong?"

"My stomach," Prabhupāda replied. "That coconut *kachaurī*—it was not cooked."

The seizure continued all night, and several devotees continually massaged Prabhupāda's body, especially his stomach. But with every breath he would moan. Piśimā was standing by, but Prabhupāda's disciples feared her presence, thinking she might want to cook something else for him, even in his illness.

Prabhupāda asked that the picture of Lord Nṛsiṁha be taken from the altar and put beside his bed. Some devotees feared that Prabhupāda might be about to pass away. The next morning, when the illness continued, the devotees called for the local *kavirāja* (Ayur-vedic doctor).

The old *kavirāja* came and diagnosed Prabhupāda's illness as severe blood dysentery. He left medicine, but it was ineffectual. Later, when Prabhupāda called Bhavānanda to his room and requested fried *purīs* with a little *paṭala* [an Indian vegetable similar to a small squash] and salt, Bhavānanda protested; such fried foods would be the worst thing for him. Prabhupāda said that this was the blood dysentery cure his mother had given during his childhood. He then called for his sister, and speaking to her in Bengali, told her to prepare *purīs* and *paṭala.* A few hours after taking the food, Prabhupāda again called Bhavānanda; he was feeling better. "My mother was right," he remarked.

A lengthy telegram arrived from Śyāmasundara, glorifying the preaching opportunities that awaited Prabhupāda in London, where he would be picked up at the airport in a helicopter and flown to the main event—the greatest Ratha-yātrā ever held. The parade would proceed down Picadilly Lane, climaxing under a large pavilion at Trafalgar Square. The telegram went on to say that millions of Englishmen—including certain very, very important people—were eager to see Śrīla Prabhupāda and that arrangements were underway for Prabhupāda to instruct the Queen's eldest son, Prince Charles, in Kṛṣṇa consciousness.

Some of the promises were exaggerated, Śrīla Prabhupāda knew, but his desire to preach again in England was strong. George Harrison had given the devotees a large estate forty-five minutes outside of London, and Prabhupāda spoke of going there and installing Deities of Rādhā and Kṛṣṇa on Janmāṣṭamī day. Yet even now, over a month before Janmāṣṭamī, he was feeling deeply affected by Śyāmasundara's invitation. Although still exhausted from dysentery, he considered flying immediately to London.

Calling in those G.B.C. secretaries and *sannyāsīs* with him in Calcutta, sitting up in bed while they sat before him on the floor, Prabhupāda asked their advice. They concluded that he should go to a healthier climate—Los Angeles or Hawaii—to rest and recuperate. Prabhupāda mildly agreed as his advisors decided Hawaii would be the best place, a place where the climate was ideal and where he would have few interruptions. Suddenly, however, he sat up straighter. He would return to the West, he said, but to London, not to Hawaii. And not to recuperate, but to preach!

"Let me strike while the iron is hot," he said. "I think that is an English maxim. If you do that, then you can keep the iron in shape. In the West, people are fed up. So we want to give them spiritual enlightenment."

Prabhupāda had immediately convinced his disciples with his forceful statements. "There are two misleading theories in the West," he continued. "One is that life comes from matter, and the other is that there is no life after death—you can just enjoy this life. They say everything is matter. So as this Kṛṣṇa consciousness movement grows, the Communists will be curbed down. People say they are trying for unity, but they have no brains to see how this will achieve unity. They have formed a big complicated League of Nations and now United Nations, but they all fail. But this simple method of Ratha-yātrā—all over the world it is spreading. *Jagannātha* means 'Lord of the universe.' So Lord Jagannātha is now international God, through our ISKCON. Therefore, I want to go to the West and give them these things."

Although Prabhupāda appeared physically unfit to immediately fly to London to the active preaching that awaited him, his disciples submitted, accepting this as another miracle by Kṛṣṇa.

* * *

London
July 7, 1973

Paravidha: *It was Ratha-yātrā day. I saw Prabhupāda coming into the temple, and he didn't look very strong. I was really amazed, but I could understand that his strength was something spiritual.*

Dhruvanātha: *At the parade site we were waiting to receive Śrīla Prabhupāda at Marble Arch, where the procession starts. The* vyāsāsana *was nicely decorated, and everybody was expecting Prabhupāda simply to sit on his* vyāsāsana *on the cart and just ride through the streets, just as he had done in the other Ratha-yātrās. So it was to our great amazement and joy that when Prabhupāda came, he refused to sit on the* vyāsāsana. *He indicated that he would dance and lead the procession!*

Yogeśvara: *They brought stairs up so Prabhupāda could mount the* ratha *cart and sit down on the* vyāsāsana. *But he waved them off and just started walking with the chariots, leading the dancing.*

Dhīraśānta: *I twisted my ankle and couldn't walk, so I rode on the cart. Therefore I could see Prabhupāda very clearly. Revatīnandana Mahārāja was chanting into the microphone from the cart, but after about fifteen minutes of the procession Prabhupāda told the devotees to tell Revatī-nandana Mahārāja and the others to come down and lead the* kīrtana *in the street with him.*

Revatīnandana: *When Prabhupāda saw his* vyāsāsana *on the cart, he said, "No, I am just a devotee. I will go in the procession." We had a big, great* kīrtana. *Haṁsadūta led, I led, Śyāmasundara led—different devotees traded off, leading this fantastic* kīrtana. *And Prabhupāda was right in the middle of the* kīrtana *with his* karatālas *the whole time. He was dancing back and forth and jumping up and down and dancing.*

Rohiṇī-nandana: *The cart was going quite slowly. Prabhupāda walked about twenty or thirty yards ahead of the cart, leading the procession. Meanwhile the* kīrtana *was coming from the* ratha *cart through microphones. Prabhupāda called them all down, and he got them all around himself, and they were chanting Hare Kṛṣṇa. Ever so often he would turn around and raise both his arms very majestically in the air and say, "Jaya Jagannātha!" Sometimes we would get a little further ahead, so then he would turn around and wait for the cart to come on. Sometimes he was dancing, and sometimes he would stand, raising his hands in the air.*

Śāradīyā dāsī: *Prabhupāda would dance, and then after a few feet he would turn around and look up at the deities with his arms raised. Then he would dance for a few moments, meditating on the deities, and then he would turn around and go on. In this way he danced the entire way. The devotees held hands in a circle around him to protect him from the crowd. It was a wonderful, transcendental affair. Prabhupāda was looking up at the deities, and all the devotees were behind him.*

Sudurjaya: *Prabhupāda surprised us. We didn't know if he was sick or not, feeling weak and dizzy or not. Sometimes he looked very ill, and sometimes he looked like an eighteen-year-old boy. He surprised us. He had his cane in his hand but raised it in the air as he danced. After a while, Śyāmasundara came up to me and said, "Listen, he's not going to make it. Prabhupāda is very ill. I want you to follow in a car. Be within thirty seconds' reach so we can put Prabhupāda in the car immediately." Prabhupāda was going down Park Lane, and from time to time he would turn back and raise his hands. He was going so fast that they couldn't pull the cart fast enough to keep up with him. He would have to wait for the cart to catch up. He would turn back, raise his hands, and say, "Haribol!" Several times he did this. He was going so fast that he had to wait. The devotees were dancing, the weather was beautiful, and the crowd was wonderful.*

Dhruvanātha: *The passersby were rooted to the spot, looking at Prabhupāda. A man of that age simply dancing and jumping in the air like a young boy was the most amazing sight! And then every five minutes or so Prabhupāda would turn around and look toward Jagannātha. The devotees would clear the way so no one blocked his sight, and he had a perfect view of Jagannātha, Balarāma, and Subhadrā. But after a while the police came and motioned that we couldn't keep stopping like this. We had to keep the whole thing going, because the traffic jams were becoming critical. Devotees were crying and chanting and dancing, and there was much commotion.*

Śrutakīrti: *When Prabhupāda was dancing, the bobbies kept on coming up and looking for someone official. Finally they came to me and said, "You'll have to tell your leader to sit down. He's causing too much of a disturbance. Everyone is becoming wild, and we can't control the crowd, you know." So I said, "All right." But I didn't say anything to Prabhupāda.*

So then they came again and said, "You must tell him he'll have to sit down." So I said, "All right," and I tapped Prabhupāda. The whole time he had been in ecstasy, dancing before the cart and encouraging everyone else to dance. He would motion with his hands and encourage the devotees to keep dancing. He kept the momentum of the festival. So I said, "Prabhupāda, the policemen want you to sit down. They say you are creating havoc in the parade." Prabhupāda looked at me, turned, and kept on. He completely ignored it and kept on dancing. And they couldn't do anything. Prabhupāda wouldn't stop, and the police wouldn't say anything to him.

Paravidha: *I was distributing* Back to Godhead *magazines along the whole parade route. I was exhausted, and I was having a lot of trouble keeping up with the procession. But Prabhupāda was just there, and he was dancing like a young boy. I was amazed at his spiritual energy.*

Dhruvanātha: *When we came to Picadilly Circus, Prabhupāda suddenly stopped the whole procession. Picadilly Circus, of course, was just packed with people. For about three minutes Prabhupāda stopped the procession and just danced and danced with the devotees all around him.*

Rohiṇī-nandana: *When we got to Picadilly Circus, Prabhupāda really started to dance. He was leaping off the ground. The car was stopped.*

It was very similar, actually, to the description in the Caitanya-caritāmṛta *of how Lord Caitanya would lead the Ratha-yātrā procession. So the cart was stopped, and then Prabhupāda would wait for it to catch up.*

Yogeśvara: *When we finally arrived at Trafalgar Square and Prabhupāda saw the big tent and the other arrangements the devotees had made, he held up his hands again. He had been dancing and walking the entire route of the parade. It must have been at least an hour that he had been walking and dancing—all the way from Hyde Park to Trafalgar Square.*

Rohiṇī-nandana: *When Prabhupāda got to Trafalgar Square, he immediately sat down on the plinth of Nelson's Column on a little* vyāsāsana *and delivered a lecture about the holy name of Kṛṣṇa. This was directly after his marathon of chanting and dancing.*

The next day's papers carried favorable news coverage of the festival, and Prabhupāda wrote of it to a disciple in Los Angeles.

> You will be glad to know the Rathayatra in London was very successful. The Daily Guardian had a picture on the front page of our cart and stated that we were competition to the monument in memory of Lord Nelson in Trafalgar Square. My health is good and I am taking daily walk and speaking at the class in the morning.

In another letter Prabhupāda wrote,

> Our festival here was very well received and I was so much encouraged by the whole thing that I was able to walk and dance the entire way from Hyde Park to Trafalgar Square.

Śrīla Prabhupāda settled into a regular routine at Bhaktivedanta Manor. "Here at Bhaktivedanta Manor," he wrote, "the place is the nicest possible. It is calm and quiet, and the village is neat and clean." Prabhupāda's room on the second floor was spacious enough to seat fifty guests comfortably, and its large windows overlooked the expansive grounds.

Prabhupāda said that if the devotees would clean out the lake and keep up the grounds, then he would stay always at Bhaktivedanta Manor and translate here in peace. They should get some cows, he said, and use some of the extra acreage for farming.

Although the devotees had not long been living in the Manor and had done little to improve the buildings and grounds, Prabhupāda pointed out a place where they could one day build a thirty-story temple, the grandest building in all of London. He proposed that he stay for at least two months and install Rādhā-Kṛṣṇa Deities on Janmāṣṭamī day; he would also oversee the construction of the temple room and altar.

Every morning at about six Prabhupāda would leave the Manor for an hour's walk. There was no restriction as to who could join him, and sometimes as many as twenty devotees would trail behind, trying to hear anything he might say. Looking off toward the horizon, he commented that Letchmore Heath reminded him of Vṛndāvana.

Prabhupāda would walk down the lane to a place called Round Bush, stroll past a wheat field, and finally return to Letchmore Heath and the Manor. A local policeman had become friends with the devotees and would regularly exchange greetings with Prabhupāda. Particularly Prabhupāda liked the cleanliness of the little village, and he would often point out even the smallest pieces of trash on the Manor grounds. The village, he said, was much neater than American towns.

Śyāmasundara had promised Śrīla Prabhupāda many interested visitors, and Śrīla Prabhupāda reciprocated, promising that as long as the interested people kept coming, he would remain in England. Each night one or two guests—including scholars, priests, and occasional celebrities—would come and visit with Prabhupāda for a couple of hours. Prabhupāda seemed especially eager to present the philosophy of Kṛṣṇa consciousness to intelligent persons. As the world's foremost Vaiṣṇava *paramparā* philosopher of the *Gītā* and the *Bhāgavatam*, he had thoroughly realized the conclusions of the Vedic literature. He was experienced in countering all challenges and atheistic philosophies and knew what to expect from Christian, Māyāvādī, atheist—anyone. If a guest mentioned the name of a philosopher or school of thought unfamiliar to Prabhupāda, then Prabhupāda would simply ask, "What is his philosophy?" Inevitably he would recognize the "new" philosophy for what it was: an old, familiar mundane philosophy—with a new twist perhaps—easily defeated or brought to its perfection with Kṛṣṇa consciousness.

Prabhupāda was always eager to glorify Kṛṣṇa and repeat Kṛṣṇa's message, and with complete, enthusiastic freshness he would present again the same points he had presented many, many times before. He said he was like a cow that gives milk in any field. Put him in India or America or England—he would always give the same nectarean milk of *Bhagavad-gītā*.

Prabhupāda's entire day—his early-morning dictation of *Caitanya-caritāmṛta*, morning walk, *Bhagavad-gītā* lecture, talks with guests—revolved around philosophy. In Scotland, when a man had challenged that God needn't be presented through philosophy, Prabhupāda had replied, "What do you expect me to talk, some fairy tales?" Philosophy was necessary, especially for the so-called intelligent persons, whose minds raised so many intellectual doubts. And besides, to always be telling others about Kṛṣṇa, Prabhupāda said, was a symptom of love.

Moved by compassion for others' suffering, Prabhupāda always spoke the message of Kṛṣṇa and never tired of repeating it. He was genuinely angered by the atheistic speculators who mislead the people, because materialistic and impersonalistic philosophies ruined a person's chances of finding the solution to life's suffering. Whenever Prabhupāda heard anyone arguing the Māyāvāda doctrine, he would become like fire. He could not tolerate it. He had to correct it. When, after one of Prabhupāda's lectures at the Manor, a boy had said he had heard someone call the chanting of Hare Kṛṣṇa "a little bit of a bluff," Prabhupāda had replied, "Who says *bluff*? Who is that fool? Who is that rascal?" He had been ready to fight the atheist to glorify Kṛṣṇa.

These were Prabhupāda's natural drives; therefore he could go on and on, without stopping. He wanted to give people Kṛṣṇa consciousness. He had no other life. Even while relaxing in the privacy of his room he always spoke of Kṛṣṇa consciousness.

The devotees had invited many prominent British citizens to meet Śrīla Prabhupāda, and the responses were good. Economist Ernst Schumacher promised to visit, as did philosopher Sir Alfred J. Ayer. When Śyāmasundara informed Prabhupāda that Mr. Ayer was well known, Prabhupāda replied, "What is his philosophy?"

"Well," Śyāmasundara replied, "he doesn't believe in the existence of God."

"I will give him evidence," Prabhupāda replied. "I will ask him what he means by 'the existence of God.' I will ask him to make a list of the deficiencies of God's existence." Prabhupāda liked to meet with philosophical men and "corner them and defeat them."

Historian Arnold Toynbee was old and invalid; therefore, Prabhupāda agreed to visit him at his residence. Interested in discussing life after death, Dr. Toynbee asked Prabhupāda about *karma*. Most people, he said, were afraid of death. Prabhupāda agreed and added that according to a certain astrologer, one of India's recent leaders had taken birth as a dog. "So they are afraid they will go down," he said. When Toynbee asked if *karma* could be changed, Prabhupāda replied yes, but only by *bhakti*, devotion to God.

Arnold Toynbee: "Not many people in the West are thinking of this."

Prabhupāda: "They are less intelligent. It is not good. If they take to Kṛṣṇa consciousness, they can continue to work and live in the city, but they can change their consciousness. Then automatically everything will come."

Śrīla Prabhupāda asked Dr. Toynbee about the book he was writing, and the professor replied that it concerned ancient Greece's influence on the Greece of today. "The Greeks came from India," Prabhupāda said. "Vedic culture was once all over the world. Gradually, a new type of culture—just like this recent partition of India and Pakistan—took place."

Prabhupāda explained how in the future the governments would fall to rascals and thieves, whose only business would be to exploit the citizens. Food would be scarce. And the governments would levy so many taxes that the people would be harassed and go to the forests for shelter. Only the God conscious people would be free. The future would be an ocean of faults, with but one saving factor: simply by chanting Kṛṣṇa's names one could be freed. Even now, Prabhupāda said, the hippies were going to the forest, and the men were separated from their wives and money and were going to the hills and forests in disappointment. "You can predict the future in this way," Prabhupāda said.

Arnold Toynbee: "In India did the politicians keep the *Vedas*?"

Prabhupāda: "No, they threw them away. Present Indian politicians are not very satisfied with the *Vedas*. They threw them in the water. I have started, among the Indians and Americans; and for the next ten thousand years Kṛṣṇa consciousness will increase. Then there will be a gloomy picture of Kali-yuga. Ten thousand years is not a short time. It is our duty on behalf of Kṛṣṇa."

Arnold Toynbee: "Do you travel much?"

Prabhupāda: "All over the world."

A bearded young priest active in social service visited Prabhupāda and, upon Prabhupāda's prodding, debated with him about meat-eating and the Bible. During the discussion, Haṁsadūta and Pradyumna were citing passages from the Bible against meat-eating. Later, after the priest had left, Prabhupāda called Haṁsadūta back into his room and said, "It was not very good for us to speak on the basis of the Bible. Better we stick to the *Gītā*. Why bother to approach them for compromise or cooperation? They will never be convinced. What is the point of meeting with the Pope?" Those inclined to meat-eating, Prabhupāda said, could always find some quote in the Bible, such as the covenant with Noah after the flood. "We do not even know what ghastly things are occurring in the slaughterhouse," he said. "No one sees these things."

The next morning on his walk Prabhupāda continued discussing his talk with the priest. "In the name of religion," Prabhupāda said, "they are killing. The *Bhāgavatam* says this cheating religion is kicked out and simply worship of God is instated."

Devotee: "The priest last night said that Jesus ate meat."

Prabhupāda: "Then Jesus contradicted himself. He also said, 'Thou shalt not kill.' One shouldn't imitate the *īśvaras*. A hippie-type mendicant in India takes *gañja* and claims to be a devotee of Śiva. No, we should not imitate the powerful controllers. That priest said also that the Bible does not say, 'Thou shalt not kill,' but 'Thou shalt not murder.' So I told him that if the word is actually 'Thou shalt not murder' in the original Hebrew, then Jesus must have been preaching to the fourth-class, tenth-class men—murderers. And the proof is that they murdered him. So such people, what can they understand about God? When I told him, the priest was silent. He could not answer."

Another priest came to see Prabhupāda, and again the question came up. Prabhupāda asked him, "Then you are in favor of killing?"

The priest replied, "Well, it is a fallen world."

"It is a fallen world," said Prabhupāda, "but we do not have to be among the fallen." The priest cited the covenant with Noah.

Prabhupāda replied, "Maybe Noah allowed it at that time, the time of devastation, but that doesn't mean you always have to do it. To live in such a time, one can eat anything to stay alive, but now so many things are in abundance to keep healthy without maintaining a slaughterhouse. In the *Bhagavad-gītā* Kṛṣṇa says, 'Protect the cows; it is the duty of the *vaiśyas*.' "

Although Prabhupāda willingly discussed with Christians, he admitted privately that to argue with them was a waste of time. "They will never agree," he said, "even if they are defeated." The best way to preach to people in general was through the chanting of Hare Kṛṣṇa, as at the Ratha-yātrā festival. Chant, dance, take *prasādam*, and invite everyone to join. "Anyway," he said, "they don't even follow their teachings. One boy came to me and said he wanted to talk. He said, 'I am a Christian,' but I told him, 'You are not a Christian. Thou shalt not kill.' "

A man from Calcutta came to see Prabhupāda. But as soon as the man began to say something about Kṛṣṇa, Prabhupāda interrupted: "Kṛṣṇa is something very difficult to understand. We are just trying to understand that there is a next life."

"But the Christians say there is no future life," the man said. "At the end of this one you either go to heaven or hell."

"But if they talk about going to heaven," said Prabhupāda, "then that is the next life. But knowledge of Kṛṣṇa is only for the most perfect out of thousands among men."

A Mr. Kumar, who sometimes lived in the London temple, visited Prabhupāda with many questions. He wanted to work for ISKCON, he said, but required money to send his mother in India. "No," Prabhupāda told him, "our men work twenty-four hours a day without a farthing." Mr. Kumar suggested ways to improve ISKCON. The devotees needed to study more, he said, especially Sanskrit, and become scholars.

Prabhupāda disagreed. "All we need is dedication," he said. "I am not a great Sanskrit scholar, but I am pulling on. And even the scholars say it is good. My Guru Mahārāja's Guru Mahārāja [Gaurakiśora dāsa Bābājī Mahārāja] was illiterate. Still, his disciple, Bhaktisiddhānta Sarasvatī Prabhupāda, was the greatest scholar of the day. But when Gaurakiśora spoke, it was exactly from the *śāstra*. Our principle is not to take time to learn something and become expert and then preach. But whatever you know, preach. Class in the morning, class in the evening, and if they read my books, that is sufficient."

One day the devotees brought Prabhupāda a newspaper clipping in which an Oxford professor, Dr. D. Zaehner, had said at a religion conference that Lord Kṛṣṇa and His *Bhagavad-gītā* teachings were "immoral." Dr. Zaehner had said that a famous murderer was perhaps influenced by the *Bhagavad-gītā*, because Kṛṣṇa says that the soul is immortal, so one can therefore kill. Śrīla Prabhupāda was disgusted at the professor's ignorance. On his morning walk he dictated to his secretary arguments to use in writing to Dr. Zaehner.

George Harrison approached Prabhupāda in a submissive mood similar to that of Prabhupāda's disciples. Prabhupāda and George took *prasādam* together, a special lunch of *samosās, hālavā,* vegetables, sour cream, and *purīs.* While they were enjoying the *prasādam*, Prabhupāda mentioned that certain Vṛndāvana *paṇḍās* (professional guides at a holy place) eat too much. Once one ate so much that he was practically dying, but he assured his son, "At least I am dying from eating, and not from starving. To die of starvation is unglorious." Prabhupāda smiled as he talked with George, gratefully acknowledging his donation of the Manor. "Have you seen my room?" Prabhupāda asked. "It is actually your house, but my room."

"No," George protested, preferring the mood of a humble disciple, "it is Kṛṣṇa's house and your room."

When George confided to Prabhupāda that by taking to Kṛṣṇa consciousness he was losing friends, Prabhupāda told him not to worry. He read to George from the *Gītā*, where Kṛṣṇa explains that He can be known only by devotional service.

"In the future," said George, "ISKCON will be so large it will require executive management."

Prabhupāda: "I have divided the world into twelve zones with twelve representatives. As long as they keep to the spiritual principles, Kṛṣṇa will help them."

Before leaving, George assured Prabhupāda that he would help him increase his temples. Later Prabhupāda commented, "George is getting inward hope from Kṛṣṇa."

One day an old acquaintance dropped by—Allen Ginsberg, wearing denims, suspenders, and a faded shirt and carrying a little Indian-made harmonium. "You are still chanting Hare Kṛṣṇa?" Prabhupāda asked.

"Yes," Allen replied, "I still chant Hare Kṛṣṇa, but I also chant other things."

Allen asked if Prabhupāda would like to hear his chanting and playing. Prabhupāda nodded. Allen began playing his harmonium and chanting *oṁ*. With each recitation of the word *oṁ*, his voice went deeper—"*Oooom*."

When the chant was over, Prabhupāda began to laugh. "You can chant whatever you want to chant," he said. "But just keep chanting Hare Kṛṣṇa. As long as you are chanting Hare Kṛṣṇa, then everything else is all right." Prabhupāda then allowed many devotees to join them for a big, blissful *kīrtana*.

Through George Harrison, another famous pop singer and musician, Donovan, was drawn to come and see the renowned leader of the Hare Kṛṣṇa movement. Donovan, accompanied by a musician friend and their two girl friends in miniskirts, sat in awkward silence before Prabhupāda. Prabhupāda spoke: "There is a verse in the *Vedas* that says music is the highest form of education." And he began to explain how a musician could serve Kṛṣṇa. "You should do like your friend George," Prabhupāda said. "We will give you the themes, and you can write the songs." Prabhupāda said that anything, even money, could be used in the service of Kṛṣṇa.

"But money is material," Donovan's girl friend interrupted.

"What do you know what is material and spiritual?" Prabhupāda said. He turned to Donovan, "Do you understand?" Donovan humbly replied that he was thickheaded but trying. Donovan's girl friend then leaned over and whispered something into his ear, whereupon Donovan stood up and said, "Well, we have to go now." Prabhupāda insisted that at least they first take some *prasādam*.

As soon as the guests left, Prabhupāda and his disciples began to laugh. Prabhupāda said, "She was thinking . . . " and he encouraged his disciples to finish the sentence.

"Yes," said Yogeśvara, "she was thinking that if Kṛṣṇa gets him, then she will lose him."

Prabhupāda so much liked preaching to important guests that he wanted to continue doing so wherever he traveled. "Wherever I shall go now," Prabhupāda wrote in a letter to a disciple, "this policy of important men being invited to talk with me about our Krishna Consciousness movement should be implemented."

A month passed at the Manor, and still several weeks remained before Janmāṣṭamī and the Deity installation. So when Bhagavān requested Prabhupāda to come for a visit to Paris and install Rādhā-Kṛṣṇa Deities, Prabhupāda agreed.

* * *

Paris
August 9, 1973

The devotees had arranged an official City Hall reception for Śrīla Prabhupāda. In the presence of the mayor of Paris and his government entourage, Śrīla Prabhupāda said that if the government leaders do not teach the citizens genuine God consciousness, then they are not responsible leaders. Reporting this talk in the next day's paper, a news writer stated that the swami even criticized Napoleon Bonaparte.

Bhagavān: *We had just moved into our new temple at 4 Rue le Sueur, Paris, and we had received forty-eight-inch Rādhā and Kṛṣṇa Deities. Prabhupāda had Pradyumna chanting the* mantras *and pouring the substances on the Deities while Prabhupāda himself looked on from his* vyāsāsana, *giving directions. I was assisting, and at one point I turned around and saw Śrīla Prabhupāda standing right next to me, taking the substances in his own hands and smearing them over the lotuslike face of Śrīmatī Rādhārāṇī. After the Deities were installed on the altar, Śrīla Prabhupāda came up and offered the* ārati, *and I assisted him by handing him the articles.*

After the installation we went up to Śrīla Prabhupāda's room and very anxiously requested him to please give a name for the Deities. He sat back in his chair and said that the Deities will be known as Rādhā-Paris-īśvara. He then went on to say that in India people look to England for education and to Paris for sense gratification. He began to laugh and said that Kṛṣṇa has come to Paris in order to get some gopīs, *some French girls, because the faces of the women in Paris are considered the most beautiful. "Rādhārāṇī is so beautiful," Prabhupāda said, "just like a Paris girl. And Kṛṣṇa has come here to find out this most beautiful of all the* gopīs. *So He is Paris-īśvara."*

* * *

August 15

Prabhupāda returned to London and the latest mail from India. A legal complication had arisen regarding the deed for ISKCON's land in Hyderabad. Prabhupāda wrote his disciple Mahāṁsa, cautioning him to avoid becoming entangled in another Bombay affair. When Prabhupāda also received word that the temple construction was progressing in Vṛndāvana, he replied,

> I am pleased to hear how you are completely absorbed in the project of our Vrindaban temple and taxing your brain how it can be carried out. I am also always praying to Krishna that He may give you intelligence to carry it out rightly.

In a letter to a disciple in Hawaii, Prabhupāda apologized for not replying to a letter.

> I was very busy in Bombay for the Juhu land of Mr. N. Now he is dead and gone, but he had created so many obstacles. . . . Still there is discrepancy. But I hope this will be squared up without delay.

Writing to Tamāla Kṛṣṇa Goswami in Bombay, Prabhupāda was as attentive as ever to the ongoing troubles there. Although the devotees remained in possession of the land and had rebuilt their temporary temple, no purchase settlement was in sight.

> If Mrs. N. is not going to sell us the land then what next step we have to adopt? . . . We fixed a criminal case against her for attempting to dispossess us from the land, and what happened to that case? The idea is that if she is not going to sell the land to us, and at the same time does not return our money with damages and interest, and occasionally tries to dispossess us from the land, then what steps we have to take? She has given us so much trouble and botheration. . . .

And Prabhupāda wrote to his disciples in Māyāpur,

> Yes, Mayapur construction must be completely finished before I return. The next time I come there must be no more workers or carpenters with their "tack-tack" sound. I would have continued to stay in Mayapur but the hammering sounds drove me away. When you are completely finished I will go there, otherwise not.

Prabhupāda also answered dozens of letters from America, where the devotees were becoming more and more keen to distribute his books. Their letters contained very crucial questions that only Prabhupāda could solve: How important was book distribution? Could the devotees abandon their robes and wear regular Western clothes to better distribute books in public? Was chanting on the streets more important than book distribution? What about taking buses and vans around the country? Could they travel with Deities in the vans? The devotees generally mentioned their own viewpoint in their letters to Prabhupāda, and yet they respectfully awaited his definitive reply.

The Kṛṣṇa consciousness movement was now big, with potential for growing much bigger. And within ISKCON, Prabhupāda's will was so powerful that a single letter from him would establish a policy for years to come. Prabhupāda appeared to be sitting quietly in his room at the Manor, following his daily routine of bathing, eating, and meeting evening guests, yet at the same time he was directing thousands of young men and women all over the world and sending them into action in the war against *māyā.*

> There is no objection to going in western clothes in order to distribute my books. It is not necessary that we always wear the robes, but we should always keep sikha and tilaka. However, a wig or a hat may be worn as you describe. We have to take whatever is the favorable position for executing Krishna consciousness. Do not forget our principles, but sometimes we may adopt such means in order to distribute books. Somehow or other distribute books and if you can impress people a little to chant then it does not matter about your dress.

The devotees continued to request clarification as to how far the ends justified the means in fulfilling Prabhupāda's order to distribute books profusely. Śrīla Prabhupāda, being free of any material motivation, could clearly see the Kṛṣṇa conscious thing to do.

> Regarding the question you have raised about traveling sankirtana parties and selling of books, yes, we want money. So that is the real preaching, selling books. Who can speak better than the books? At least whoever buys, he will look over. The real preaching is selling books. You should know the tactic how to sell without irritating. What your lecture will do for three minutes, but if he reads one page his life may be turned. We don't want to irritate anyone, however. If he goes away by your aggressive tactics, then you are nonsense and it is your failure. Neither you could sell a book, neither he would re-

> main. But if he buys a book, that is the real successful preaching. That is the certificate of my Guru Maharaja, if someone, brahmacari, would sell a one paise magazine, if one of our brahmacaris would go and sell a few copies, he would be very very glad and say, "Oh, you are so nice." So distribution of literature is our real preaching. Now if you cannot handle the matter nicely, that is your fault. But the success of your preaching will be substantiated by how many books are sold. Anything you want to sell, you have to canvass a little, so he gives some money for the service of Krsna. That is his good luck and he gets the chance to read some transcendental knowledge. But if you only irritate and he goes away, that is your less intelligence.

Prabhupāda's instructions were so important to his disciples that a letter from him was as effective as a personal visit. By such letters he maintained the lives and affairs of his disciples all over the world. Each day in the late morning he would have his secretary read aloud each incoming letter, and usually he would dictate the answer without delay. He had often said that the *vāṇī*, or order, of the *guru* was more important than the *vapuḥ*, or personal presence. Thus by his letters he established and illuminated the path of Kṛṣṇa consciousness for his sincere followers.

In America now Prabhupāda's preaching was primarily through the distribution of his books, whereas in India it was through establishing temples. Yet both methods were one and the same to him. And although his vision encompassed the whole world, he felt and described himself as only the humble servant of his spiritual master. Whether sitting peacefully on the lawn of the Manor and teasing one of the little children or directing one of his lieutenants to "drop thousands and millions of books into the laps of the conditioned souls," whether meditating with great energy on the next phrase in his *Śrīmad-Bhāgavatam* purports or worrying about what Mrs. N. was conspiring in Bombay—he always tried to serve his Guru Mahārāja.

Śrīla Prabhupāda received an emergency phone call from Bombay. Girirāja wanted him to come and personally settle with Mrs. N. the purchase of the Juhu land. Girirāja had consulted a new lawyer, Mr. Bakhil, who felt that Prabhupāda must be present for there to be a settlement. Another ISKCON lawyer, Mr. Chandawal, also advised that Śrīla Prabhupāda come immediately to Bombay. Girirāja, therefore, had telephoned Prabhupāda, begging him to please come and settle the matter with Mrs. N. once and for all. Prabhupāda agreed. He would remain in London one more week, until Janmāṣṭamī. Then he would return to Bombay.

August 21

M. Rasgotra, the Indian ambassador to England, attended the Janmāṣṭamī day celebration and introduced Śrīla Prabhupāda, expressing his appreciation of Prabhupāda's great work. Prabhupāda spoke, describing the advent of Kṛṣṇa as the key to peace for the troubled material world. "Especially in India," he said, "we have got so much asset for understanding God. Everything is there, ready-made. But we won't accept. So what is the remedy for such disease? We are searching after peace, but we won't accept anything which is actually giving us peace. This is our disease. So the Kṛṣṇa consciousness movement is trying to awaken the dormant Kṛṣṇa consciousness in everyone's heart. Otherwise, how could these Europeans and Americans and other countrymen who had never even heard of Kṛṣṇa four or five years ago be taking to Kṛṣṇa consciousness so seriously? Therefore Kṛṣṇa consciousness is there in everyone's heart."

Prabhupāda recited prayers from *Brahma-saṁhitā* describing the sublime, eternal existence of Kṛṣṇa on His eternal planet, Kṛṣṇaloka. "But Kṛṣṇa is also everywhere," he explained, "and if you are a devotee, then you can catch Him. If you want to catch Him, He comes forward ten times more than your desire. Therefore we simply have to receive Him. This Deity worship in the temple means worshiping Kṛṣṇa, the Supreme Personality of Godhead. He has very kindly accepted to assume a form which you can handle. Therefore do not think that we have installed a marble statue. The rascals will say, 'They are heathens.' No, we are worshiping Kṛṣṇa personally. Kṛṣṇa has kindly assumed this form because we cannot see the gigantic Kṛṣṇa or how Kṛṣṇa is everywhere. Remain twenty-four hours a day in Kṛṣṇa's service. This is the purpose of installing the Deity."

* * *

Bombay
September 15, 1973

The day after his arrival, Śrīla Prabhupāda met with Mrs. N.'s solicitors and heard their offers. The situation had begun to look hopeful, and yet the conclusion eluded them. Mrs. N. had become changed by the public reaction to her attempt to demolish the temple. If Prabhupāda would pay the full balance of twelve lakhs of rupees for the land in one payment, she told her lawyer, she would agree. Prabhupāda was agreeable, but did not want to arrange to collect his money until he was certain that Mrs. N. was actually serious.

Mr. Asnani, a Bombay lawyer and ISKCON life member, regularly met with Mrs. N., persuading her to cooperate with Prabhupāda. Her lawyers concurred. Yet after Prabhupāda had been in Bombay for several weeks, no meeting with Mrs. N. had taken place. Once Mr. Asnani went to bring Mrs. N. to meet with Prabhupāda, but she was not feeling well. Day after day Mr. Asnani would tell Prabhupāda, "Mrs. N. will come tomorrow." Prabhupāda became disappointed at the procrastination, and seeing this, his secretaries told Mr. Asnani that although they knew he meant well, they were inclined to have their other lawyers handle the case. Mr. Asnani asked for another forty-eight hours to close the deal and execute the conveyance.

Mrs. N. was at her other home, where she had just recovered from her illness, when Mr. Asnani visited. "Mātājī," he begged, "my Guru Mahārāja is leaving tomorrow. If you don't come tonight, the problem with the land will go on another year." Mrs. N. agreed, and around nine P.M. she and Mr. Asnani arrived at the home of Mr. Bogilal Patel, where Śrīla Prabhupāda was holding a program of *kīrtana* and *Bhāgavata* discourses. Prabhupāda was on the roof preparing to lecture, but hearing that Mrs. N. had arrived, he interrupted the meeting and came down to his room to talk with her. They talked briefly, and Prabhupāda excused himself and returned to the roof to lecture.

Around midnight, he returned to his room again. Mrs. N. was still waiting. She burst into tears and bowed at Prabhupāda's feet. "I am sorry for everything I've done," she sobbed. "Please forgive me." She promised to do whatever Prabhupāda wanted.

Prabhupāda looked at her compassionately and understood her heart. "You are just like my daughter," he said. "Don't worry. I will take care of you. I will see to all of your needs for the rest of your life." And Prabhupāda said he still accepted the very terms she had proposed: that he pay the remaining balance of twelve lakhs plus fifty thousand rupees compensation for the delay.

Prabhupāda and Mrs. N. had set November 1 as the tentative deadline for the final signing of the conveyance. Shortly after their meeting, Prabhupāda moved from Bogilal Patel's to the home of Mr. Sethi, where working intensely he tackled the remaining problems—such as getting C. Company to withdraw their claim.

Next he moved to the home of Mr. C. M. Khatau, just two blocks from Hare Krishna Land, where he lived in a summer cottage, a simple structure with a bamboo frame and *chāṭāi* walls. Usually, conveyances had to be signed in the presence of the city registrar at his office downtown, but Mr. Asnani had arranged for the registrar to come to Prabhupāda's place.

At six-thirty in the evening Śrīla Prabhupāda was seated at his low desk between two windows, his back against the wall. Mrs. N. and her lawyers, the registrar, Mr. Asnani, Mr. and Mrs. Sethi, and about eight devotees were present, and the full room grew warm and stuffy. Mrs. N. sat at Prabhupāda's right as the registrar prepared the papers for signing. Śrīla Prabhupāda sat gravely. The room was silent except for the sound of papers rustling and a pen's scratching. Preparing and signing the conveyance papers took more than twenty minutes. Prabhupāda paid Mrs. N., who then signed the conveyance. The land was legally ISKCON's.

Girirāja: *The room was hushed during the signing, and everyone felt as if a momentous event was taking place—just as if two great world powers were signing a treaty. After Mrs. N. signed the document, everyone silently watched the papers being passed. She started to cry. Tamāla Kṛṣṇa Goswami quietly asked her why she was crying, and Mrs. N. replied that just that day Mr. Matar had come and told her he had found a buyer for the land for many more lakhs than we were paying. Actually, as we were watching Mrs. N., we were thinking that she must be remembering all the events that had taken place, the wrongs that she had done, the death of her husband. It was very intense, like a combination of months of struggling. So for Prabhupāda, the devotees, and Prabhupāda's well-wishers, their dreams and desires and efforts over the past many years were being fulfilled.*

Śrīla Prabhupāda asked that the devotees inform the newspapers, and he invited everyone into the hall outside his room for a feast. Mats were rolled out in two lines, and devotees brought leaf plates and placed them in front of everyone. The devotees began serving the various dishes to the two rows of seated guests.

Prabhupāda was standing. "Now let us start," he said, as he supervised the serving. The devotees had prepared several courses: rice, *dāl,* many varieties of *pakorās* (such as potato, cauliflower, and eggplant), potato *sabjī*, wet cauliflower *sabjī, papars, barfī, laḍḍus, camcam* (a milk sweet), vermicelli *khīr, hālavā,* and a lime drink. It was a festive and happy occasion.

Mrs. Warrier (a tenant on Hare Krishna Land): *The devotees were all saying "Jaya" after the signing, and all of them were very happy. Then Prabhupāda gave a lecture about the Bombay project. He gave an idea to all the people of how it would be all marble. There wouldn't be a single thing that wasn't built from marble. Some were asking how it would be possible for everything to be marble, and Prabhupāda explained that it was possible and could be done. He was visualizing the project, and everyone was thrilled to hear the way he was describing it. It would be like one of the seven wonders of the world. People would be attracted from all over to come and see it. It would be a landmark in Bombay. Prabhupāda explained the whole project as if he saw it in his mind's eye, and he said that after it was constructed it will be more than what we could visualize. It would be fantastic!*

After the late feast, when everyone had departed, Prabhupāda returned to his room. Leaning back at his desk, he exclaimed, "It was a good fight!"

Later Prabhupāda would cite the story of the fight for the Bombay land as evidence that a person in Kṛṣṇa consciousness has no problems. "Now we have spent in Bombay eighteen to twenty lakhs of rupees," he said months later while on tour in Europe. "The property is actually worth fifty lakhs. People are surprised, and some of them are envious. But if you come, you will find that it is a very, very fine place. It is just like a paradise garden, twenty thousand square yards, and we have got six buildings. So actually, when we come to Kṛṣṇa consciousness there are no problems."

Surely the land was full of potential, but how could he say there had been no problems? "No problems" meant that Śrīla Prabhupāda saw how Kṛṣṇa personally arranged things for His devotees. When he had needed money, it had come, in an amount that ordinarily would have been impossible to collect. And the formidable opposition Kṛṣṇa had removed. Prabhupāda had no organized means of income and little political influence to fight persons like Mr. and Mrs. N., but because he was surrendered to Kṛṣṇa there was no problem. All the problems of the world were created by the nondevotees, who defied the injunctions of the Supreme. "Anyone who is in *bhakti-yoga*," Prabhupāda said, "he can understand that all problems are solved. We can practically see."

And yet he had had to tolerate the problems created by the nondevotees. For almost two years he had struggled to secure the land for Kṛṣṇa's service. Whether in Bombay or elsewhere, he had had to worry over how to help his inexperienced disciples, who were ill-equipped to handle the ploys of the opposing party. It had been an ordeal, a test of patience, a challenge of courage. But because he had not been bewildered by *māyā*, illusion, there had been "no problem."

Prabhupāda showed by his example that if one strictly follows *bhakti-yoga*, one is not touched by the modes of nature, by *māyā*. The same transcendental science he constantly taught in his lectures and informal discussions, he also personally demonstrated. He was faithful in Kṛṣṇa consciousness, and all his problems had been adjusted. Kṛṣṇa says in the *Bhagavad-gītā* that if one surrenders to Him, one easily overcomes all problems. The devotee understands that the problems of *māyā* can be overcome by surrendering to Kṛṣṇa, by surrendering to the orders of Kṛṣṇa's representative, the spiritual master.

Now that the land was ISKCON's, Prabhupāda could proceed to enact his vision. In attempting to construct buildings and propagate Kṛṣṇa consciousness, he would meet more *māyā*-created problems, no doubt, but the greatest struggle had been won. The gorgeous temple of Śrī Śrī Rādhā-Rāsavihārī would manifest. In the future, devotees and guests could come to India's gateway and stay in a first-class hotel at Hare Krishna Land and conveniently imbibe the spiritual atmosphere of the temple. And the devotees, as long as they did not forget Prabhupāda's example and instruction, could successfully utilize the facility in the spirit of service to Kṛṣṇa. The price Prabhupāda had paid in tolerance and dependence on Kṛṣṇa would never go in vain.

What Śrīla Prabhupāda produced by his tolerance was not only the facilities and the ongoing mission at Hare Krishna Land but a monumental living example of the behavior of a *sādhu*. In the *Śrīmad-Bhāgavatam*, Lord Kapiladeva describes the *sādhu*:

titikṣavaḥ kāruṇikāḥ
suhṛdaḥ sarva-dehinām
ajāta-śatravaḥ śāntā
sādhavaḥ sādhu-bhūṣaṇāḥ

"The symptoms of a *sādhu* are that he is tolerant, merciful, and friendly to all living entities. He has no enemies, he is peaceful, he abides by the scriptures, and all his characteristics are sublime."

Because the *sādhu* is tolerant (*titikṣavaḥ*), he is undisturbed by the difficulties imposed by material nature. In Prabhupāda's attempts to secure the Juhu property, he had met with enemies and difficulties, and he had been tolerant. Prabhupāda had sometimes said, "You have to tolerate."

And a *sādhu* is not only tolerant but merciful (*kāruṇikāḥ*). When ISKCON's provisional temple had been attacked by the police, Prabhupāda could have considered it a signal to leave the place and give up trying to help such ingrates by bringing them Kṛṣṇa consciousness—"Why go to such botheration? What's the use of trying?" He had already nearly a hundred temples outside of India. If the people of Bombay didn't like Kṛṣṇa consciousness, then why not go away and leave them to their fate?

But no. As a genuine *sādhu*, Prabhupāda was merciful. Because he had come to deliver the compassionate message of Kṛṣṇa consciousness, he had to tolerantly give that message to everyone. People were misguided and were living like animals, only for sense gratification, and by the laws of *karma* they would suffer in their next life. Seeing this unhappy predicament, Prabhupāda had felt moved to help these fallen souls, even if they were unappreciative.

Śrīmad-Bhāgavatam also describes a *sādhu* as *suhṛdaḥ sarva-dehinām:* the only desire in his heart is the welfare of all others. Being unbounded by nationalism, he thinks of himself not as Indian or American or even as human being, but as eternal spiritual soul, meant to benefit all living entities.

A *sādhu, Śrīmad-Bhāgavatam* describes, is *ajāta-śatru,* because he never creates enemies. Although envious persons may declare themselves a *sādhu*'s enemy, a *sādhu* behaves as the best friend of everyone, trying to bring everyone to Kṛṣṇa. Because Prabhupāda was trying to spread Kṛṣṇa consciousness, envious persons would continue to oppose him. But as he sublimely showed in Bombay, "What can be done? We have to tolerate." Thus, even before any foundations were laid for buildings, Prabhupāda had already fully demonstrated all the ornaments of the *sādhu.* Remaining peaceful (*śānta*) and dependent on Kṛṣṇa, he had become victorious. And for whoever serves such a great personality, *Śrīmad-Bhāgavatam* states, the door to liberation is open.

CHAPTER SEVEN

April 1972

Śrīla Prabhupāda was meditating on constructing his Krishna-Balaram Mandir. In April of 1972 he asked his disciple Surabhi, who had drawn the plans for the Bombay center, to execute drawings, basing the design on Indian renaissance architecture. Prabhupāda liked the Govindajī temple, located near the original Govindajī temple constructed by Rūpa Gosvāmī. He liked its open courtyard surrounded by many arches and its front steps leading up to the Deity *darśana* area. He suggested that some features of the temple be incorporated into his temple. Surabhi, with the assistance of a Vṛndāvana architect, executed the plans, and Prabhupāda approved.

> This will be the grandest temple in Vrndavana. Many high-class gentlemen in Delhi who are also devotees will relish the chance to live with us on weekends and it will be for them just like Vaikuntha. You must construct something wonderful. Otherwise it will be a discredit to you American boys. That will absolve the position of America and India. And this Vrndavana project is one of the most important of ours in ISKCON.

Although Guru dāsa had been careful to keep in touch with Prabhupāda by mail, he had neglected certain important matters in Vṛndāvana, such as digging a well and getting city approval—things Prabhupāda had repeatedly asked for. In the summer of 1972 Prabhupāda wrote,

> From the beginning I said I simply wanted a temple built in Vrndavana just like Govindaji's temple. And there have been so many letters, but that has not been done. Never mind, now I like that plan of Surabhi's.

Two weeks later Prabhupāda again wrote Guru dāsa on the same point.

> I wanted a temple like Govindaji. Is it so difficult that for the last six months you have consulted so many engineers? Any ordinary

> engineer could draw up the papers and get it passed. There has been so much unnecessary correspondence.

To build a temple in Vṛndāvana should not be so difficult, Prabhupāda thought, and he became impatient with the delays. Concerned that the devotees and architects not make the building too costly, he said that they should go ahead with the plans he had approved, even if the building were to be a little cheaper than in the original plan. He was concerned that a competent disciple oversee the work so that ISKCON didn't get cheated.

As early as April of 1972, Prabhupāda had asked that the Deities in Vṛndāvana be Kṛṣṇa and Balarāma. "Krsna may be black, Balarama of white, and the pose in the back of the *Back to Godhead* magazine is very nice." He asked that a sign be put out front announcing, "Shri Krishna Balaram Mandir."

One reason Prabhupāda chose Kṛṣṇa and Balarāma as the presiding Deities was that most of the Vṛndāvana temples were of Rādhā and Kṛṣṇa; ISKCON's temple would be unique in Vṛndāvana. Another reason was that the ISKCON land was located in Ramaṇa-reti, an area of forest and soft sands where Kṛṣṇa and Balarāma had enjoyed Their childhood pastimes five thousand years ago. To celebrate and worship the youthful sports of Kṛṣṇa and Balarāma in Ramaṇa-reti was fitting.

Although thousands of years had passed since Kṛṣṇa's advent in Vṛndāvana, the same atmosphere and many of the same sights and sounds still prevailed. Peacocks ran across the sands or sat on rooftops or in trees. The cooing and chirping of pigeons and cuckoos and the sweep of the parrots' green wings were eternal sounds and sights of the Vṛndāvana forest. In *Kṛṣṇa, the Supreme Personality of Godhead* Prabhupāda had described how Kṛṣṇa and Balarāma and Their cowherd friends played in Ramaṇa-reti and similar places.

> "My dear friends, just see how this river bank is extremely beautiful because of its pleasing atmosphere. And just see how the blooming lotuses are attracting bees and birds by their aroma. The humming and chirping of the bees in the forest is echoing throughout the beautiful trees in the forest. Also, here the sands are clean and soft. Therefore, this must be considered the best place for our sporting and pastimes."

According to *Śrīmad-Bhāgavatam*, the playing of the cowherd boys with

Kṛṣṇa and Balarāma as friends in Vṛndāvana is the highest spiritual realization, far beyond the ordinary religionist's understanding of God. The Supreme Truth, whom some meditated upon as impersonal Brahman, others worshiped as the Supreme Almighty, and still others considered an ordinary living entity, was the eternal, loving friend of the cowherd boys of Vṛndāvana. Only after many, many lifetimes of pious activities had they become eligible to join in the loving pastimes of Kṛṣṇa and Balarāma in Ramaṇa-reti.

In establishing a temple of Kṛṣṇa and Balarāma, Prabhupāda wanted to offer the peaceful, transcendental atmosphere of Ramaṇa-reti to all people, including visitors from abroad, commuters from Delhi, and his own disciples. Already he had received a letter from a major international travel agency requesting that he provide accommodations for tourists so that the ISKCON guesthouse could be included in official tours of spiritual India. People were always coming to India to tour the holy places; unfortunately most of the places were unauthorized or overrun by cheaters. ISKCON's center, therefore, would be very important. Prabhupāda wrote,

> Have a European preaching center, and try to enlist all the tourists and hippies who come to Vrndavana. Give them nice prasadam and engage them in chanting, cleaning the temple, and reading our books, give them all facility for becoming devotees.

There was another particular significance in Prabhupāda's choosing Kṛṣṇa and Balarāma as the central object of worship in his Vṛndāvana temple. Lord Balarāma is the first expansion from Lord Kṛṣṇa, and in His incarnation of Saṅkarṣaṇa, He upholds all the universes. The Vaiṣṇavas, therefore, worship Balarāma for spiritual strength. "You can pray to Lord Balarāma," Prabhupāda said, "to help you in your deficiency." As the source of spiritual strength, Lord Balarāma is also known as the original spiritual master.

As in Prabhupāda's other large ISKCON temples, there would be three altars, and beside Kṛṣṇa and Balarāma would stand the Deities of Lord Caitanya and Lord Nityānanda. Lord Caitanya is Kṛṣṇa Himself, and Lord Nityānanda is Lord Balarāma, a fact the Krishna-Balaram Mandir would proclaim to the world. Lord Nityānanda is especially referred to as the *kṛpā-avatāra,* the form of God most merciful to the fallen conditioned souls. Thus the worship of Kṛṣṇa and Balarāma as Lord Caitanya and Lord Nityānanda would emphasize distributing Kṛṣṇa consciousness to others. Prabhupāda also wanted to install Deities of Rādhā-Śyāmasundara along with Their two attendant *gopīs*, Lalitā and Viśākhā.

Śrīla Prabhupāda could not possibly stay full-time in Vṛndāvana, and yet whenever he was away, progress slowed. Guru dāsa, the temple president, had little money and little expertise in managing finances. Prabhupāda called him "Damn Cheap Bābu," a name given by Indians to Westerners who think they have won a "damn cheap" bargain, although they are actually being cheated.

Since Prabhupāda did not trust his devotees' spending habits, he arranged for a complicated system whereby he would have to approve all ISKCON Vṛndāvana checks, even while traveling. When Guru dāsa wanted to spend, Tejās, the Delhi temple president, would come to Vṛndāvana and approve the expenses. Then a check would be made out and mailed to Śrīla Prabhupāda for his signature. When the check returned to Delhi, Tejās would add his own signature and give the check to Guru dāsa.

Although Prabhupāda generally preferred not to burden himself with managing his temples, he insisted on supervising all spending in Vṛndāvana, down to the last rupee. But even with such controls, Guru dāsa would misspend money, taking funds earmarked for construction and using them for other temple purposes—usually getting cheated by the merchants.

After Prabhupāda's 1972 visit during Kārttika, he was away from Vṛndāvana for an entire year, directing things through correspondence. With the Kṛṣṇa consciousness movement growing quickly on all continents, he had many places to visit. Still, his three main projects—Bombay, Vṛndāvana, and Māyāpur—were his major subjects of correspondence and his greatest financial investments.

One reason he did not come more often to Vṛndāvana was that Guru dāsa's letters had been very optimistic, promising a temple opening by Janmāṣṭamī 1973. Surabhi was in charge of the construction and knew well that the work was going too slowly, yet Guru dāsa would write to Prabhupāda, painting a picture of eminent completion of the construction and opening of the *mandira*. Prabhupāda was enlivened to hear the good news, and he held Guru dāsa to his promise, though with reservations.

> If you can finish the work by Janmastami next, that would be a very great credit for you, and I shall come from any part of the world

> just to install the deity. But now you must work very, very hard to make good your promise to me, otherwise I shall be very disappointed and become very, very angry upon you.

Prabhupāda warned the devotees in Vṛndāvana that they would have to work diligently, finishing before the monsoon season arrived in June if they were actually to fulfill their promise.

But anyone visiting the construction site in Vṛndāvana could understand that the building would never be finished in time. The temple area consisted of foundation lines and steel rods. Only three or four devotees were living there, struggling to organize laborers and to obtain funds and building materials. That summer was extremely hot, and each day the devotees were forced to spend the afternoon lying down in their huts, exhausted from the heat. Prices for cement and steel had doubled. Yet Prabhupāda continued to respond to Guru dāsa's glowing reports, encouraging him to continue with determination.

But Prabhupāda could also read between the lines, and he cautioned Guru dāsa, "I simply want to see that the work is being carried on vigorously, and the money shall not be used to pay bad bills. The money should simply be used for construction." Talk of a temple opening by Janmāṣṭamī gradually disappeared, but Prabhupāda did not express his disappointment. Rather, he continued to encourage and push the devotees onward, asking that at least his own room be completed, so that when he visited in October of 1973, he would have a place to stay.

When Prabhupāda arrived, however, his quarters were far from completion, and he had to live for a week in the home of a Vṛndāvana friend. He did not remove Guru dāsa, but he tried to teach him better management and accounting. He also wrote to his India G.B.C. secretary, Tamāla Kṛṣṇa Goswami, to get more funds for the Vṛndāvana project.

> So I have arrived here in Vrindaban, but so far the project is concerned, why the money is so irregular? Tejiyas reports that in the past three months you have sent Rs. 5,000/- and since then nothing. How will the project go on?

Inspired by Prabhupāda's presence, the devotees rallied. They held a little festival on the land, erecting a tent and decorating the foundation posts with banana trees and flowers. For several evenings Prabhupāda lectured before a crowd of about fifty local people sitting on folding chairs in between the foundation lines.

Prabhupāda was determined in his desire. He wanted a temple as much as ever, and the small band of disciples in Vṛndāvana were convinced of their mission to erect that temple. They knew they were building a temple not merely as their own local project, but as something very important for the whole world. Prabhupāda set the next Janmāṣṭamī, August 1974, as the new grand opening.

Surabhi had considerable architectural and construction experience, but he had never worked with such an ornate building before. He doubted, therefore, whether they could finish in a year's time. Tejās wondered whether they could raise the funds in time. Guru dāsa was becoming more competent, and he assured Prabhupāda that they would meet their deadline.

Subala had wanted to stay in Vṛndāvana, but only on the condition that he be relieved of management, free to chant and wander in the groves. But he had long since departed for the West. Those devotees who remained committed to Vṛndāvana knew that, at least for the present, the real spiritual path in Vṛndāvana was one of hard labor, anxiety, combating the elements, and working as pure instruments in the service of Kṛṣṇa's pure devotee.

In February 1974, as Prabhupāda was traveling eastward from Los Angeles, he wrote Guru dāsa that he would like to come to Vṛndāvana as soon as his residential rooms were completed—and he asked when that would be. Guru dāsa consulted Surabhi, who said one month. Trying to be more positive, Guru dāsa invited Prabhupāda to come and move into his new quarters in three weeks, but Śrīla Prabhupāda telegrammed back that he would be coming in *two*!

At that time Prabhupāda's house had no roof or floor, and only portions of the outer walls. Surabhi began a marathon construction effort and hired two work crews, one for day and one for night. Two weeks nonstop they worked, drastically cutting corners. They plastered and painted simultaneously, and as a result the walls remained wet. A few days before Prabhupāda's arrival they put down a temporary floor: bricks, covered with cow dung, covered with rugs, covered with sheets. The weather was cold, and the house had no heating.

The morning Prabhupāda arrived, the devotees all gathered with him as he sat happily before his desk, praising their achievement. He said if they could keep working like this, they could finish everything before Janmāṣṭamī.

Almost immediately upon his arrival Prabhupāda began to manifest the symptoms of a cold, but he would not hear of moving to another place. "This is my first house," he said. "Now I am going to stay here."

The large brick-and-stone room was simple and austere and remained dark during most of the day, but Prabhupāda considered it his Vṛndāvana residence. Soon local distinguished visitors began calling on him, and he received them warmly, discussing Kṛṣṇa consciousness hour after hour in his room. In the evenings he would lecture there and hold a *kīrtana*.

Prabhupāda had a problem to face in Vṛndāvana. Guru dāsa had informed him that Mr. S. wanted to take back fifty feet of the donated land, claiming the construction was not going quickly enough and that he had never intended to give the front portion. He was thinking of using it for shops, maybe even a petrol pump. Prabhupāda was alarmed. For Mr. S. to take back the front part of the property would ruin the temple scheme and make a farce of the gift. What good was land without proper access to it?

On further inquiry Prabhupāda learned that Guru dāsa had not yet received the actual deed. Prabhupāda was greatly disturbed, yet he proceeded calmly and intently. Guru dāsa, he said, should immediately secure the deed from the registrar and construct a high brick wall around the property. Prabhupāda's secretary wired Mr. S., who was away from Vṛndāvana: "HARE KRSNA. PRABHUPADA NOW IN VRINDABAN UNTIL THE 13TH. NOW SETTLE UP FRONT PIECE AS PROMISED."

Mr. S. wired his reply: "FRONT PART OF LAND WILL BE USED FOR OTHER PURPOSES AS DECIDED EARLIER. LETTER FOLLOWS." Suddenly it seemed that Prabhupāda had another Bombay case on his hands.

Mr. S.'s action, however, confirmed Prabhupāda's urgency for completing the construction. Had the land been already walled and the temple built, there would have been no question of Mr. S.'s taking the land back. Prabhupāda's followers could now see clearly his reasons for pushing them. He had been vigilant, even heavy and critical, but for good reasons. *Māyā's* opposition to Kṛṣṇa consciousness was always present, so that if the devotees let up for even a moment, they could suffer great losses. The question "Why hurry? Why be so anxious to build a temple right away?" should never have been asked. It was the question of the naive, the lazy. As long as the Kṛṣṇa consciousness movement had no temple in Vṛndāvana, the threat would exist that there might *never* be a temple.

Prabhupāda wrote to a friend in Calcutta,

> This statement of K. has given me much concern. He said personally to me that under dictation of Srimate Radharani he has given the land to us in charity. We have invested already lacs of rupees for constructing a temple, and now if he uses the front portion for other purposes there will be great damage to the view of the temple. . . . Kindly see Mr. N. S., brother of K., and settle this up so we can go on in our progressive construction work. Kindly treat this as very urgent.

In Mr. S.'s absence from Vṛndāvana, Prabhupāda took the opportunity to speak with Mr. S.'s brothers as well as with Mr. S.'s lawyers. What had been given in the name of Śrīmatī Rādhārāṇī, he informed them, could not be taken back. Mr. S.'s associates agreed, at least for the moment, that Mr. S. had no substantial position. Meanwhile, the laborers were working quickly to build a twelve-foot-high wall around the property.

It was four A.M. Prabhupāda sat in the cold darkness, with a small desk lamp shining before him. Having risen from bed at two and come into his main room to dictate *Śrīmad-Bhāgavatam* purports, he now sat silently. He wore a wool knit hat pulled over his ears, a sweater, and a gray wool *cādar* around his shoulders.

On the other side of the double doors sat his servant, peeking in to see what his spiritual master was doing. On Prabhupāda's last visit to the United States, he had acquired a new secretary-servant, Satsvarūpa dāsa Goswami. Despite the cold, Prabhupāda's new assistant was happy to be in Vṛndāvana and so intimately situated close to his spiritual master.

Prabhupāda rang his bell. The servant jumped up, opened the double doors, and entered the room. In the far corner of the large room, seated at the desk, he saw Prabhupāda, looking grave and mystical, his beautifully intense eyes sparkling. As Satsvarūpa offered obeisances, he thought of his great fortune in being there with his spiritual master. When he sat up, he saw Prabhupāda nod slightly, and he felt that Prabhupāda was acknowledging his servant's good fortune.

Sitting on the floor on the other side of the desk, Satsvarūpa faced Śrīla Prabhupāda. In awe and reverence he tensed, prepared to do whatever Prabhupāda requested, yet fearful that the request might be something he wouldn't know how to do.

"Get the *Kṛṣṇa* book, Volume Two," Prabhupāda said. His servant ran and got it from the shelf, returned, and again sat down.

"Read the story of King Nṛga," Prabhupāda said. Though terse, Prabhupāda's commands were complete. His servant paused, wondering if there was anything else. He opened the book, then hesitated. "Out loud?" he asked. Prabhupāda nodded, and his servant began to read aloud.

Soon, however, Satsvarūpa became puzzled as to why Prabhupāda was having him do this so early in the morning when he was usually dictating *Śrīmad-Bhāgavatam*. As Satsvarūpa read aloud, Prabhupāda sat motionless, giving no indication that he was pleased, or even listening. In that silence, Satsvarūpa became very aware of his own voice reading, and he listened intently to the story.

King Nṛga, the story explained, gave many cows in charity to the *brāhmaṇas*. One day, however, one cow wandered back and entered among King Nṛga's herd, and so the king unknowingly gave it in charity to another *brāhmaṇa*. But as the new owner was leading the cow away, the former owner returned to claim it. An argument ensued between the two *brāhmaṇas*. Coming before King Nṛga, they charged that he had taken back a cow previously given in charity—a great sin. The puzzled King Nṛga very humbly offered each *brāhmaṇa* one hundred thousand cows in exchange for this one cow. Neither accepted, however, since according to Manu's law, a *brāhmaṇa's* property can't be taken under any condition, even by the government. Consequently, both *brāhmaṇas* left in anger, and as a result King Nṛga had to take his next birth as a lizard.

As Prabhupāda's servant read on, he suddenly got the feeling that Prabhupāda had asked him to read this story to expose the cheating of his own servant. In a panic, he tried to think of how he had committed the offense of stealing from his spiritual master. He couldn't think of anything wrong—until he recalled having taken a pair of socks which had been given to Prabhupāda as a gift. Prabhupāda was always receiving gifts wherever he went, and it was his practice, after collecting socks and scarves and so on, to give them to his disciples. Prabhupāda would use only a fraction of the things given to him. So because it was cold in Vṛndāvana, Satsvarūpa, who had no socks, had taken one inexpensive-looking pair that he was sure his spiritual master would never want to use. He had assumed that Prabhupāda would not object, but now his cheating was indirectly exposed.

After the story was completed, Prabhupāda remained silent, as did his servant. "Perhaps Prabhupāda is sleeping," Satsvarūpa thought, though he dared not say anything or even move. They both sat motionless, Satsvarūpa looking down at the book and sometimes up at Prabhupāda, waiting for an indication.

Five minutes passed. Finally Prabhupāda said, "Now take this chapter and type it up." His servant acknowledged the instruction and got up to leave. But still it wasn't clear. Why had he read the story, and why type it? Prabhupāda then spoke again. "Now I want to dictate one letter." Satsvarūpa had a notepad with him, and he sat down and immediately began writing Prabhupāda's words.

The letter was to Mr. S., and Prabhupāda referred to Mr. S.'s donation of the land and to his desire to take back the front fifty feet. He reminded Mr. S. that, according to the original agreement, he had given the entire land with the sanction of Śrīmatī Rādhārāṇī. How could he say that now he was taking it back? Mr. S. should please reconsider what he was proposing. In this connection Prabhupāda was enclosing the story from *Śrīmad-Bhāgavatam* of King Nṛga. Mr. S. should read it and consider the implications.

Prabhupāda's servant felt relieved. But he also felt that his guilt was valid and that he should be wary of becoming too familiar with his spiritual master's possessions. And he had learned another lesson as well: his own viewpoint of Prabhupāda was entirely subjective. Although he had been with Prabhupāda, he had not correctly understood Prabhupāda's thoughts and motives. He felt that perhaps he was not the only disciple who sometimes made that mistake. One may try to comprehend the many aspects of Śrīla Prabhupāda, but one should not expect to understand completely. Even G.B.C. secretaries and other leading devotees who were right with Prabhupāda in his dealings could not know what Prabhupāda was thinking. Satsvarūpa Mahārāja decided that it was best to always follow Śrīla Prabhupāda's instructions, and going back to the adjoining room, he began typing the story of King Nṛga.

At sunrise Prabhupāda stepped out of his house onto the dusty lane, and the devotees of ISKCON Vṛndāvana joined him on his morning walk. As he walked he began saying that one of the devotees had complained that the electricity was always going off. The devotee had said that India was advanced in spiritual knowledge and the West in material knowledge and that the two should combine. Prabhupāda agreed. "Yes," he said, "that is my mission. To combine them."

Prabhupāda reached the Chhatikara road in front of the property and began walking down the middle of the road in the direction of Delhi. Large *nīm* trees lined the road. "The material side of life is also necessary," Prabhupāda continued. "In the West, even for shaving they have a machine. This is very good, but it is also being misused. It is all for the itching sensation, sex, which is insignificant and abominable. The whole intelligence is being employed like the dog's or cat's."

Prabhupāda paused, and a devotee asked, "Prabhupāda, how can we understand that Vṛndāvana is Kṛṣṇa's abode? There seems to be so much contamination in Vṛndāvana."

"This is because your senses are impure," said Prabhupāda. "But when your eyes are smeared with the salve of love, then you can see Vṛndāvana. Don't judge Vṛndāvana by this external manifestation."

As Prabhupāda walked along the road, many persons greeted him and his disciples, calling, "Jaya Rādhe!" "Hare Kṛṣṇa!" Some even stepped out of their shoes and prostrated themselves before Prabhupāda, who returned their respects with folded palms, nodding his head, and saying, "Hare Kṛṣṇa."

The tightly gathered group walking in the cold morning air passed fields, *āśramas*, and groves. They heard the singing of many varieties of birds: sparrows, parrots, cuckoos, pigeons, and peacocks. Sugarcane stood high and ready for harvest. As Prabhupāda walked farther, the large *nīm* trees gave way to small thorny acacia trees, and herds of cows and buffalo grazed in the fields. For half an hour Prabhupāda continued. Then, turning, he retraced his route.

On the roadside he passed a man dressed in the simple white cloth of a *bābājī*, warming himself before a fire of twigs. Prabhupāda said that the *Ṣaḍ-gosvāmy-aṣṭakam*, by Śrīnivāsa Ācārya, defines the actual qualities of a person in the renounced order. The song glorifies the six Gosvāmīs, who gave up their posts as government ministers and became mendicants, accepting only one cloth and thinking always of Kṛṣṇa and the *gopīs*.

"Vṛndāvana is the gift of Rūpa and Sanātana Gosvāmī," Prabhupāda said. "They wrote many books so poor people could take advantage and become Kṛṣṇa conscious. We see many imitations of Rūpa Gosvāmī in Vṛndāvana today. But they should never take the dress of Rūpa Gosvāmī, especially if they cannot give up this cigarette-smoking habit. It was the gift of Bhaktisiddhānta Sarasvatī that we should not jump and try to change our garb all of a sudden. We should try to hear of the Absolute Truth from realized souls." Prabhupāda said that especially his disciples living in Vṛndāvana should become *gosvāmīs*. Whether *gṛhasthas* or *sannyāsīs*, they should live simply and austerely and engage twenty-four hours in the service of Kṛṣṇa.

Prabhupāda sat in his room talking with Guṇārṇava about finances. "Where are the bills?" Prabhupāda asked.

"I am keeping duplicates, Prabhupāda," Guṇārṇava explained, showing him how he had attached the bills to the vouchers. "Tejās is keeping the originals in Delhi."

"This is just an explanation," Prabhupāda replied. "I am an auditor. I am not A. C. Bhaktivedanta Swami. Don't you understand? The auditor wants to see the bills, not just your excuses."

Throughout the day, Prabhupāda would call in Guru dāsa, Surabhi, Mr. Lahadi (the engineer), even the contractor, Mr. Alibuchs. Although the contractor was Muhammadan, Prabhupāda requested him, "Please do a nice job, because this is Kṛṣṇa's temple. If you work very nicely, Kṛṣṇa will bless you." Prabhupāda assured him that money would not be a problem. He would arrange that ten thousand dollars a month would come from his temples in America until the construction was finished.

"It will be finished by Janmāṣṭamī?" Prabhupāda asked.

"Yes," Guru dāsa said firmly. "It will be done."

* * *

Māyāpur
March 1974

While traveling from Calcutta to Māyāpur, Prabhupāda stopped as usual at the pleasant, secluded mango grove and, sitting on a straw mat, took a breakfast of fresh fruits. A group of his disciples and his sister, Bhavatāriṇī, were also present, and Prabhupāda saw that everyone received *prasādam*. He then returned to his car, and the caravan continued to Māyāpur.

As Prabhupāda's car approached the Mayapur Chandrodaya Mandir, he was met by a "roadblock" of ISKCON devotees waiting at the spot known as Śrīvāsāṅgana, over two miles from the ISKCON property. Four hundred devotees from America, England, Europe, South America, Australia, India, and other parts of the world sang Hare Kṛṣṇa, following Prabhupāda as he rode slowly toward the Mayapur Chandrodaya Mandir.

Prabhupāda smiled. Looking out from the back seat of the car, he recognized many faithful disciples, all hankering for his merciful glance of recognition. The car, surrounded tightly by devotees, inched its way through the gates and up the long drive to the temple. Along the roadside and around the temple buildings, colorful marigolds and *tagar* were abloom, enhancing Śrīla Prabhupāda's joyous reception.

The temple room was completed, its sparkling marble floor, freshly painted walls, and crystal chandeliers all having been readied just a few days before. After offering obeisances before the resplendent golden forms of Rādhā-Mādhava on the altar, Prabhupāda turned and walked the long temple hall to sit on his *vyāsāsana* and address this first truly international gathering of disciples. He welcomed them to Māyāpur, acknowledging that on this day, Bhaktivinoda Ṭhākura's prediction had come true. The devotees shouted triumphantly, "Jaya! Jaya, Śrīla Prabhupāda!"

Bhaktivinoda Ṭhākura had written,

> Oh, for that day when the fortunate English, French, Russian, German and American people will take up banners, mṛdaṅgas and karatālas and raise kīrtana through their streets and towns. When will that day come?

Bhaktivinoda Ṭhākura's prophecy had come to pass. He had also predicted, "Soon a great saint will come and establish Lord Caitanya's movement throughout the world." That great personality—empowered to create devotees of all races and backgrounds and to rally them together in Māyāpur, thousands of miles from their homes—was Śrīla Prabhupāda. And although he saw himself as an instrument of the *ācāryas,* his disciples saw him as the personification of Lord Caitanya's and Lord Nityānanda's mercy. As stated in the *Caitanya-caritāmṛta, yadyapi āmāra guru—caitanyera dāsa / tathāpi jāniye āmi tāṅhāra prakāśa:* "Although I know that my spiritual master is a servitor of Śrī Caitanya, I know him also as a plenary manifestation of the Lord."

Leaving the temple room, Prabhupāda went upstairs and retired to his room, satisfied that the building was now fulfilling its purpose by giving shelter to hundreds of his spiritual children. He began greeting leading disciples from various parts of the world, hearing the encouraging news of book distribution and dealing with problems. He asked that everyone take advantage of the holy *dhāma* by maintaining *kīrtana* in the temple room around the clock, stopping only for scheduled classes in *Śrīmad-Bhāgavatam*.

The devotees were very happy to be together in the *dhāma*. Those with experience of India, like Jayapatāka Swami and Acyutānanda Swami, led groups of devotees on *parikrama* (pilgrimage) to local holy places. This visit to Māyāpur would constitute the first half of the devotees' Indian pilgrimage; after ten days they were scheduled to go to Vṛndāvana.

Almost all of the devotees assembled in Māyāpur preached in areas of the world where the modes of ignorance and passion predominated. Daily they had to mix with materialistic people, and it was inevitable that they would become worn down. This pilgrimage, therefore, was a chance for purification. Although they were not advanced in birth or in knowledge of the Sanskrit *Vedas*, Prabhupāda had accepted them, and that was their certification as devotees. They were bona fide candidates for understanding the meaning of the *dhāma*.They would become refreshed by bathing in the Ganges in Māyāpur and the Yamunā in Vṛndāvana, and they would return to their respective centers throughout the world, purified and renewed for more active preaching.

One song by Narottama dāsa Ṭhākura described the pilgrims' eligibility to realize the *dhāma:*

gaurāṅgera saṅgi-gaṇe, nitya-siddha kari' māne,
se yāya vrajendra-suta-pāśa
śrī gauḍa-maṇḍala-bhūmi, yebā jāne cintāmaṇi,
tāra haya vraja-bhūme vāsa

"Those whose intelligence has come to understand that the eternal associates of Vṛndāvana-dhāma are nondifferent from those in Navadvīpa can attain the service of the son of Nanda Mahārāja [Kṛṣṇa]. Such fortunate persons perceive the holy *dhāma* as an object of service because their transcendental eyes have been opened by the mercy of the eternal perfect associates of Navadvīpa-dhāma. Therefore, those who are enthusiastic realize the touchstone of the holy *dhāma* of Navadvīpa through their transcendental eyes. Thereafter, they reside in the holy *dhāma* of Navadvīpa which they know to be nondifferent than Vṛndāvana and serve in their eternally perfected spiritual bodies."

The devotees' main reason for coming to Māyāpur, however, was to associate with Śrīla Prabhupāda. He was always traveling, and his disciples could only expect to see him briefly from time to time as he passed through their area. To see him in Māyāpur and Vṛndāvana, where they could be with him daily on walks and in the temple, was the most ecstatic part of the festival.

Prabhupāda's happiness to be in Māyāpur was increased many times by the large gathering of his international family. He wanted this. Māyāpur was for the devotees. Prabhupāda even thought that, if possible, all the devotees should stay here permanently and simply go on chanting, although he admitted that it was not practical in terms of world preaching. He derived great satisfaction from sitting in his room above the temple hall and hearing the constant rousing *kīrtanas.* "Bhaktivinoda Ṭhākura has said," he remarked, "there is nothing of value in all the fourteen worlds except the chanting of the holy names."

At Prabhupāda's request, his Governing Body Commission members had gathered in Māyāpur. Their purpose was to discuss ISKCON's preaching activities around the world and then to pass resolutions to direct that preaching. This was the first time they had met as a body in Prabhupāda's presence, and he instructed them how to conduct their meeting. They should not simply talk, he said. Rather, someone should present a proposal, which should then be discussed and voted on. All resolutions should be listed in the minutes.

"Chalk out your plans for the year," Prabhupāda said. "And then whatever you decide, do not change it, but carry it out. Then next year you can meet and discuss again." He was not in favor of prolonged meetings, but he was satisfied to see his G.B.C. secretaries seriously confronting all items on the agenda for the sake of a growing Kṛṣṇa consciousness movement.

One of the main features of the Māyāpur festival was the arrival of advance copies of the recently published volume of the *Caitanya-caritāmṛta.* The volume contained chapters Seven through Eleven of the *Ādi-līlā* and included color illustrations by Prabhupāda's disciples. Chapter Nine especially glorified the *saṅkīrtana* movement begun by Lord Caitanya, and verse after verse ecstatically confirmed the authenticity of Śrīla Prabhupāda's movement.

Kṛṣṇadāsa Kavirāja describes Navadvīpa-dhāma as the place where Lord Caitanya had planted the seed of the Kṛṣṇa consciousness "tree." In one verse he states, "Thus the branches of the Caitanya tree formed a cluster of society, with great branches covering all the universe." And Śrīla

Prabhupāda had written a conclusive one-sentence purport to this verse: "Our International Society for Krishna Consciousness is one of the branches of the Caitanya tree."

Prabhupāda's *Caitanya-caritāmṛta* translation and commentary was the fruit of the Caitanya tree. It was fully authoritative and *paramparā,* but never merely academic or technical. Its teachings stressed that Caitanya Mahāprabhu's desire to widely distribute devotional service should be the desire of everyone. It left no doubt about what Prabhupāda expected from the members of the Kṛṣṇa consciousness movement.

> The only purpose of the preachers of the *saṅkīrtana* movement must be to go on preaching without restriction. That is the way in which Śrī Caitanya Mahāprabhu introduced the *saṅkīrtana* movement to the world.

This volume also contained one of the most important verses of the *Caitanya-caritāmṛta: bhārata-bhūmite haila manuṣya-janma yāra/ janma sārthaka kari' kara para-upākara.* "One who has taken his birth as a human being in the land of India should make his life successful and work for the benefit of all people." In his purport to this verse, Prabhupāda explained the special piety of the Indians, who were always ready to take part in a *saṅkīrtana* festival. Unfortunately, the present leaders of India were leading the people away from God, away from distinguishing pious and sinful acts, and away from belief in a next life. The Indians had the special duty of educating the world in Vedic principles.

"If all Indians had taken to this path as advised by Lord Caitanya Mahāprabhu," Prabhupāda wrote, "India would have given a unique gift to the world, and thus India would have been glorified." Moreover, it was not only the duty of the Indians but the duty of everyone to help the Kṛṣṇa consciousness movement: "One should know definitely that the best welfare activity for all of human society is to awaken man's God consciousness, or Kṛṣṇa consciousness."

Prabhupāda stayed with his disciples in Māyāpur for a full week, lecturing daily and meeting with smaller groups for many hours. On the day of Gaura-pūrṇimā he went down to the Ganges and took the sacred water on his head, while his men dove off the high bank and swam. The next day he left for Vṛndāvana, where he would again meet his disciples and introduce them to the *dhāma.*

*　　　　*　　　　*

Although many of the Western devotees, inexperienced in living and traveling in India, were afflicted with indigestion, dysentery, and even, in some cases, culture shock and homesickness, they nevertheless traveled, a somewhat bedraggled group, from Māyāpur to Calcutta to Delhi, and finally to Vṛndāvana.

Since the Vṛndāvana temple and guesthouse was still mostly a construction site, the devotees had to stay at the nearby Fogel Ashram, while Prabhupāda again took up residence in his newly constructed rooms near the site of the Krishna-Balaram Mandir. The devotees would see him regularly on morning walks and during the morning *Bhāgavatam* class, and he would also come in the evening sometimes to speak under an outdoor pavilion at Fogel Ashram.

Noticing that not many devotees attended his first evening meeting in his room, Prabhupāda inquired and learned that many of them were out visiting Vṛndāvana's famous old temples and other pilgrimage sites, while others were shopping in the bazaar, and still others were sleeping. "Bring them all back," Prabhupāda said, annoyed. "Coming to pilgrimage means to come where the *sādhus* are. I am here, so why is everyone going elsewhere?" On hearing this, so many devotees came to Prabhupāda's room that they could not all fit.

Prabhupāda began talking about *tapasya*, austerity. "The *tapasvīs* in Vṛndāvana go naked," he said, "even in the cold. They are determined not to take birth again for material life." He described how the living entity before birth remains cramped within the womb, a condition much like being tied by the hands and feet and thrown in the ocean. Worms within the mother's body bite the skin of the embryo, and the living entity suffers. Because *māyā* deludes us into thinking we are happy, Prabhupāda explained, we have to again enter the womb of a mother. And although in one lifetime we may be a wealthy human being, in the next life we may be a bug or hog or dog.

"So this life is for *tapasya,*" Prabhupāda said. "But we cannot execute severe penances in this age. So our penance is to try to reform poor crazy persons. One should take voluntary pains for Kṛṣṇa. Kṛṣṇa comes to save the fallen souls, so if you help a little, He will be pleased. Kṛṣṇa comes Himself and He sends His devotee and He leaves books, and still we are mad for sense enjoyment. Our penance, therefore, is to try to reform the fallen souls."

Prabhupāda's preaching uplifted his disciples, whose duty was to preach to the citizens of many lands. They had come, at Prabhupāda's bidding, to visit Māyāpur and Vṛndāvana, but their real work was to save the fallen souls of their native countries, and Prabhupāda's preaching filled them with determination.

Later, one of the devotees told Prabhupāda that dealing with the devotees was sometimes more difficult than dealing with the materialists, and he mentioned a well-known problem case, a devotee named Makhana-cora. "That is your penance," Prabhupāda said. "Your penance is to work with Makhana-cora. We should take anxiety. For a sane man to work with a crazy man is not pleasurable, but the service to Kṛṣṇa is pleasurable." Prabhupāda described how he had left his peaceful life in Vṛndāvana to take on so much burden and anxiety for Kṛṣṇa. Just as he had taken a risk by going to America in old age, so his disciples should accept whatever difficulties were required in preaching Kṛṣṇa consciousness. "The work is not pleasurable," Prabhupāda said, "but making so many devotees is pleasurable."

Although the devotees had been visiting the various temples of Vṛndāvana, eager to imbibe the Vṛndāvana spirit, the real nectar came when Prabhupāda, sitting in his room, spoke about Vṛndāvana. "Vṛndāvana is for *paramahaṁsas*," he said. "You cannot see Vṛndāvana with *viṣaya*, or material spirit. The test is how much you have conquered over eating, sleeping, and mating. Don't think you can just come to Vṛndāvana and become a *gosvāmī*. One who comes to Vṛndāvana with a material spirit will take birth as a dog or a monkey in Vṛndāvana. That is his punishment. But the dogs here are also Vaiṣṇavas.

"People come to Vṛndāvana to give up all material anxieties and family life. So one should not be afraid. He should never mind what is going to happen. There are many devotees in Vṛndāvana who are not disturbed by heat or cold. But another risk in Vṛndāvana is to meet those who talk of the *gopīs* but are not free from smoking *biḍis*. They are *sahajiyās*. We have to see who is a devotee by his personal behavior. If one is seeking money and *biḍi* and women and talking of the *gopīs*, then what is his position? Śrī Caitanya Mahāprabhu never talked of the *gopīs* publicly. The real Vṛndāvana is not to eat *prasādam* and sleep but to follow the advice of Vṛndāvana-candra [Kṛṣṇa] and broadcast His message. That is His message. That is Vṛndāvana. Vṛndāvana-dhāma is worshipable. Don't commit an offense here. Take it as *cintāmaṇi-dhāma*, Kṛṣṇa. Narottama dāsa Ṭhākura says to see Vṛndāvana is not possible with *viṣaya*. So we should take the shelter of Gaura-Nitāi, become cleansed of eating, sleeping, and mating. Then you will see Vṛndāvana. Don't commit offenses here. There is a special influence in Vṛndāvana."

Prabhupāda said that Vṛndāvana's spiritual quality was such that devotional service performed here had one hundred times the effect of service performed elsewhere. But an offense in Vṛndāvana also had one hundred times the effect. Ordinary persons, therefore, were advised to visit a holy place like Vṛndāvana for no more than three days; otherwise they would become slack and return to their sinful activities. "Better to come," Prabhupāda said, "become purified, and leave on the fourth day. And the worst offense to Vṛndāvana is to commit illicit sex here. So do not come and play hide-and-seek with Kṛṣṇa. He sees with His eyes, the sun, and He is also in your heart. Kṛṣṇa knows everything. Those who want to be devotees have to be sincere. They shouldn't play tricks, because Kṛṣṇa knows everything. Be sincere with Kṛṣṇa and His representative. Preach the gospel of *Bhagavad-gītā* as it is. Become a spiritual master."

After his evening lecture, Prabhupāda mentioned how some of the *sahajiyās* had walked out during his lecture. "They are so advanced," he said, "that they want to hear only of the embracing and kissing of Rādhārāṇī and Kṛṣṇa. They take my talks as ordinary." Prabhupāda explained that his process of lecturing was to speak on only one verse per lecture, but that that speaking was the same as Kṛṣṇa's speaking. He said that his own Guru Mahārāja had lectured for three months on the first verse of *Śrīmad-Bhāgavatam*, and for that he had gained great respect.

Prabhupāda learned one day that one of his disciples had left the company of the ISKCON devotees to live among the *bābājīs* at Rādhā-kuṇḍa. Prabhupāda became angry and sent for the boy to come immediately. When the boy arrived, Prabhupāda went out to see him. Dressed in only a *dhotī*, Prabhupāda spoke sternly to his disciple, saying that the monkeys of Vṛndāvana also live simply but are interested only in eating and sex. "Don't become a monkey!" Prabhupāda said, trembling as he spoke. "Why don't you come and live with me?"

The boy replied, "The *bābājīs* have given me some facility to chant."

"You come with me!" Prabhupāda exclaimed. "I will give you facility. But don't become a monkey." The boy surrendered before Prabhupāda's compassionate concern.

Prabhupāda heard from his disciples living in Vṛndāvana that some of the local *gosvāmīs* had a complaint about him. They had read an article published in *Back to Godhead* and considered it insulting. The article, written by Prabhupāda's disciple Hayagrīva, contained a statement that *gosvāmīs* in Vṛndāvana who misbehaved would become hogs and monkeys in Vṛndāvana in their next life. Prabhupāda replied that the statement was accurate. The article, he said, had not specifically referred to the present *gosvāmīs* but to any *gosvāmī* who lived sinfully in Vṛndāvana. This was not merely an opinion but was the authoritative conclusion of the original *gosvāmīs* of Vṛndāvana.

Although Yamunā dāsī lived in Vṛndāvana with her husband, Guru dāsa, Prabhupāda rarely saw her. So one day he sent for her and inquired why she was not coming to hear him and serve him. Yamunā admitted that she was afraid because Prabhupāda seemed to be in a chastising mood of late. (She was referring to Prabhupāda's insistence and pushing to get the Vṛndāvana temple built.) Prabhupāda said that only by his pushing was the temple being built. But Yamunā again confessed her fear of Prabhupāda's anger.

"You may be afraid of your spiritual master," Prabhupāda said, "but that doesn't mean you shouldn't come and see him." He then narrated the story of how Lord Balarāma had once forced the River Yamunā to come before Him. As he spoke, all the devotees present became aware that Prabhupāda was not only telling the *līlā* of Lord Balarāma's frightening the River Yamunā, but he was also speaking indirectly about his disciple Yamunā. Absorbed in the pastimes of Lord Balarāma, Prabhupāda described how the Lord, intoxicated from drinking honey, had threatened the River Yamunā, forcing her to come. But when the Yamunā did not come, Lord Balarāma had cut into the earth with His plow, forcing her to flow to Him. "In this way," Prabhupāda said, "I will drag you to come and see me." Yamunā dāsī agreed to stop her foolish reluctance and come and cook for her spiritual master.

Although the afternoons were warm in Vṛndāvana, the early mornings were chilly. Dressed in a sweater, a wool *cādar*, and a fuzzy wool cap that buttoned under his chin, Prabhupāda led his disciples on a pre-dawn walk along Chhatikara Road. With the ISKCON leaders and *sannyāsīs* staying close to catch his words, he walked and talked in Vṛndāvana. His walks were so long that most of the devotees became tired, and some joked that Prabhupāda was going to walk all the way back to Delhi. When the sun rose, gradually the air would begin to warm.

Some of the devotees had expected that in Vṛndāvana Prabhupāda would talk more about the places of Kṛṣṇa's pastimes and about Kṛṣṇa and the *gopīs* and that Prabhupāda himself would want to see the places of Kṛṣṇa's pastimes. But Prabhupāda seemed far more concerned to hear of the preaching of his disciples or to discuss the construction of the Krishna-Balaram Mandir. Often when devotees raised the topic of Vṛndāvana, Prabhupāda would criticize the cheating of certain Vṛndāvana *bābājīs* and the corruption within Vṛndāvana. Or he would speak of the special vision required before one could properly see Vṛndāvana. He said Vṛndāvana was wherever a pure devotee lived. And he stressed that the devotees' main business was to go out of Vṛndāvana and preach.

As they walked along the road, the main traffic was pedestrians, workers carrying milk on bicycles, or men riding on bullock carts; only occasionally an automobile would speed by, its horn honking. Almost every person who approached would respectfully greet Prabhupāda with "Jaya Rādhe!" or "Hare Kṛṣṇa!" Or they would hold up their hands or bow their heads and say *namas te.* One young man driving a bicycle ricksha approached from the opposite direction and, just before reaching Prabhupāda, stopped his ricksha, got down, stepped out of his shoes, and prostrated himself on the road. Prabhupāda smiled and said, "Very good boy."

Prabhupāda paused. "This is Vṛndāvana," he said. The simple habit of the ordinary people in Vṛndāvana to offer respect to a saintly person was, to Prabhupāda, an expression of Vṛndāvana's essence. Vṛndāvana was one of the few remaining places in India where even a common man would chant the name of Rādhārāṇī and Kṛṣṇa as he passed by on the road. To fully understand this extraordinary phenomenon was to understand Vṛndāvana.

One devotee asked Prabhupāda that if so many residents of Vṛndāvana were fallen souls, then what was the meaning of the statement that to be born in Vṛndāvana was to be liberated? "It says in the *Kṛṣṇa* book," the devotee said, "that the people in Vṛndāvana don't need a spiritual master. Kṛṣṇa is their spiritual master."

"Yes," Prabhupāda replied, "they have an excellent spiritual master. But one may have a spiritual master and not obey him. Then what is his position? So they are fallen who do nonsense things in Vṛndāvana. But their fortune is also there—that they are born in Vṛndāvana. But they misuse that fortune."

The land was very dry. Prabhupāda said that Vṛndāvana was becoming like a desert and would become more so in the future. He said this was because of impiety. "In the West," he said, "I see in America, Germany, there is so much green. But not here."

The devotees then questioned Prabhupāda. "Wasn't the West more impious than Vṛndāvana?"

"Yes," Prabhupāda said. "I came to you in the West, and you did not know anything about Kṛṣṇa. You did not even know that these things were bad—meat-eating and illicit sex. But when I told you to stop, you did it. But this is Kṛṣṇa's land, Vṛndāvana, and they are doing these things here. Therefore it is even worse. And they are being punished directly by Kṛṣṇa."

Prabhupāda's morning walks in Vṛndāvana were as exciting and enlightening as his formal lectures. On two consecutive morning walks, he outlined a comprehensive plan for starting an ISKCON *varṇāśrama* college. *Bhagavad-gītā* explains how society should be divided into four orders, according to a person's nature and occupation. Prabhupāda said that although the members of the Kṛṣṇa consciousness movement were above the social divisions—*brāhmaṇa, kṣatriya, vaiśya,* and *śūdra*—they should teach others by acting perfectly within these divisions. Not everyone would become a *brāhmaṇa*, but everyone could attain the same perfection by doing his particular duty—for the pleasure of Kṛṣṇa. "We will teach military art," said Prabhupāda, to the amazement of his disciples. "Soldiers will wear *tilaka* and march, saying, 'Hare Kṛṣṇa, Hare Kṛṣṇa.' They can march with military band and fight."

To Prabhupāda, establishing *varṇāśrama-dharma* did not seem difficult. ISKCON should begin by starting a college based on the *varṇāśrama* conception. "There should be no unemployment," Prabhupāda said. "We will say, 'Why are you sitting idly? Come onto the field. Take this plow. Take this bull. Go on working. Why are you sitting idly?' This is the Kṛṣṇa consciousness movement. Nobody should be allowed to sit down and sleep. They must find out some employment. Either work as a *brāhmaṇa*, or as a *kṣatriya,* or as a *vaiśya.* Why should there be unemployment?

"Just as this body is working—that means the leg is working, the hand, the brain, the belly. So why should there be unemployment? You stop this unemployment—you will see the whole world is peaceful. There will be no complaint. They will be happily chanting Hare Kṛṣṇa. Just like this field here. No one is working it. They have all gone to the cities to work in the factory. It is a condemned civilization."

On a morning walk near the end of the Vṛndāvana festival one of the devotees mentioned that the festival was almost over and that the devotees would be going back to their centers. "Yes," said Prabhupāda, and he stopped walking. "Yes, that is our real business—to go and preach."

As the devotees were making travel arrangements for Delhi and onward, Girirāja arrived in Vṛndāvana with upsetting news from Bombay. The municipality of Bombay had denied them permission to begin construction of a temple. According to Girirāja, two permissions were required: permission to build according to rules and regulations and a No-Objection Certificate from the police commissioner. In issuing the No-Objection Certificate the police must consider two points: whether the temple would create a traffic problem and whether the presence of a temple would cause community or religious tensions. The municipality had been delaying their permission, saying they first required an NOC from the police. And the police had been saying that they needed the sanction of the municipality before they would consider giving the NOC. Girirāja had been pursuing this bureaucratic matter, but now a commissioner from the police had written a letter flatly refusing to give an NOC. According to the commissioner, the *kīrtana* in the temple would produce a "nuisance."

The report from Girirāja deeply disturbed Śrīla Prabhupāda. "You should immediately object," he told Girirāja on his walk the next morning, "that the government is completely unqualified. The pure devotees are always engaged in *kīrtana*, and the government calls it a nuisance. He could at least be a gentleman and say that the sound should not be amplified while people are trying to take rest. But instead he has said the *kīrtana* is simply a nuisance." Prabhupāda said that there were many learned persons in Bombay, and they also would not stand for this judgment.

"You have to organize all the Vaiṣṇavas," Prabhupāda continued. "In the *Bhagavad-gītā* it is said, *satataṁ kīrtayanto mām*: one has to chant Kṛṣṇa always. Śrī Caitanya Mahāprabhu says, *kīrtanīyaḥ sadā hariḥ*. And this rascal is saying '*bhajana* is nuisance'? Hmm? Is it not possible to invoke an agitation against this? What right has he got to say 'nuisance'? He could have spoken in sweet language that, 'The *bhajana* may be very good for the devotees, but it creates disturbance to the others. Therefore we cannot allow.' Say like that. But they cannot still stop *bhajana*. But his remark is that the *bhajana* is nuisance! Chanting Hare Kṛṣṇa is the culture of India. We must make propaganda and organize *kīrtana* parties and fight this."

One of the G.B.C. men proposed that instead of going back to the West some of the devotees stay, go to Bombay, and hold massive protests. At first Prabhupāda approved this spirit, likening it to Lord Caitanya's protest against the Kazi, who had stoped the *saṅkīrtana* movement in Navadvīpa. But on reflecting, he decided it would not be wise to fight with the government. The devotees could not hope to win such a fight, nor would the people appreciate it. Prabhupāda suggested the devotees hold massive *kīrtana* programs and preach positively to the people of Bombay, convincing them of the value of Kṛṣṇa consciousness. "When the people of Bombay are convinced of the importance of Kṛṣṇa consciousness," Prabhupāda said, "they will see that the temple is built."

In an urgent mood, Śrīla Prabhupāda left Vṛndāvana for Bombay. His last instruction to Guru dāsa and the others in Vṛndāvana: "An ideal *gosvāmī* should remain here to challenge any false *gosvāmīs*. But if you also become false, then you cannot challenge."

* * *

Bombay
March 20, 1974

Disciples and ISKCON life members continued to discuss with Śrīla Prabhupāda about confronting the police commissioner's refusal to grant ISKCON permission to build a temple at Hare Krishna Land. Ironically, ISKCON's property was bordered on one side by a large cinema hall, and every evening, both before and after the movie, a long line of traffic would form. The honking horns and the hundreds of pedestrians coming and going created much noise and congestion. If the neighborhood and government could tolerate a cinema, then how, without prejudice, could they call the Kṛṣṇa *kīrtanas* a nuisance?

Although addressing the specific issue of government permission, Śrīla Prabhupāda also preached on the greater principle of how governments in Kali-yuga restrict religious life. "The government policy," he said, "is that religion is an opiate of the people. They think religion is just a sentiment. They want to open slaughterhouses and kill these mischief, loitering cows. Their conclusion is that religion has no value. Therefore, their decision is to not encourage these temples and this *bhajana.* From their point of view it is useless."

Some of Prabhupāda's Bombay friends suggested he work through the Jan-Sangh political party, which supported Hinduism, and thus form a strong political coalition. But Śrīla Prabhupāda was more concerned to use this opportunity for preaching. "I suggest that we make vigorous propaganda," he said. "Hold meetings in big halls so that the public may understand, at least, that this movement is very important. Let there be advertisements that we will speak on different subject matters, and then I will come and speak.

"In that meeting, make a nice gentleman the president. Create public opinion so that they will come and sign, 'Yes, here must be one temple.' We will prove from śāstric evidence. As it is stated in *Bhagavad-gītā, catur-vidhā bhajante māṁ janāḥ sukṛtino 'rjuna.* This word *bhajana* from *bhajante* is used with reference to the very pious men, *sukṛtinaḥ.* The opposite kind of man is *duṣkṛtinaḥ*, the miscreants. So *bhajana* is for the pious man, as recommended in the *Bhagavad-gītā.* And *Bhagavad-gītā* is held in great estimation all over the world. And yet he has accused *bhajana* as nuisance? How rascal and ignorant! We have to make it clear that *bhajana* is so important. *Bhagavad-gītā* is meant for solution of all material problems, but the people of India are not accepting it.

"My disciples can also speak and say, 'You please come with us. We are foreigners, but we know Kṛṣṇa is not for this or that. So why are you Indians lacking? You accept your culture. We have taken to Kṛṣṇa, and Kṛṣṇa says that simply by *kīrtana* one becomes free from all contamination. So why not join with us? What is the wrong there? It is stated in your *śāstra*, and we have adopted it. And we are feeling better. So why you are so callous, you educated youth and gentlemen?' This kind of propaganda has to be made."

Śrīla Prabhupāda had abandoned the idea of direct political agitation, but he continued to speak against the police commissioner's decision and to deliberate on overcoming it. He considered the matter from all possible angles, pro and con. At one point he said that if they could not get sanction to build a temple, then they should build a hotel. "I am trying to get sanction," he said. "If you don't give permission—then hotel."

"Build a hotel in the front and a temple in the rear," suggested Tamāla Kṛṣṇa Goswami.

"Yes," Prabhupāda replied. And he instructed his men further on dealing with opposition. As with the struggle to acquire the land, the present struggle also threatened to become a long legal battle. Prabhupāda remained always transcendental, however, even while fighting. And he maintained his normal activities in Bombay, enjoying the mild tropical climate.

Although ISKCON owned a number of tenement buildings on the Juhu land, the devotees had not been able to use a single one, since all were occupied. But recently when tenants had vacated one of the apartments, the devotees had prepared it for Prabhupāda. It was a modest place, two small rooms with a little kitchen, but now for the first time Prabhupāda had his own residence at Hare Krishna Land.

Prabhupāda liked to sit on the narrow veranda outside his apartment and take his massage in the sun. Surveying the Juhu land, with its many tall coconut trees, their long palm leaves rustling pleasantly in the breeze, Prabhupāda said Hare Krishna Land was a paradise. The devotees were happy.

One day during his massage Prabhupāda saw that the contractors, whom he had allowed to come and take coconuts for a set price, were also taking away the leaves to sell in the marketplace. Leaping to his feet, Prabhupāda called from the veranda, "Caityaguru!" Soon the devotee in charge of grounds management appeared before Prabhupāda. "I cannot close my eyes!" Prabhupāda said. "No one else sees these things! You are being cheated!"

Every morning several Indian gentlemen would join Prabhupāda as he walked along Juhu Beach. Whenever Prabhupāda would criticize so-called great political and spiritual leaders of India, exposing their poor understanding of *Bhagavad-gītā*, these men would become disturbed. Similarly, Prabhupāda's disciples became disturbed to hear these men argue with Prabhupāda.

One day when Prabhupāda criticized a favorite hero, a certain doctor argued back, criticizing Prabhupāda's statement that the Absolute Truth was Kṛṣṇa, the Supreme Personality of Godhead. The doctor and others asserted that the Absolute Truth was many things and that ultimately everything was one. The devotees could barely restrain themselves, but still Prabhupāda always treated these men as his friends.

Early the next morning in his room, however, Prabhupāda told his disciples that these men were actually Māyāvādīs. "We will now have a program," he said, "where we will walk on the beach, but we will only chant Hare Kṛṣṇa. If they want to talk, we will just chant, and we will all chant only. If they wish to, they can walk with us."

"Prabhupāda," a devotee said, "they will be restless if we do that."

"Even if they don't chant," said Prabhupāda, "if they only hear, it will be beneficial for them. Māyāvādī philosophy is very dangerous. Śrī Caitanya Mahāprabhu said that whoever hears it is doomed."

A devotee asked why a Māyāvādī would disguise himself as a *kṛṣṇa-bhakta.* They do it, Prabhupāda said, to get popular reception for being liberal to all. But if a woman says that she is very liberal and accepts *any* man, that may seem to be a liberal proposal, but it is not good. "We will read the *Kṛṣṇa* book on the walk," Prabhupāda said. "I am walking with my disciples. If these men like, they can join and hear. But if they want to ask questions, they must accept the *guru's* answer without argument. Is that all right?"

The next morning, although the usual challengers did not join the walk, Prabhupāda had Girirāja read aloud from the *Kṛṣṇa* book. Suddenly, Prabhupāda sighted the familiar group of speculators approaching from the opposite direction. But as they drew closer, they purposely turned aside so as to avoid Prabhupāda. One of them came over, however, and, representing the entire group, informed Prabhupāda they were not going to walk with him any more; they had met and decided that their conversations with him created too much argument and criticism. "India has many saints," the man added.

"I am the policeman," Prabhupāda said, "and I have to catch the thief." After a few days, the same group rejoined Prabhupāda on his walk, and the discussions continued as before. Some of Prabhupāda's disciples remained disturbed, but Prabhupāda was jolly, correcting his friends like an older brother, teaching them pure Kṛṣṇa consciousness.

Prabhupāda would take a breakfast of fruit and nuts. Around eleven A.M. he would sit on the veranda in his *gamchā* while his servant massaged him with mustard oil. During the massage, Prabhupāda would often speak with one or two of his Bombay devotees, giving them pertinent instructions. After lunch he would rest an hour or two and, on arising, take a glass of fresh coconut water or sugarcane juice. In the evening he would meet guests and then around ten P.M. take rest. At one A.M. he would rise and sit at his desk, beneath a tentlike covering of mosquito netting, and dictate his translations and purports to *Caitanya-caritāmṛta* until time for his morning walk.

Several times a day, Prabhupāda would call for Girirāja and other Bombay managers to confer on the latest strategy in securing permission to build the temple. When Prabhupāda's Bombay friends would visit, they would often find him on the roof of the tenement, sitting on white cotton sheeting and leaning on white bolsters, preaching the philosophy of *Bhagavad-gītā* by the hour. He would ask his visitors to help him solidly establish Kṛṣṇa consciousness in Bombay.

One day during the massage Prabhupāda confided to his servant, "Most men are retired at my age. I do not want to manage any more. I just want to do some writing." Prabhupāda asked if there was some place in the world he could go for six months, a place where he would be all alone, where no one would come to disturb him, and where he would not get any mail.

Prabhupāda's servant suggested Tehran. Prabhupāda considered it, then suggested New Vrindaban. He spoke of Mahatma Gandhi, who could not even sleep at night because people were always after him, even though he traveled incognito.

That very day a letter came from Bhagavān in Paris, inviting Prabhupāda to tour his ISKCON centers in Europe. Immediately Prabhupāda was enlivened at this invitation. He said he would go.

"But earlier today," his servant said, "you wanted to go away and be alone."

Prabhupāda laughed. "That will not be possible for me in this lifetime. Better I keep traveling and die on the battlefield. For a warrior, it is glorious to die on the battlefield. Is it not?"

Traveling around the world once or twice a year had become Prabhupāda's routine. In describing his own spiritual master, he had written, "Hindus are not allowed to cross the ocean, but you send your devotees overseas to preach." The injunction for Hindus not to cross the ocean was to protect them from leaving the pious land of India, since so many Indians gave up their culture when they went abroad. When Prabhupāda had been a small child, one of his uncles had suggested he one day go to London and become a lawyer, but Prabhupāda's father had protested; he did not want his son to be exposed to the sinful ways of the West.

Years later Prabhupāda *had* gone to London, as a preacher, to change the ways of the sinful. For this reason the Vaiṣṇava should travel.

Just before starting his European tour, Prabhupāda explained to several devotees in his room that they also should travel and preach. He said they should do so while they were young, and then when they were old and matured in Kṛṣṇa consciousness, they could go to Māyāpur, retire, and simply chant Hare Kṛṣṇa. "Of course, for myself," Prabhupāda added, "I'm not so mature."

The devotees were silent a moment, but then one ventured, "But Śrīla Prabhupāda, if you say that you're not mature, then how can we ever think that we are old or mature enough to retire?" Prabhupāda smiled and said that they would have to decide for themselves. But he was not mature enough.

Tamāla Kṛṣṇa Goswami said, "Then we also will never become so mature that we can retire."

* * *

April 18

Before going to Europe, Prabhupāda responded to an invitation from his devotees in South India to attend a three-day *paṇḍāl* festival in Hyderabad. No sooner did he arrive at the airport in Hyderabad, however, than a group of reporters asked him for a press conference.

Prabhupāda consented, and a reporter opened with a technical philosophical question, inquiring whether Prabhupāda's philosophy was *advaita* or *dvaita.* South India was so steeped in the ancient philosophical debate between the Vaiṣṇavas and the Śaṅkarites that here an ordinary news reporter was concerned with comparative philosophies.

Prabhupāda scoffed at the question. "What is the point of discussing such things," he challenged "—whether one is *dvaita* or *advaita*? Kṛṣṇa says, *annād bhavanti bhūtāni. Anna* means 'grains.' The people have no grains. Grains are produced from the rains, and rains from sacrifice. So perform sacrifice. You have to divide the society into four orders. You may be *dvaita* or *advaita*, but you need grains."

Prabhupāda's secretary wrote to Bhagavān in Paris, keeping him informed of Prabhupāda's location and schedule.

> You can contact us here until the 29th or 30th of April after which we will be back in Bombay. Your idea for festivals sounds nice. Here they had a three-day pandal. Last night about a thousand people came,

> sat very silently through his whole lecture, and then pressed forward to receive blessings from Srila Prabhupada. Devotees had the Deities on stage and a vyasasana and lots of prasadam for the guests.

April 25

From Hyderabad Śrīla Prabhupāda flew to Tirupati. There in mountainous Tirumala stands the richest temple in India, where a Deity of Viṣṇu known as Bālajī resides.

The temple managers respectfully welcomed Śrīla Prabhupāda and his party, providing them with two cottages on the mountainside. According to the temple policy, people usually have to wait in a long line before seeing the Deity—since fifteen thousand people enter the temple daily—and they are given only a brief *darśana.* Non-Hindus are usually not allowed. But Śrīla Prabhupāda and his disciples received the special honor of a private *darśana* of Bālajī.

At the end of a long inner sanctum, its entrance guarded by two large figures of Jaya and Vijaya, the gatekeepers of Vaikuṇṭha, the Deity was enthroned. The only light in the inner sanctum came from flaming torches affixed to the walls or held by the *pūjārīs.* When approaching the Deity in the hallway, many pilgrims would traditionally call out, "Govinda!" But as Prabhupāda entered, he sang, "*Govindam ādi-puruṣaṁ tam ahaṁ bhajāmi.*"

Later in his cottage Prabhupāda remarked that the millions of people going to see Bālajī were proof that the masses are still attracted to God, despite government propaganda. Although most people may go to the Lord for alleviating material distress or for getting money, still they called out the holy name, "Govinda!"

A devotee asked Prabhupāda why the Deity was called Bālajī. "*Bālajī,*" Prabhupāda said, "means 'child'—Kṛṣṇa as a cowherd boy, not in His Vaikuṇṭha aspect."

Prabhupāda was pleased to stay in the cottage and take the Deity's *prasādam.* He suggested that in New Vrindaban they build cottages like this and that ISKCON build temples like the temple of Bālajī, with its gold dome and extensive facility for visitors.

One day an official of the Tirupati temple, while visiting Prabhupāda, mentioned that their collection was about forty lakhs of rupees per month. Prabhupāda inquired how the temple's income was being spent. When the priest indicated that most of the money went for renovation of the buildings, Prabhupāda replied that temple renovation was good, but propagating the message of Kṛṣṇa all over the world was better. "Bālajī is Kṛṣṇa," Prabhupāda said. "His message should be spread. He descended as Caitanya Mahāprabhu to teach us."

Prabhupāda told the priest of how so many old churches in London were not being used. "How will the spirit of the temple be maintained without preaching?" Prabhupāda asked. The priest then boasted that they were building another temple and installing *pañcopāsanā* (five deities recommended for worship by the impersonalist Śaṅkarācārya). Prabhupāda was surprised. "Your leader is Rāmānuja," he said. "He never recommended *pañcopāsanā*!"

For the two days in Tirupati, Prabhupāda went three or four times daily to see the Deity of Bālajī. And whenever he went, the *pūjārīs* would clear the inner sanctum of all other visitors and allow him a private *darśana* for as long as he liked, standing in the torchlight before the mystical, bejeweled form of Bālajī.

* * *

Bombay
April 29

Although in a few days Prabhupāda would be leaving for Rome, a problem now faced him and the management of his Indian projects. Tamāla Kṛṣṇa Goswami was requesting that Prabhupāda allow him to go to America; after four years of management in India, he was eager to try a different kind of preaching. His Godbrother-friend Viṣṇujana Swami had pleased Prabhupāda with his bus-touring in America and had convinced Tamāla Kṛṣṇa that this was the most opportune preaching. Śrīla Prabhupāda had accepted the proposal, although reluctantly. Certainly it would be good for the preaching in America, and it would be good for Tamāla Kṛṣṇa. But what about India? Once again Prabhupāda was faced with the fact that the only manager for ISKCON in India was himself.

Carefully he reviewed a recent report of the spending and accounts in Māyāpur. Concerned that all money be handled very carefully and spent exactly for the purpose it was intended, he had written to Jayapatāka Swami,

> Money for the land must be spent for land purchase; if I send money for constructing of a kitchen it must be spent for that.
>
> Also, if you purchase land it must be properly utilized. . . . And if

> you actually produce some grains and vegetables, then where is the necessity for further money for maintenance. For maintenance we require 100 rupees per head without any risk for purchasing lands and cultivating the same. I understand there are only 20 men there at present, so utmost 2,000 rupees is necessary for maintenance. I am not competent to understand everything concerning what you plan to do, but that is my rough estimate.
>
> You have tried to explain by long letter which I have not gone through yet. In the meantime go on the above principle: money spent must be used for that purpose intended. That will keep it very clear.

From a previous letter from Śrīla Prabhupāda, Bhavānanda and Jayapatāka had become a little despondent, thinking that they may have displeased their spiritual master. But Prabhupāda reassured them,

> I know you are working hard and sincerely. I have no business to criticize but as head of the institution or your spiritual master, it is my duty to find out your faults. Even Caitanya Mahaprabhu presented Himself as faulty before His spiritual master. To remain faulty before the spiritual master is a good qualification so he is subjected to rectification. But if one thinks he is all perfect then there is no scope for rectification. Don't be sorry when I find fault. That is my primary duty. Canakya pandit says one must find fault with disciples and sons, it is good for them.

Prabhupāda also scrutinized the finances in Vṛndāvana, where Guru dāsa was president and Tejās, in Delhi, was financial supervisor. Reviewing Tejās's latest request, Prabhupāda wrote back,

> I am enclosing the list of checks requested by you by Registered post except I am not sending one check for Rs 3,000 for Deity clothes to be paid to the tailor Lalit Prasad of Vrindaban. Deity paraphernalia is supposed to be collected separately by Gurudasa and Yamuna, not come out of the construction fund as you have requested. Besides, I have advised Gurudas not to pay any tailor but to make clothes by our own devotees for the deities.

Prabhupāda also found a serious inconsistency in the accounting, which he pointed out to Tejās for correction.

> According to my check book, after writing the last check for Rs 17,600.00 there is a balance of only Rs. 18,745.81. But you are

> indicating a balance of Rs. 100,313.64. Where is the difference? Send me a complete statement of account.

Guru dāsa and Tejās had assured Prabhupāda that the Krishna-Balaram Mandir would be ready to open by July 1974. Prabhupāda designed the invitation cards himself and asked that they be printed and sent to important persons.

> The founder-acarya and the members of the International Society for Krishna Consciousness requests the pleasure of Mr. and Mrs. ______'s company to visit the installation ceremony of the Krishna-Balarama temple from August 8 to 10 and accept prasadam.
>
> Guru dasa Adhikary
Local President
>
> A.C. Bhaktivedanta Swami
Founder-Acarya
>
> Surabhi dasa Adhikari
Secretary

With only three months left, Prabhupāda's plans were to travel from May through July. Giving permission for transferring funds from Delhi to Vṛndāvana, he left. He would return in three months for the grand opening.

CHAPTER EIGHT

Śrīla Prabhupāda's first two stops in Europe were Rome and Geneva. In both places devotees had arranged many outside speaking engagements as well as meetings with important guests in Prabhupāda's room. The Rome temple was a small house at a busy intersection near Piazza Lodi. Traffic was relentless, its noise penetrating into Prabhupāda's quarters within the temple building. "I hope the noise of the traffic doesn't bother you too much," Dhanañjaya, the temple president, apologized.

"No," Prabhupāda replied, "this sound is very pleasing. It means this is a very important part of Rome. This is a very good location."

At the Villa Borghese, in a hotel hall built to seat five hundred people, Prabhupāda spoke before a crowd of more than one thousand. Prabhupāda was pleased by the enthusiastic gathering of Italians, who behaved as if coming to receive the blessings of the Pope. They were pious, but they had not been taught properly how to engage in the Lord's service. This, he said, was the one defect. Although the devotees had arranged a meeting between Prabhupāda and the Pope, the Pope was ill, so Prabhupāda met with Cardinal Pignedoli, who was in charge of non-Christian liaisons.

In flying to Geneva, Prabhupāda and his secretaries viewed the snow-covered Alps. "This is a very dangerous spot," Prabhupāda remarked as the plane flew above the alpine peaks. "Many planes have crashed here."

In Geneva the mayor offered Prabhupāda an official reception. Everything went smoothly, according to diplomatic protocol. Afterward, the mayor asked frankly, "If everyone became like you are saying, wouldn't the economy be threatened?"

Prabhupāda said no. And he quoted the same verse he had given to press reporters in Hyderabad: *annād bhavanti bhūtāni.* Grains are produced by rains, which are produced by sacrifice to Viṣṇu. Prabhupāda proposed that if men cultivated their own land and kept cows, they would have no economic problems. Kṛṣṇa conscious devotees could work in all ways of life within society; in fact, they could teach how to organize society according to God conscious principles.

While returning to the temple, Prabhupāda asked, "Were my answers all right?" One of the devotees replied that he thought the mayor considered the devotees beggars. "Therefore," Prabhupāda said, "I told him about tilling the land. We are not beggars. We are giving the highest knowledge. I gave him a copy of *Bhagavad-gītā*, the highest knowledge. He could not give us anything. So who is the beggar?"

Prabhupāda accepted an invitation in Geneva to speak at the World Health Organization of the United Nations. He also met at the temple with Indologist Jean Hurbert and with several scientists and professors.

One of Prabhupāda's leading disciples, Karandhara, came to visit him in Geneva. Karandhara had left the movement four months before, being unable to follow strictly the four regulative principles. Up to that time he had been the leading manager of ISKCON in the United States, and Prabhupāda had depended heavily on him to deal with his Dai Nippon printers, to coordinate book distribution, and to collect funds from all the temples in the U.S. Since leaving, Karandhara had felt great remorse, had had a change of heart, and had telegrammed Prabhupāda that he wanted to come and surrender at his lotus feet once again. Śrīla Prabhupāda had welcomed him back, and Karandhara had flown immediately to Geneva.

After speaking for a few hours with Karandhara, Prabhupāda decided he would be just the man to take up the heavy responsibilities of G.B.C. of India. He should make his headquarters in Bombay and help the devotees there get the No-Objection Certificate. It was a bold move for Prabhupāda, based on trust in his disciple and on the immediate need for Kṛṣṇa conscious leadership in India. He had his secretary immediately type a letter to the leaders of the temples in Hyderabad, Bombay, Calcutta, Māyāpur, Delhi, and Vṛndāvana, authorizing Karandhara's appointment as the new Governing Body Commissioner for India. "It is a great relief for me," wrote Prabhupāda. "Please give him all cooperation and work together for advancement of our mission to make the people of India Kṛṣṇa conscious."

Paris
June 8

Twenty-five hundred people in the audience as well as fifty devotees onstage awaited Śrīla Prabhupāda's appearance at La Salle Pleyel in Paris.

After *kīrtana*, Prabhupāda began his lecture by having a devotee read in the Bible from the Gospel of St. John: "In the beginning was the Word, and the Word was God." Prabhupāda then spoke on the power of the holy name as transcendental sound.

Many persons in the crowd were student radicals, who specifically came to cause trouble. And Śrīla Prabhupāda gave an analogy that agitated them, comparing the conditioned soul's existence in the material world to a citizen's punishment for breaking the laws of the state. As soon as Prabhupāda said that disobedient citizens would be punished, the students began to boo and yell. He was speaking in English, and his disciple Jyotirmayī-devī dāsī was translating each line over the microphone. When the students began shouting, Prabhupāda turned to Jyotirmayī and asked, "What are they saying?"

"They don't like the example you have given," she replied, "because they don't like the government here."

Śrīla Prabhupāda then spoke back to the challengers, "You may not like it, but the fact of the matter is that if you break the laws you will be punished." He was speaking of the absolute law of *karma*, but the student radicals took it politically. They continued shouting at Prabhupāda. One man jumped up and shouted loudly in French, "You may be speaking spiritual things, but one thing I would never do is sit on a throne and demand that people bow down to my feet!" At these words the audience began applauding and whistling and chanting the words "*Par terre! Par terre! Par terre!*" Prabhupāda again asked for a translation. Jyotirmayī told him they were shouting, "Get down!"

Returning the challenge, Prabhupāda spoke strongly into the microphone: "I could speak to you from the floor also, but that does not mean you would understand any better. If you know the science of God consciousness, then you also can sit on the *vyāsāsana*, and they will bow down at your feet."

Prabhupāda's strong reply brought silence to the hall, as if his answer had satisfied the challengers. Suddenly a black man jumped up on the stage and addressed himself to the theater audience. He began by speaking in defense of Prabhupāda and the devotees, but then he began speaking against them. Finally he began speaking incoherently, and Prabhupāda turned to his disciples onstage and said, "All right, have *kīrtana*." The devotees rose with drums and *karatālas* and began a rousing *kīrtana*. Most of the people in attendance joined also, and the protests were drowned out.

After this tumultuous scene, while riding back to the temple, Prabhupāda said that in the future they should not give him a *vyāsāsana* to sit on before public audiences; in the future they should give him a simple cushion to sit on. He also doubted the value of explaining philosophy to such large audiences. For the balance of his stay in Paris he spoke to smaller groups who were actually interested to hear him.

Frankfurt
June 18

When Śrīla Prabhupāda arrived, Haṁsadūta and a large group of devotees accompanied him in a procession of twenty cars and vans to the outskirts of the city to the ISKCON center, Schloss Rettershof, a castle on a hill. "My heart becomes engladdened when I hear a *mṛdaṅga* in a German village," Śrīla Prabhupāda said.

The devotees showed Prabhupāda the Schloss. The central room was a large ground-floor hall with a ceiling two stories high. A second-floor gallery, overlooking the hall, led to Prabhupāda's quarters. While Śrīla Prabhupāda was in his room, the assembled devotees from centers all over Germany and from Amsterdam gathered downstairs, where they held a wildly enthusiastic *kīrtana*. After half an hour Haṁsadūta appeared at the railing and motioned to the devotees to come up to Prabhupāda's room.

Somehow the devotees managed to squeeze into Prabhupāda's quarters or to at least stand in the hallway and watch, as Prabhupāda sat, relaxed, speaking informally. "I worked hard my whole life," he said. "I never liked to sit idle. So devotional service means to be always engaged in Kṛṣṇa's service. Not like the servants in Calcutta. They get an order, and then they go to Dalhousie Park and sleep all day. Then when they come back late, the master asks them, 'Where have you been all day?' And they reply, 'I was busy working for you.' Not like that, you see?"

Prabhupāda laughed, and all the devotees also began laughing, although most of them understood very little English. Prabhupāda then quoted Lord Caitanya's prophecy that His name would be heard in every town and village. The devotees' chanting in the villages of Germany, he said, was fulfilling that prediction.

"But unfortunately," he added, "people object, just like the man who is being saved from danger." He gave the example of a man on a roof flying a kite. When another man, seeing him about to walk off the roof, called out to him, "Look out, you're in danger!" the man on the roof became angry and said, "What, you have checked my movement?" Any gentleman, Prabhupāda said, will speak out if he sees another in danger, even though the one in danger may object.

Prabhupāda's German devotees accompanied him on speaking engagements in nearby towns, and although he was not very enthusiastically received by most people, the devotees became more dedicated than ever to give their lives in the service of Prabhupāda and Kṛṣṇa. For his public engagements he sat on a small cushion, so as not to again arouse the indignation of people who could not understand the tradition of the *guru*.

At one engagement a wealthy businessman, two of whose sons were Prabhupāda's disciples, questioned Prabhupāda. "How can a crocodile of the Nile swim in a German river? In other words, how can you transplant a foreign culture with Indian ways and dress to Germany?"

"You can become Kṛṣṇa conscious in a tie and suit," Prabhupāda replied.

"Isn't this chanting self-hypnosis?" asked another man.

"*No,*" Prabhupāda replied staunchly, "it is purification." And so it went—mostly challenges, with a few sincere inquiries.

While Prabhupāda was in Frankfurt, two interested, distinguished visitors came to see him: a Benedictine monk, Father Emmanuel, and Baron von Dürkheim, a prominent German philosopher and spiritual writer. Both men were attracted by Prabhupāda's philosophical explanations and accompanied him on his morning walks for several days.

* * *

Śrīla Prabhupāda's next stop was Australia. He had worked out a schedule whereby he would attend three Ratha-yātrā festivals in three cities: first in Melbourne, then a week later in Chicago, and two days later in San Francisco. He would then go to Los Angeles, Dallas, and New Vrindaban, timing everything for his return to Vṛndāvana by July 25 for the Krishna-Balaram Mandir opening two weeks later.

He was now regularly referring to the opening date of the Krishna-Balaram Mandir as a time when many devotees from around the world could gather at Vṛndāvana to be with him. On June 17 he had written from Germany to Jayahari in London.

> I am presently traveling through Europe and in the past weeks have held many programs in Rome, Geneva, Paris and now Germany. I,

therefore, have no time to carefully study and decide on your proposals. The best thing is if you can come and meet with me personally after I have finished this present tour. I am planning to go to Vrindaban for Janmastami, for the opening installation ceremonies of our Krsna Balaram Temple. If you can come to see me in Vrindaban I would be glad to discuss and plan with you what is best for your devotional service engagement.

After a twenty-hour flight from Frankfurt to Australia, Prabhupāda was picked up at the Melbourne airport by devotees in a borrowed Rolls Royce. The newspaper reporters were quick to notice the car. "DIVINE GRACE COMES ROLLSING IN," read one headline. The story began, "Sixty young Hare Krishna devotees yesterday welcomed their earthly leader to the city with obeisances—but official Melbourne met him coolly."

Another story began, "A chauffeur-driven Rolls Royce will meet the founder of the materialistic-shunning Hare Krishna sect, Bhaktivedanta Swami Prabhuapda, at Tullamarine today." Another newspaper showed a large picture of Śrīla Prabhupāda smiling and bore the headline "H.D.G. IS HERE TO HOUND US." The story began,

His Divine Grace A. C. Bhaktivedanta Swami Prabhupada, the founder of the Hare Krishna movement, is here to save us from the dog's life. Unless we cultivate some spiritual knowledge, warns HDG, we are left with "the dog's mentality".

News coverage of Prabhupāda's visit didn't end with reports on his arrival at the airport. The next day, while the devotees were preparing the Ratha-yātrā carts, an extraordinary incident resulted in front-page headlines in *The Herald.*

Krishna sect uses canopy to save women from blazing office

MONKS from the Hare Krishna sect held the painted canvas canopy of their religious wagon as a safety net so five screaming women could jump to safety from a blazing three-story building in Melbourne yesterday.

The article was accompanied by two large pictures showing "Hare Krishnas" holding the large canvas canopy.

Although the news media was unable to understand the disciples' love for Śrīla Prabhupāda, the rescue was something everyone could relate to. Wrote a columnist in *The Australian,*

> The fact that makes the rescue doubly impressive, was the use of a HOLY rug—not just an ordinary bedroom one—for the rescue mission. The rug was being sewn for use at a religious festival in Melbourne tomorrow.

The columnist coyly speculated whether the devotees' "holy rug" was still usable in the religious festival as a canopy for His Divine Grace A. C. Bhaktivedanta Swami Prabhupāda.

> You see, the Swami is not one of your ordinary swamis. He is the founder of the Hare Krishna, and the group describes him as the Lord Of The Universe. Devotee spokesmen had reported, however, that the "rug" would be used in the festival.

The incident proved to be good publicity for the festival the next day, when Lord Jagannātha, the Lord of the universe, and His pure devotee, Śrīla Prabhupāda, held a Ratha-yātrā procession through the main streets of Melbourne. Regarding media coverage, Prabhupāda had said that simply the printing of the holy names Hare Kṛṣṇa greatly benefited the readers, regardless of whether the names were mentioned in reverence or disrespect.

Amogha: *Prabhupāda met Lord Jagannātha at City Square by Town Hall. There was a* vyāsāsana *on the cart, but he chose to walk before the carts, in front of the Deity of Lord Caitanya. Prabhupāda was wearing a gold wool cap, a peach-colored turtleneck jersey, and an effulgent silk saffron* dhotī *and* kurtā. *Around his shoulders he wore a white silk* cādar, *and he wore a garland of orchids and many yellow flowers. It was winter in Melbourne and quite cold, but he put his hands up and chanted and danced.*

We had about eleven new mṛdaṅgas. *There were also three men playing big bass drums. And we all formed a circle around Śrīla Prabhupāda. It was ecstatic, all playing drums, chanting Hare Kṛṣṇa, and Prabhupāda himself chanting in the parade, going on through the city. Prabhupāda marched with transcendental power, just taking over the city, walking right down Swanson Street.*

Sabhāpati: *From the point of view of weather, it wasn't a very nice day. Prabhupāda met the* ratha *cart at the corner of Swanson Street and Burk Street, and he led from there on. He walked about two miles. All the devotees had been having* kīrtana *in three different groups, but when Prabhupāda met the Ratha-yātrā procession we all gathered around him. He was leading the procession. Behind him was a fourteen-foot* mūrti *of Lord Caitanya, followed by three* ratha *carts. Every now and again in the procession Prabhupāda would stop and turn around and stare up at Lord Caitanya. He would simply stand and look up at Lord Caitanya for a minute or two, and then he would turn around again and lead the procession. It was such an ecstatic experience that one gets the feeling that Prabhupāda had conquered Melbourne, and Australia.*

Gaura Gopāla: *I was right next to Prabhupāda through the whole ceremony, playing the drum. He particularly liked to sing one tune through the whole time. He put his hands up in the air. He was dancing.*

Vaikuṇṭhanātha: *The Ratha-yātrā parade was going, and Prabhupāda was walking, and at one point he asked me, "Get me some water." I became panic-stricken because there was nowhere to get water. So I just depended on Kṛṣṇa and ran over to a house as fast as I could and asked the people for some water. They gave it, and I ran back to Śrīla Prabhupāda. When I was getting that water, though, there was this big rainbow out, and it had actually begun to rain a little bit. It was a very vivid rainbow, and the end of the rainbow came right down on top of the huge building where the Ratha-yātrā ended.*

Hari-śauri: *There is a huge place, the Exhibition Buildings, and we had rented one section of it where the roof was about eighty feet high. So the* ratha *carts were taken in with the tops lowered, and then the tops were put up again inside the hall. All three* ratha *carts were brought in, and the tops were pulled up. Then Śrīla Prabhupāda came in, and everyone was seated. About a thousand people were there. Śrīla Prabhupāda sat up on the* vyāsāsana *on the* ratha *cart itself and gave a lecture from there.*

Sabhāpati: *Although it was a cold and rather nasty day, there were a thousand people in that Exhibition Building. Prabhupāda's lecture was brief. He thanked everyone for coming along and joining in the* saṅkīrtana *movement of Lord Caitanya Mahāprabhu. He told everyone he was very appreciative of how they had come to see Lord Jagannātha and of how they were taking part. He said that actually all these activities of singing and dancing were due to Śrī Caitanya Mahāprabhu.*

The Melbourne newspapers duly reported the Ratha-yātrā: "A day for cymbals and chants," "Chariots top the Swami." One newspaper reported, "Don't let Krishna alarm you: cleric."

> The sight of the Hare Krishna youths in Melbourne streets should not alarm Australians or cause them to mock, the Rev. Gordon Powell said in Scots Church yesterday.
>
> He said the sect could be a sign of the swing of the pendulum back to spiritual values and traditional virtues on the part of modern youth.

The article praised the devotees' "reaction against extreme materialism" and reported the events of the Ratha-yātrā parade. Reverend Powell, head bishop of the Anglican Church in Melbourne, had paid Śrīla Prabhupāda a visit, and this had resulted in the bishop's Sunday sermon comment that "Hare Krishnas" were not alarming. Śrīla Prabhupāda took the bishop's comments as very significant.

During his week's stay in Melbourne, Prabhupāda attended a large program at the Town Hall, where he inspired a long and ecstatic *kīrtana,* with one thousand people dancing in a circle before the Deity of Lord Caitanya. He also visited St. Pascal's Teaching College, a Franciscan seminary, and was very well received by the monks there. The seminarians asked intelligent philosophical questions, one of them inquiring about what Prabhupāda thought of their founder, Saint Francis of Assisi. The seminarian described briefly how Saint Francis saw everything in the universe in relation to God and addressed nature's creations as Brother tree, Brother bird, and so on. Saint Francis's attitude, Prabhupāda replied, was first-class God consciousness.

That same evening in his room Prabhupāda met with the vicar-general of the Roman Catholic Church in Australia, Reverend J. A. Kelly. Prabhupāda played a recording of his morning's lecture at St. Pascal's, and afterward the Reverend asked if Prabhupāda would pose with him for a picture to be printed in their religious periodical. Again, the newspapers picked it up: "Swami spreads unity message."

> The normally serene cloisters of the Roman Catholic Yarra Theological Union echoed to the chants of Hare Krishna yesterday. . . .
>
> "It does not matter what religion you belong to as long as you love

and serve God,'' said His Divine Grace A. C. Bhaktivedanta Swami Prabhupada.

''We must be delivered from the disease of materialism, or else there will always be want.''

After the discussion, the president of the institute's Student Representative Council, Franciscan seminarian Patrick McClure, 25, said that there seemed to be a consensus in many areas.

''In particular we agree with the need to reject materialism,'' he said.

Mr. McClure said the informal meeting reflected an openness and tolerance in the church.

''Maybe they have something to tell us,'' he said.

July 1

In Melbourne Prabhupāda dictated a letter to Guru dāsa in Vṛndāvana. It was less than six weeks before the scheduled opening of the Krishna-Balaram Mandir, and Śrīla Prabhupāda had not received regular reports from Vṛndāvana. He was concerned that everything be ready on time for a gorgeous ceremony.

My dear Gurudas,

Please accept my blessings. I am spending my last two days in Australia and after this I shall go to the U.S.A. In the meantime, I wish to give you some instructions regarding our Janmastami installation in Vrindaban.

The main thing is the ceremony shall be conducted by our own men. We do not have to be dependent on taking help from persons who will not even eat with us, thinking us inferior. All over the world, in Paris, New York, Australia, etc., our men and women are worshiping the deity very nicely and I am very proud of their worship. There is no reason why we have to think we are dependent on any Indian goswami in order to conduct our ceremony in Vrindaban. So you understand this and be convinced of it, and let them come as invited but we shall conduct the affair ourselves.

You can also arrange to have the Her Govinda dramatical players and our own players as well. There should be abundant prasadam for whoever comes all day long. The kitchen should go on. So see there is sufficient stock of rice, attar [flour], ghee. The life members should be especially cared for and invited. We shall manage our own affairs.

If they come that is good but if not we shall manage. From our side everything should be done nicely.

All big officers in Mathura and Vrindaban should be invited. Goswamis and godbrothers also. Also invite local Marawadis and invite Parthak also. Practically by distributing a general invitation card we shall invite everyone. All the inhabitants of Vrindaban will be invited to come and see the deity and take prasadam. There should be special arrangement for life members, Mr. Birla and many other respectable visitors. There is no question of money. Let it be a first-class, 1-A arrangement. Krsna will provide all expenditures so try to make it gorgeous. Gorgeous means sufficient stock of prasadam and temple decorations as gorgeous as possible. The internal management of dressing can be done by Yamuna, Madira and Jayatirtha they are all expert. The shastric direction can be from Pradyumna. . . .

Also Mr. Jai Purna of Karnapur came to see me, so invitation should be extended to him. Invite all local asramas and sannyasis as well. I do not hear of Pranava; I sent him a telegram but there is no reply.

The whole management should be done combinedly. Do not fight amongst yourselves, that is my only anxiety. I shall leave for Vrindaban by 25th July. In the meantime, reply to me at L.A.

Your ever well-wisher,
A. C. Bhaktivedanta Swami

While Guru dāsa got direct instruction on the ceremony, almost every other devotee Prabhupāda wrote received his personal invitation to the Krishna-Balaram Mandir opening. In a letter to Cyavana Mahārāja in West Africa, Prabhupāda wrote,

You want to see me and I also have some important things to discuss with you, so the best thing is if we meet at the end of July in Vrindaban, India. Today I am leaving for the United States to attend Rathayatra in Chicago and San Francisco but at the end of July I will reach Vrindaban. We are having a very big festival there on Janmastami when we will open our Krsna Balaram temple by installing the deities. So you must also attend to help in conducting the ceremonies. I will therefore see you in Vrindaban by the end of July.

Śrīla Prabhupāda's engagement at La Trobe University in Melbourne was like a repeat of the unpleasant incident with the radicals at La Salle

Pleyel in Paris. It was, again, a large, free-admission audience of students, and again the disciples had prepared Prabhupāda a standard *vyāsāsana*. Devotees held a *kīrtana* onstage and introduced Śrīla Prabhupāda, who began speaking very basically about the distinction between the soul and the body and about how this education is required for all people. But after no more than ten minutes, a young man in the audience stood up and began to shout profanities at Śrīla Prabhupāda. "And how do you explain your Rolls Royce?" he added.

The audience, which had been quiet until the interruption, now became noisy and restless. Three of Śrīla Prabhupāda's more aggressive disciples left the front row and went to the back, where the man was shouting. Meanwhile Śrīla Prabhupāda stopped speaking and sat tolerantly, waiting. The shouting stopped, and he began again. "As I was explaining, in material life we have been changing from one body to another. This is not a very good condition of life. Nobody wants to die, but he is forced to die."

After five minutes, the abusive language again broke out. This time Śrīla Prabhupāda's three disciples pushed the shouters out the back door. In the fight, one of the students pulled a knife from his boot, but a devotee disarmed him.

The atmosphere inside the auditorium was tense, and many people were talking loudly. Some got up to leave. Madhudviṣa Swami, taking the microphone, pleaded with the students to remain calm and continue hearing from Śrīla Prabhupāda. Some students in the audience seemed on the verge of violence, and the devotees feared for Prabhupāda's safety. But Prabhupāda was willing to continue. He called for questions.

Student: "I am a Christian, and I would like to know what is your opinion of Jesus Christ."

Śrīla Prabhupāda: "We respect Jesus Christ as you do, because he is representative of God, son of God. We are also speaking of God, so we respect him with our greatest veneration."

Question: "You are a son of Jesus too?"

Śrīla Prabhupāda: "Yes, I am a servant of Jesus. I don't say I am Jesus."

Question: "I want to know if you have the power of Jesus?"

Śrīla Prabhupāda: "No, I have no power of Jesus."

Question: "Well, I've got the power of Jesus![Laughter.] Because I'm a Christian."

Śrīla Prabhupāda: "That's all right. You are Christian. We are Kṛṣṇian. It is practically the same thing." (Laughter and applause.)

Student: "I have one other question. I believe Jesus is coming back, and not Kṛṣṇa. What are you guys going to do when you see Jesus?" (Laughter.)

Śrīla Prabhupāda: "When he is coming, welcome. We shall welcome. It is very good news that Jesus is coming."

Student: "Jesus had no reputation. He wore sandals and was crucified between two thieves. And your spirituality is on a Rolls Royce and a padded seat, and you're all into money—you Kṛṣṇas, you want money."

Śrīla Prabhupāda: "I don't want money."

Student: "And you say violence is violence, that's what you believe. Jesus turned the other cheek, and he expected his followers to." (Applause.)

Śrīla Prabhupāda: "This Kṛṣṇa consciousness movement is not a sentimental religious system. It is science and philosophy." Prabhupāda explained that understanding the science of God was transcendental to Christianity or Hinduism. The real goal was to learn to love God.

Second student: "I have a question about Krishnamurti. Krishnamurti stresses that when you are speaking in the Western world, you should speak and present yourself as a Westerner, not as an Indian or as you would speak in India. Instead of sitting on a raised dais and dressing in the robes of a monk, Krishnamurti would say dress in Western clothes and sit on a chair. What is your opinion of this?"

Śrīla Prabhupāda: "Actually a God conscious person is neither a Westerner nor Easterner. So anywhere the devotee goes, as they receive him, he accepts. These devotees have arranged a raised seat, so I have accepted the raised seat. If they wanted me to sit down on the floor, I would have gladly accepted. I have no objection to this or that. But as devotees receive and give honor, that is good for them, because actually we should honor the Supreme Lord God and His representative. Nowadays it is different. Students are not learning to honor. But that is not actually the system. According to the Vedic system, the representative of God must be honored as God."

Another student (loudly): "Do you consider your movement the major form of enlightenment emanating from the United States today? What particular role does your movement play in the White House psychological warfare department? Will you be coming to our Fourth of July demonstration against the United States this year and take up the real political issues?"

Again many students began shouting. Madhudviṣa Swami took the microphone. "I can answer if you like. Our movement is not from the

United States. If you have some paranoia that everything is coming from the United States, well, that is your hang-up, not mine. [Applause.] And second of all, our spiritual master came to the United States to start this Kṛṣṇa consciousness movement because he got a free ticket on the boat to go there. If you would have sent him a free ticket, he probably would have come to Australia first. So he is trying to spread love of God. He is not trying to start any kind of political movement. He is trying to spark a revolutionary consciousness. I think you are also interested in revolution. We are interested in revolution also. But we are interested in revolution which will help people to feel peace themselves, whether they are Communists or Marxists or whatever it is you like. We are trying to help people attain happiness whether they are— "

Madhudviṣa Swami's remarks triggered the largest vocal protest yet. The commotion rose as students all over the hall began to shout. There was no possibility of a peaceful philosophical discussion.

The devotees' greatest concern became getting Prabhupāda out of the hall unharmed. Prabhupāda rose from his *vyāsāsana* and, escorted by his disciples, left by a side exit. A large crowd of students had gathered outside the door as Prabhupāda emerged, but he entered his waiting car without incident. As he rode slowly through a cluster of students a girl kicked at the car with her booted foot. And as the devotees were getting into their vans students threw stones. Finally, as the devotees drove off the campus, they had to pass under an elevated walkway where some waiting students threw black paint down onto the vans.

Riding in his car, Prabhupāda was mostly silent, but he seemed disgusted. He said that in the future, he would only give lectures in classes where he was invited; no more wide-open lectures.

* * *

Śrīla Prabhupāda flew from Melbourne to Chicago, stopping overnight in Hawaii. His schedule allowed him only a couple of days in Chicago, where he would attend that city's first Ratha-yātrā festival.

He was very keen on holding Ratha-yātrās in big cities around the world. And although large crowds often could not hear Kṛṣṇa conscious philosophy without becoming restless, angered, or even violent, everyone could enjoy and benefit from a Ratha-yātrā festival. Śrīla Prabhupāda had written in *The Nectar of Devotion,* quoting from the *Bhaviṣya Purāṇa,* "A person who follows the Ratha-yātrā car when the *rathas* pass in front or from behind, even if born of a lowly family, will surely be elevated to the position of achieving equal opulence with Viṣṇu."

In Jagannātha Purī, India, the original home of Jagannātha worship, a Westerner could see Lord Jagannātha only during the yearly Ratha-yātrā festival when the Deity would come out of the temple and ride on His cart. And besides, very few Westerners would actually go to Jagannātha Purī. But Śrīla Prabhupāda and his Kṛṣṇa consciousness movement were making Lord Jagannātha available to everyone by bringing the Ratha-yātrā right down the main street of their city. It may seem odd to the average American or Australian, but from the viewpoint of Lord Jagannātha and His followers, it was perfectly proper. Lord Jagannātha, "the Lord of the universe," was for everyone, everywhere, regardless of nationality or religion.

This year's festival, 1974, would mark the eighth annual San Francisco Ratha-yātrā. And now, at Prabhupāda's urging, devotees in more and more cities were beginning to hold the festival. Śrīla Prabhupāda wanted to give utmost prestige to this kind of preaching, and so he had gone out of his way to come to Chicago, where he had never been before, just to ride an hour down State Street on Lord Jagannātha's cart. Prabhupāda felt that his disciples, by holding Ratha-yātrās in cities on every continent, would defeat false religion. And spontaneously people would be attracted to Kṛṣṇa, simply by enjoying a festival of singing, dancing, feasting, and seeing the Lord.

Prabhupāda stood in downtown Chicago before the large, elaborately decorated car, eager to ascend to the seat where he would ride during the procession. But there was no ladder, so he waited while devotees ran to a hardware store and got one. Then he mounted the cart and sat on his *vyāsāsana.*

The city was busy with thousands of shoppers and workers. Many members of Chicago's large Indian community had turned out to receive the Lord's blessings and to observe this tradition so well known to them. And hundreds of Prabhupāda's disciples from throughout the Midwest had gathered to pull on the ropes of the cart, lead *kīrtanas*, and distribute *prasādam* and *Back to Godhead* magazines, as the big cart plied down one of the busiest streets in America.

Although several policemen on motorcycles led the procession, their mood was hardly that of the King of Orissa, who had traditionally led the Ratha-yātrā procession in India. Each year the king would present himself as a menial servant, leading the parade by sweeping the road before Lord Jagannātha with a gold-handled broom. The Chicago police, however, seemed intent only in getting the parade over with as soon as possible. With stern anxiety they dedicated themselves to keeping open the flow of ordinary automobile traffic. They acknowledged that the devotees had an official permit for the parade, but they continually prodded them to pull the cart faster, threatening to terminate the parade entirely.

By Kṛṣṇa's grace, however, everyone, including the Chicago police, became satisfied as the procession moved along peacefully for several miles, finally arriving at the Civic Center Plaza. Amid skyscrapers and city noise, Śrīla Prabhupāda addressed the outdoor audience. Immediately following the lecture, the devotees began *prasādam* distribution and *kīrtana.* Prabhupāda was pleased by the festival.

* * *

San Francisco
July 7

Thousands followed the three carts for several miles through Golden Gate Park. Śrīla Prabhupāda, riding on the second cart, beneath the deity of Subhadrā, wore the same golden wool cap he had worn in Australia, a white bulky knit sweater, and a garland of red roses. Despite his recent extensive traveling, he was alert and well. He looked out at the sea of devotees and parade-followers and took great satisfaction in the transcendental scene.

In his speech before a crowd of ten thousand, Prabhupāda said that the Americans should lead the world in propagating Kṛṣṇa consciousness. "I know that all American ladies and gentlemen here are educated and intelligent," he said, "and I am very much obliged to the Americans who have helped me make this movement popular all over the world. When Śrī Caitanya Mahāprabhu first introduced the Hare Kṛṣṇa movement, He said, *bhārata-bhūmite haila manuṣya-janma/ yāra janma sārthaka kari' kara para-upakāra.* He thus expressed His desire by saying that anyone who has taken birth as a human being in Bhārata-varṣa, or India, should understand the Kṛṣṇa consciousness movement and spread it all over the world for the benefit of all humanity. He also predicted that in all the villages and towns of the entire world the Kṛṣṇa consciousness movement will be known.

"So with the cooperation of you young Americans who are kindly helping to spread this movement, it is now factually becoming well known all over the world. I recently went to Melbourne, Australia, where we held a similar festival in which many thousands of people joined and chanted and danced with us. Then I went to Chicago, where we held the same ceremony. Now this morning I have come here, and I am so glad to see that you are also joining this movement."

Prabhupāda's fingers tapped lightly against his *karatālas* as he spoke, his eyes half closed. He chose his words with confidence, and those words echoed across the meadow. Prabhupāda requested his audience not to think that Kṛṣṇa consciousness was sectarian; it was meant for everyone, because the real nature of the self was spiritual. Chanting the holy name and dancing, he said, were not ordinary.

"It is open to everyone who will simply chant the *mahā-mantra:* Hare Kṛṣṇa, Hare Kṛṣṇa, Kṛṣṇa Kṛṣṇa, Hare Hare/ Hare Rāma, Hare Rāma, Rāma Rāma, Hare Hare. You are generally young, whereas I am an old man who may die at any moment. Therefore I request you to take this movement seriously. Understand it yourselves, and then preach it throughout your country. People outside America generally follow and imitate what America does. I am traveling all over the world, and everywhere I see other countries building skyscrapers and in other ways imitating your country. Therefore if you kindly become Kṛṣṇa conscious and chant and dance in ecstasy, in emotional love of God, the entire world will follow you. Thus the entire world can become Vaikuṇṭha, a spiritual world in which there will be no more trouble. Thank you very much."

* * *

Guru dāsa had sent a letter to all ISKCON centers inviting devotees to attend the opening of the Krishna-Balaram Mandir in Vṛndāvana. He had invited life members from Bombay and Calcutta and had reserved cars for them on the trains. Prabhupāda also was inviting his disciples to come to Vṛndāvana for Janmāṣṭamī. Lecturing before hundreds of devotees in Los Angeles, he said, "I invite all of you to come to Vṛndāvana to the opening of the Krishna-Balaram Mandir."

Prabhupāda had also mailed invitations to his Godbrothers, and when one of them, Śrīdhara Mahārāja of Navadvīpa, accepted the invitation, Śrīla Prabhupāda replied, assuring him of comfortable accommodations and suggesting the easiest way to travel from Calcutta to Vṛndāvana. Śrīla Prabhupāda also told Śrīdhara Mahārāja of his preaching.

> You will be glad to know that our books are selling very nicely. Last year we sold about four million books, and this year within six months we have completed last year's quota, and therefore we can reasonably expect to double the sale of last year. The only difficulty is that we are expanded worldwide organization, and it requires very acute management to keep up the status quo. So by Krishna's grace everything is going on nicely.
>
> Regarding preaching tour, it has become a little difficult for me because I have got the same heart trouble as you have, and still I am moving just to encourage these young boys and girls who are working on my behalf.

On July 15, only ten days before Prabhupāda's proposed arrival in Vṛndāvana, he wrote almost identical letters to his *sannyāsī* disciples, inviting them to come and resolve the many personal matters and items of business that had been pending during his busy tour.

> I cordially invite you to attend our opening ceremony in Vrindaban because all of our sannyasis will be present there. You also come there as a regular sannyasi and take part. That is my desire.

When Karandhara, the newly-appointed G.B.C. for India, began to express doubts that everything would be ready on time, Prabhupāda replied from Los Angeles,

> The festival must be gorgeously done. It should not be poor. If there is a scarcity of money, it will be supplied. There must be full prasadam for all the guests. You plan for that, and I will supply the funds. Complete prasad distribution must go on.
>
> Regarding the temple not being finished on time, that is your responsibility. What can I do?

Although Prabhupāda had responded to Karandhara forcefully, the note of uncertainty from his head manager in India disturbed him. He wrote to Surabhi, who was in charge of the Vṛndāvana construction, "I am a little agitated in mind because Karandhara's letter says that there may be some work to be done even during the time of our festival."

While in Los Angeles, Prabhupāda also received word that the London Ratha-yātrā, scheduled for later that month, had been canceled by the local authorities; the previous year's parade, officials said, had seriously interfered with traffic. Prabhupāda insisted that the devotees protest this unreasonable ruling. "It is religious discrimination," he said. And he advised that sympathetic Indians in London approach the ambassador and request him to present the matter before the queen. The recent statements of the Reverend Powell of Melbourne could be used to demonstrate that Christians should not be alarmed by the Kṛṣṇa consciousness movement. "The police objection means that the whole religious ceremony should be stopped?" Prabhupāda challenged. "What is this? Simply for some technical mistake, now they will stop our whole religious ceremony?"

Prabhupāda said that if the City continued to prohibit the parade, the devotees should erect a stationary cart in Hyde Park and hold a festival there, without a procession. "After holding our ceremony," said Prabhupāda, "we shall take the deity in a palanquin and go to Trafalgar Square. The *ratha* will stay. It will not move. But we shall take the deities on palanquin and go to Trafalgar Square. In this way, take police permission and, after going there along with the ceremony, protest. They cannot object. But the *ratha* must be seen. And the people must know that the rascal police government has stopped it."

Prabhupāda repeated his instructions several times. He was in a grave mood as he instructed his followers. "My Guru Mahārāja used to say, *prāṇa āche yāṅra sei hetu pracāra:* one who has got life, he can preach. The dead man cannot preach. So you become with life, not like dead man. Just like all my Godbrothers, they are dead men. And therefore they are envious of my activities. They have no life. If you want to make an easygoing life, showing the Deity and then sleep, then it is a failure movement."

Prabhupāda could not bear to hear that such an important festival as Ratha-yātrā was being stopped. "We shall abide by all the rules," he said, "but we must have this festival. They saw last year that in the open sunshine thousands of people, tens of thousands of people, stood in

Trafalgar Square for three hours. And they do not go to the church. So they have seen there is something. Otherwise, how people have taken so much interest?"

Brahmānanda Swami: "Yes, just like in the San Francisco paper, they admitted, 'This is the most popular festival.' "

Prabhupāda: "Yes, fifteen thousand people attended my lecture silently in San Francisco. So they are seeing there is something in the movement. But sometimes some parties do not want us to go on without objection, or else they will be finished."

On the day of Prabhupāda's departure from Los Angeles, he addressed the assembled devotees in the temple, encouraging them to remain faithful in Kṛṣṇa consciousness. And he revealed his own feelings of urgency. His constant traveling was for his disciples—so they would remain strong. And if they remained strong, following the simple programs he had given them, then their success was guaranteed. "Some way or other," he said, "we have introduced this program in the Western countries. And you are so intelligent, you have very soon captured it. So stick to the standard. Then your life is successful. It is not at all difficult. But don't deviate. Then you are *pakkā. Pakkā* means 'solid': *mām eva ye prapadyante māyām etāṁ taranti te.* If you remain solid in Kṛṣṇa consciousness, then *māyā* cannot touch you.

"So that is my request. I am traveling all over the world. I am going to see how things are going in Dallas and New Vrindaban. So my touring is natural. I have started this movement. I want to see that it is going nicely. *Don't deviate.* That is my only request." Prabhupāda began to cry, and simply concluded, "Then you will remain solid. Thank you very much."

New Vrindaban
July 18, 1974

A letter from Karandhara reached Śrīla Prabhupāda, informing him of his resignation as G.B.C. for India. The responsibilities were too great for him, for he had only recently come back to Kṛṣṇa consciousness. He would continue to follow the spiritual program, but he could not be the G.B.C. Again Śrīla Prabhupāda was set back, and before several G.B.C. men in his room at New Vrindaban he asked, "What to do? What shall we do? So maybe I should just give up these projects in India."

"But Śrīla Prabhupāda," the devotees replied, "those India projects are very dear to you."

"But what can be done?" Prabhupāda asked.

Except for Guru dāsa, none of the devotees in Vṛndāvana thought that the building would be ready by the scheduled grand opening. Work was going along slowly, as usual, and except for the Deity hall area, the land was still a construction site. There were no altars, no Deities. Tejās thought Guru dāsa so feared displeasing Prabhupāda that he could not bear to admit that the building would not be ready. The date had been set, and Prabhupāda did not want excuses. "It has to be done by Janmāṣṭamī," he wrote. "There is no question of delay." Guru dāsa admitted that the temple construction wouldn't be *completely* finished by Janmāṣṭamī, but he reasoned that the opening ceremony could still take place, even if the final touches on the temple weren't done.

Because there was no regular G.B.C. secretary for India, Prabhupāda did not receive accurate reports on the Vṛndāvana temple construction. When Tamāla Kṛṣṇa Goswami had left in April to preach in the West, several months had passed before Prabhupāda had appointed a replacement, Karandhara. Now, after only a few weeks, Karandhara had resigned. Guru dāsa's version, therefore, was the only one Prabhupāda had received. The end of July grew near, and devotees prepared to travel to Vṛndāvana—for a fiasco.

* * *

Vṛndāvana
August 4, 1974

When Prabhupāda's car pulled up at the ISKCON property in Ramaṇa-reti, a group of devotees greeted him with *kīrtana* and flowers. Some twenty-five devotees from temples around the world had already gathered for the grand opening celebration, and along with the Vṛndāvana devotees they crowded happily around Śrīla Prabhupāda. No formal walkways had been constructed, and Prabhupāda walked through the half-constructed walls, past piles of sand and bricks, making his way toward the Deity house. Even here the lack of ornamentation and finishing was apparent, and rubble lay all around.

"What is this?" Prabhupāda demanded as he toured the construction site. "There is nothing here. Where is the temple? You told me the temple was finished." Guru dāsa, Surabhi, Guṇārṇava, and others directly responsible were unable to answer. Their faces went white.

Prabhupāda was furious. "How can you open this?"

The visiting devotees also began speaking among themselves: "It's not ready. How can we open?"

"But Prabhupāda," said one devotee, "devotees from all over the world are coming."

"Stop them immediately!" Prabhupāda said. "There will be no opening!"

Prabhupāda had burst the bubble, the illusion that they would be ready for the grand opening. Prabhupāda's anger was frightening, and the devotees who surrounded him were no longer carefree and joyful. "You were going to open this temple?" Prabhupāda scoffed.

"The altar is ready," said Harikeśa, who had come from Japan to attend the opening. "We can install the Deity and—"

"You cannot open this temple!" Prabhupāda shouted. "This temple is not completed!"

Prabhupāda then walked into his house, followed by the Vṛndāvana managers and a few other leaders. Whoever could keep his distance from Prabhupāda in this mood considered himself spared. Surabhi's wife ran off to pray to Kṛṣṇa, afraid of Prabhupāda's ferocity.

In his room Prabhupāda's anger only increased. He yelled at Guru dāsa for mismanagement. He yelled at Surabhi. He yelled at all of them. No one dared to offer suggestions or excuses. There was nothing to do but turn white and become depressed. Prabhupāda suddenly inquired whether the temple could be opened, despite the mess. "Can you have the Deity rooms ready at least?" He turned to Surabhi. "This is an insult to our Society. What will people think? We have announced it everywhere!"

"Nobody actually knows about it, Śrīla Prabhupāda," Surabhi replied fearfully, exposing himself for another blast.

"Oh?" Prabhupāda somewhat changed his tone. "You have not made any propaganda about it? No invitations?"

"Not yet, Prabhupāda. Not to the people in Vṛndāvana. They do not expect it to open, because everyone who has been here can see that it is not possible to open. They know it's not ready."

"This is a farce," Prabhupāda scowled. "It is a fiasco." Disgusted, he looked at his Vṛndāvana managers. "We have to open. How can we open on Janmāṣṭamī?"

"Śrīla Prabhupāda," Surabhi said, "the doors are not ready. They are still cutting the wood." Prabhupāda inquired about the Deities from Yamunā, who explained that Their paraphernalia had been purchased but that the thrones were not ready.

"What is your opinion?" he asked her.

"I am totally unqualified to speak," Yamunā said, "and although I have no right to speak, I see it as almost impossible to actually open the temple. There is no *pūjārī.*"

With a sense of finality and failure, Prabhupāda said, "Then we won't do it. But we have invited so many people from all around the world to come, and I was not informed of this. Now you all decide.

"*When* can we open?" Prabhupāda asked. "Can we open on Diwali? When is Diwali?"

"October, Śrīla Prabhupāda."

"How about Bhaktisiddhānta Sarasvatī's appearance day?" a devotee suggested. "That's at the end of December."

Prabhupāda was silent, looking displeased. Surabhi spoke up. "It will take six months, actually seven months." Then Prabhupāda chose the day of Rāma-navamī, in April; the opening could coincide with the annual gathering of devotees in Māyāpur and Vṛndāvana.

Surabhi spoke again. He had grown pessimistic from his experiences with construction in India. "It depends on whether we can get the cement, Śrīla Prabhupāda," he said. "We have to get it from the government. That was the main obstacle preventing us from opening now. We could possibly have the opening in three months, if we could get cement."

"All right," Prabhupāda said, resigned—there was no use trying to set a date. "It will be done before next Janmāṣṭamī." His tone was sarcastic. "And if the cement can be obtained, it can be done after three months."

Later, while meeting with various individuals, Prabhupāda continued to express his displeasure, especially to Guru dāsa. He asked questions but was dissatisfied with the answers. He asked Guru dāsa to bring the financial records, and then he reprimanded him more. Finding a receipt for Guru dāsa's stay in an expensive hotel in Jaipur, Prabhupāda made an issue of it. Guru dāsa became aloof. When Prabhupāda finished talking with him, Guru dāsa returned to his room, staying there unless Śrīla Prabhupāda called for him.

Prabhupāda began talking about changing the temple presidents in Vṛndāvana; he suggested Harikeśa. Guru dāsa and his wife, he said, could be in charge of the guesthouse, which was as yet only a hole in the ground. He called Guru dāsa again and asked what he thought of his managing the Vṛndāvana guesthouse, suggesting he go to the Jaipuria Guesthouse in Vṛndāvana for ideas about management.

"But Prabhupāda," Guru dāsa said, "they charge such low rates at the Jaipuria Guesthouse. I'm sure those rates must be subsidized."

"This Mr. Jaipuria is a Marwari businessman," Prabhupāda replied. "He's not losing money on the guesthouse. He's making money. That is the art of management. That you have to learn by going there and seeing." But Guru dāsa felt too exhausted by the austerities of living and managing in India, where Prabhupāda's attention and criticism were so demanding and intense and where everything was so difficult. He and his wife began to think of leaving Vṛndāvana.

Prabhupāda continued to pressure Surabhi, calling him in at different times of the day. "Why aren't these Deity doors up?" Prabhupāda demanded.

"I am trying, Śrīla Prabhupāda," Surabhi replied. "There are so many things to do."

"Never mind," Prabhupāda said, "you have to get it done. These hired men are all cheating you. Don't let them cheat you. It is not easy for all these devotees to collect money. It is all Kṛṣṇa's money and can only be used for Kṛṣṇa's projects. Protect that money and see it doesn't go in the hands of the wrong people. I don't want the contractors to become rich men because of our projects. And I want marble on that building. Where is the marble?"

"Where can I get marble?" Surabhi asked.

"Why are you asking me these questions?" Prabhupāda shouted. "You are the expert. I don't know. Use your intelligence."

Ultimately, Prabhupāda's anger with his disciples was incidental, the reaction due them for their foolishness. It was also a way of instructing them and testing them. But deeper was Prabhupāda's transcendental impatience and frustration that his devotional service in Vṛndāvana was still not manifested. He wanted a wonderful temple for the glory of the Kṛṣṇa consciousness movement, a temple that would establish Kṛṣṇa consciousness all over the world. It was an offering to his spiritual master, and he had promised it to Kṛṣṇa. But still it was not completed.

As for Prabhupāda's disciples' failure to do the job, Prabhupāda had to take the burden and the agony of that failure. His disciples were his instruments in his service to Kṛṣṇa. If the instruments didn't work properly, then he suffered, just as when one's arms and legs fail to function, the whole body suffers. His disciples' failure to carry out his desires was his loss. In this way, he felt transcendental lamentation over their failure to open the Krishna-Balaram Mandir on Janmāṣṭamī day.

Prabhupāda's disturbance, though transcendental, was nonetheless real; it was not feigned merely for instructing. Nor could the devotees cheaply "cheer up" their spiritual master. For Prabhupāda's disciples to properly assist him, they would have to understand his transcendental mood and serve him accordingly. Prabhupāda wanted practical, down-to-earth service from his disciples. They should not expect to serve him sentimentally but should work hard. Devotional service was dynamic. Prabhupāda wanted his disciples to help him with his projects to serve his Guru Mahārāja—projects which, if successful, could save the world from misery.

Getting concrete was a big problem. Surabhi, Guṇārṇava, Tejās, and others were always meditating and striving, "How to get cement?" Yet it seemed no cement was available in the whole of India, as month after month they waited for government permission. Daily, since Prabhupāda's arrival for the so-called temple opening, the devotees had been traveling by bus and ricksha to Mathurā to see if cement—even a few bags—was available.

Sometimes they were cheated. One shipment of twenty bags had been cut with other materials, and when they used it in casting a column, it remained soft for four days and finally crumbled. When at last enough cement arrived to complete the work, the devotees felt sure it had happened only because of Śrīla Prabhupāda's presence.

Prabhupāda had Guṇārṇava count every bag of cement as it arrived. From eight in the morning until nine-thirty at night the shipment kept coming on trucks, each truck with four coolies to carry the heavy bags on their backs into the storage shed. Guṇārṇava stood outside all day with pad and pen, marking the receipt of each bag. Śrīla Prabhupāda came out of the house several times and watched gravely. In the evening, when they were finished, he called Guṇārṇava in. "So how many bags?" Prabhupāda asked, and Guṇārṇava gave the exact figure.

"Everything is locked away now?" Prabhupāda asked.

"Yes, Śrīla Prabhupāda."

Prabhupāda talked about the cement as if talking about a shipment of gold.

August 12

Prabhupāda felt very weak. It was on the afternoon of his appearance day, and he was sitting at his desk in the main room of his house. He lay down on his seat and put his head against one of the arm pillows. The following day he felt so weak he could not walk or stand. He had no appetite and ran a fever of 104 degrees. A local doctor arrived and examined Prabhupāda—malaria. He prescribed some medication, which Prabhupāda took once or twice and then refused. A second doctor came and prescribed different medicines. "Stop bringing these doctors," Prabhupāda said. "No doctor can cure me."

It was August, the monsoon season, and many devotees fell sick. When Śrutakīrti, who had recently returned to his post as Prabhupāda's personal servant, contracted malaria, Kulādri, who had come to Vṛndāvana to attend the temple opening, volunteered to assist. Then Kulādri got malaria. Other devotees became ill with malaria, jaundice, dysentery, and various digestive problems.

The weather was overcast, hot and humid, and thousands of varieties of insects began appearing. For several days at a time the sky would be cloudy, the temperature in the nineties. Then the sun would come out and steam everything up with almost intolerable heat. It was Vṛndāvana's most unhealthy season.

As Prabhupāda's condition worsened, the devotees became morose and even fearful for their spiritual master's life. They brought Prabhupāda's bed out where it was cooler, on the small patio outside his house. His servants would massage or fan him. Days passed and Prabhupāda didn't eat, except for a few grapes and some slices of orange. This was the way his father had died, he said—by not eating. Such remarks frightened Prabhupāda's disciples all the more, and they began visiting the *samādhis* of the Gosvāmīs to pray that Prabhupāda would be cured.

One evening Harikeśa stayed up all night near Prabhupāda's room, chanting softly a continuous *kīrtana* of Hare Kṛṣṇa. Prabhupāda liked it. "This *kīrtana*," he said, "is what actually gives us life." After that devotees took turns, so that there was always *kīrtana*.

Prabhupāda explained that his illness was due to the sins of the ISKCON leaders, eighty percent of whom were not strictly following the rules and regulations, he said. Even in Vṛndāvana some of the devotees weren't regularly rising at four A.M.. Since Prabhupāda was speaking little, he had only briefly mentioned this cause of his illness. But brief as it was, it crushed his disciples. As for who was guilty, each disciple would have to say for himself. But in a mood of "Oh, God, what have we done?" all the disciples in Vṛndāvana immediately became very attentive to the rules and regulations.

In the morning *Bhāgavatam* class the devotees who lectured regularly discussed the subject as explained in Śrīla Prabhupāda's books: At the time of initiation Kṛṣṇa absolves the initiate of all karmic reactions due for past sinful acts. The spiritual master, however, as the representative of Kṛṣṇa, also shares in removing the disciple's *karma.* Kṛṣṇa, being infinite, can never be affected by such *karma,* whereas the spiritual master, although completely pure, is finite. The spiritual master, therefore, partially suffers the reactions for a disciple's sins, sometimes becoming ill. Jīva Gosvāmī warns that a spiritual master should not take too many disciples, because of the danger of accepting an overload of *karma.* Not only does the spiritual master accept the previous *karma* of the disciples, but if the disciples commit sins after initiation, then for those also the spiritual master may sometimes become ill.

Prabhupāda said that his "misdeed" was accepting so many disciples, but he had no choice for spreading Kṛṣṇa consciousness. The spiritual master sometimes suffers, he said, so that the disciples may know, "Due to our sinful activities, our spiritual master is suffering," and this always had a sobering effect on any would-be offender. But now, for the first time, Prabhupāda was specifically blaming his disciples for a serious illness. By neglecting their spiritual master's most basic instructions, they were causing him great distress. They understood that their spiritual master was no ordinary malaria victim, and they knew they had to correct their mistakes and pray to Kṛṣṇa that Prabhupāda would get better.

Prabhupāda's condition was so critical and the implications of his statements so broad that his secretary, Brahmānanda Swami, thought it best to notify the entire International Society for Krishna Consciousness. Because Prabhupāda was pleased by the twenty-four-hour *kīrtana,* Brahmānanda Swami thought that this program might be introduced in every ISKCON temple in the world. A few telegrams were sent, and word quickly spread that every temple should hold continuous *kīrtana,* petitioning Kṛṣṇa for Prabhupāda's recovery.

It reminded some of the senior disciples of 1967, when they had stayed up all night chanting and praying for Prabhupāda's recovery from an apparent heart attack. At that time Prabhupāda had encouraged them to chant a hymn to Lord Nṛsiṁhadeva and to pray, "Our master has not finished his work. Please protect him." Due to the sincere prayers of the devotees, Prabhupāda had said, Kṛṣṇa had saved his life. Now, in 1974, there were many more devotees than in 1967, and all of them were praying for Prabhupāda's recovery; but now also, from what Prabhupāda had said, there were also more devotees to misbehave and cause him pain. *That* message—"Eighty percent of the leaders of my disciples are not following the rules and regulations; this is why I am suffering"—was not telegrammed. It was too heavy.

Prabhupāda had come to Vṛndāvana for a celebration, but there had been none. Now he was very sick, and his servant was carrying him in his arms to and from the bathroom. Other devotees were also massaging and serving him very sincerely. And there was always *kīrtana* for him. Meanwhile he simply depended on Kṛṣṇa and waited to get better so that he could go on with his work.

While he tolerated his condition as the mercy of Kṛṣṇa, he suddenly received word that the governor of Uttar Pradesh was coming to visit him. The governor, a Muslim named Akbar Ali Khan, was traveling in the area, and Seth Bisenchand, a friend of Prabhupāda's and the governor's, had recommended that the governor visit the temple.

Prabhupāda thought that perhaps the governor would agree to help the devotees, at least in such matters as getting government permission for steel and cement. Therefore, despite his failing health, he insisted that the devotees hold a reception in the courtyard; and he would personally go out and greet the governor. Lying on his back and speaking in a faint voice, he ordered a feast to be cooked and tables and chairs to be arranged in the courtyard.

The devotees pleaded with Prabhupāda to allow them to do everything themselves and tell the governor that Prabhupāda was very ill. "He has come," Prabhupāda said. "I have to go out and meet him."

Śrutakīrti dressed Prabhupāda in a fresh silk *dhotī*. Prabhupāda tried to apply the Vaiṣṇava *tilaka* to his forehead, but even that was a struggle and took more than five minutes. When they were ready to go, Prabhupāda asked his servant, "Have I put on my *tilaka*?" He seemed almost delirious from the fever and was unable to stand. Śrutakīrti and others carried him in a chair and placed him in the middle of the courtyard, where they had arranged several tables with *prasādam* and Prabhupāda's books.

Just before the governor's arrival, many policemen and soldiers arrived, roping off the area, directing traffic in front of the temple, and holding people outside until the governor arrived. Guṇārṇava had rolled a long red carpet from the edge of the property into the temple courtyard, and devotees lined both sides of the carpet, chanting with *karatālas* and *mṛdaṅgas*. When the governor arrived, Surabhi presented him with a garland. Immediately removing the garland, the governor walked down the red carpet and into the courtyard. Prabhupāda stood.

The devotees were amazed to see Prabhupāda standing straight and shaking the governor's hand. Prabhupāda and the governor stood together for a while and then sat down. Except for the guests, everyone present knew that Prabhupāda was not capable of much exertion. They saw him shivering and trembling, yet trying to smile and be gracious with his guest. The devotees were in great anxiety, thinking that Prabhupāda's life might end at any moment, and yet they took part in the sociable pretense along with their spiritual master. The governor, on invitation, gave a speech, talking about how India's future lay in industry.

Then Prabhupāda stood to speak, leaning against his chair. His eyes were very dark, and he was barely able to focus his vision. Although he had spoken very little for almost two weeks, he now spoke for twenty minutes, while the governor listened politely. Afterward Prabhupāda sat and honored *prasādam* with the governor and his entourage of fifteen ministers. After the governor left, the devotees carried Prabhupāda back to his room, where he collapsed with a 105-degree temperature.

The political guests and military escort gone, the temple site returned to its usual quiet, and the devotees resumed their soft *kīrtana*, chanting by Prabhupāda's bedside. Amazed at Prabhupāda's strength and determination, they realized how little they themselves were actually putting forth in Kṛṣṇa consciousness.

After two full weeks Prabhupāda's fever finally broke. A great ordeal was now over. The monsoon was ending, but the same problems of temple construction persisted.

And so did Prabhupāda's determination. His disciples also felt determined, and they resolved to work through all the bureaucratic delays and slow labor conditions. Now no one was going to neglect spiritual regulation.

Prabhupāda spoke no more about his illness, and devotees around the world were informed of his improvement; they could stop the emergency *kīrtanas* and go on with work as usual. Prabhupāda also resumed his usual duties regarding the temple construction.

One thing was clear, however; Prabhupāda was completely spiritual. And the devotees working with him had engaged in a spiritual contract, a contract based on love and trust. He was taking their *karma*, and they had promised to follow his instructions. Now, despite his disappointment in them for their failures, that contract was still in order. If he continued to give his causeless mercy, then they could carry out his orders. Otherwise they were without spiritual strength. For Prabhupāda there was never a question of not continuing. Even when he had suffered illness on his disciples' account, he had never thought to abandon them.

After more than two weeks of not translating, Prabhupāda resumed his work. He had been working quickly on the *Caitanya-caritāmṛta* and was up to the discussions between Lord Caitanya and Sanātana Gosvāmī in *Madhya-līlā*. Taking up where he had left off, Prabhupāda again began rising early and studying the Bengali translations and commentaries. He would turn on his dictating machine and begin to speak, his voice a faint, harsh whisper. But as he continued his voice grew stronger, until by the end of an hour he was speaking normally. By the time he left Vṛndāvana he was working unusually fast, producing two tapes a day.

* * *

Bombay

From November 1974 through January 1975 Śrīla Prabhupāda stayed in Bombay. During this time he persistently but patiently tried to obtain the No-Objection Certificate, which would enable him to start construction of Rādhā-Rāsavihārī's beautiful temple. His close involvement with this project impressed Girirāja and others who were dedicating their lives to Hare Krishna Land. As Śrīla Prabhupāda had written in *Bhagavad-gītā*, "One has no goal in life save and except acting in Kṛṣṇa consciousness just to satisfy Kṛṣṇa. And, while working in that way, one should think of Kṛṣṇa only: 'I have been appointed to discharge this particular duty by Kṛṣṇa.' While acting in such a way, one naturally has to think of Kṛṣṇa. . . . That order of Kṛṣṇa comes through disciplic succession from the bona fide spiritual master."

To serve in a particular project, dedicating oneself to giving the local people Kṛṣṇa consciousness, was an opportunity Śrīla Prabhupāda offered every disciple. His field was the entire world, and he was like an emperor who wanted to award vast lands to loyal sons. But his awarding of lands and projects was not for material ownership (which is always illusory) but for service to the Lord. Kṛṣṇa was the proprietor of everything; therefore a preacher could remain in a particular area of Kṛṣṇa's domain and try to free the residents from the clutches of *māyā*. Hare Krishna Land in Bombay was one of Prabhupāda's major plans, but it was only gradually evolving, as if Kṛṣṇa first wanted to see the devotees pass many tests of obedience to Prabhupāda's order before allowing the project to manifest.

Although ISKCON owned a half-dozen tenement buildings on the Juhu land, law prohibited them from evicting any of the tenants. But no law said that the owner could not add another story onto his buildings. So Śrīla Prabhupāda had requested Mr. Sethi, a loyal life member and a construction contractor, to build rooms on the top of at least two of the tenement buildings. Eagerly, Mr. Sethi had undertaken this order and had obtained permission for the construction.

Now that the work was completed, the rooms were being used for *brahmacārī* quarters, offices, and book storage. At last the devotees had vacated the straw huts that had been their residence from their first days on the land. This move not only relieved them from living in nasty, rat-infested quarters, but also allowed them to tear down the huts. And demolition of the huts had been a stipulation before the city would issue the NOC.

Another major objection from the city had been that the temple's *bhajana* would create a nuisance, and that point had to be satisfied first and foremost. When the police saw Prabhupāda's drawing of the projected temple and hotel, they admitted that within such a big temple the *kīrtana* would not create as much noise as it did at present. So they agreed to accept the master plan for Hare Krishna Land and remove their objections based on "nuisance," provided ISKCON tear down the straw huts and widen the access road so the tenants could approach the back portion of the land. Each of these legal demands involved many detailed points of contention; it was like a long, drawn-out chess game. But Prabhupāda was experienced, cautious, and determined. He proposed to stay at Hare Krishna Land for several months to help Girirāja, Mr. Sethi, and the others.

Meanwhile, Prabhupāda insisted that the spiritual program at Hare Krishna Land go forward unabated. Even without a permanent temple, five to seven hundred guests were coming for the Sunday feasts. Girirāja had reported to Prabhupāda that Janmāṣṭamī in Bombay had been a great success, with several thousand people coming to see the Deities and take *prasādam.*

For Śrīla Prabhupāda, who was now accustomed to staying in places like New York or Los Angeles for a week or less, to stay in Bombay for a three-month period confirmed again that Hare Krishna Land was very dear to him. It was his special child. When danger threatened, he became alarmed and protective, and when success came, he was very proud and wanted to tell the world.

Prabhupāda seemed satisfied that at least *some* construction was always going on. He asked that Mr. Sethi build a brick wall around the property, even though parts of the wall were sometimes torn down at night by *guṇḍās.* "Build something," Prabhupāda said, "even if it is just one brick, but go ahead with construction." Just as when, in acquiring the Bombay property, Prabhupāda had understood the great value of possession even before attaining the deed, so with construction he insisted they go ahead, even without full permission. "The work must begin," Prabhupāda said, "whether you have got sufficient men and bricks or not. Begin even little, little, so it can be understood that we have begun."

Śrīla Prabhupāda had received word from Vṛndāvana that the newly elected governor of Uttar Pradesh, Dr. Channa Reddy, had visited the temple site. Hearing this, Prabhupāda decided to invite him for the rescheduled opening of the Krishna-Balaram Mandir.

> Your Excellency:
> . . . Tentatively the date is fixed up on Sri Ram Navami, the Birthday of Lord Ramachandra. Probably it will be the fixed up date because we are depending on the progress of the construction work. If you kindly give me your consent, we can print your Excellency's name on the invitation card as the Chief Guest and Inaugurator of the temple.
>
> You are already our member as well as a great devotee of Lord Krishna, so we shall feel it a great privilege if you kindly agree to this proposal.

Prabhupāda followed his invitation to the governor with a letter to Surabhi in Vṛndāvana.

> . . . *Everything* must be cent per cent completed by the end of March. Is the contractor cheating? That means it will never be finished. Simply

> we have to put money. From the photos I have seen, there is not very much progress. What to do?
>
> I want no explanations. I want to see everything finished. If there is still doubt please tell me frankly.

Invitations were coming in for Śrīla Prabhupāda to travel to different places, and another world tour was developing. Prabhupāda wrote to Hṛdayānanda Goswami, who was inviting him to visit Mexico City and Caracas.

> . . . Yes I want to come there very much. Now we are in Bombay trying to get permission from the government to build our temple. And it appears that we will possibly be getting the permission next week. If this works out then I will immediately be going to Honolulu and from Honolulu I can go directly to Mexico City, then Caracas, and then to Australia by the end of Jan. If the Bombay situation is not settled up I may have to stay till mid-Jan. or so and then in mid or end of Jan. I will be going to Australia to stay for one month.

By mid-January of 1975 the city finally issued the NOC. Prabhupāda was jubilant and immediately called for a cornerstone-laying ceremony. He had already held a ground-breaking and cornerstone-laying ceremony in March 1972, on first moving to the land. Nevertheless, he wanted another one, as this would actually signify the beginning of the construction of the temple. He therefore devised a festival involving all life members and friends of ISKCON in Bombay.

Śrīla Prabhupāda was ready to travel, and this time, more than ever, he impressed on his leaders in Bombay that the temple construction should go ahead without interruption. No doubt there would be new opposition from the government. But such opposition would be overcome, as in the past, by Kṛṣṇa's grace. The devotees, however, would have to be very determined. This was the reward of working for Prabhupāda in Hare Krishna Land—that one gained determination in the face of trouble and knew that by staying with one's service he was pleasing Kṛṣṇa and Kṛṣṇa's pure devotee.

* * *

During February and March of 1975, Śrīla Prabhupāda toured widely again, traveling eastward via Tokyo and Hawaii to Los Angeles. While traveling, he received word that Governor Reddy had accepted the invitation to attend the Vṛndāvana temple opening on Rāma-navamī. He also received an encouraging report from Surabhi, assuring him that this time the temple opening would definitely take place. "I am encouraged that you expect to have everything completed on time," Prabhupāda wrote. "This I want."

Prabhupāda traveled to Mexico and Caracas. Again, in answering his mail, he was saying he would soon meet everyone in Vṛndāvana. To an Indian life member who wrote him for advice in touring foreign temples, he wrote,

> By the 20th of March I will be in Calcutta and you can see me there. I shall advise you personally. You are also invited to participate in our Mayapur festival during Sri Caitanya Mahaprabhu's appearance day ceremony, as well as the opening celebration of Krishna-Balaram temple in Vrindaban on Rama-Navami day. The Governor of U.P. will also come there to participate and many other important and respectable gentlemen will also be coming. I hope you will also come with your wife and son and mother, and encourage us by taking part in the festival.

Leaving South America, Prabhupāda moved quickly, stopping in Miami, Atlanta, Dallas, and New York—all within a month of his departure from India. He then went to London, stopped in Tehran, and returned to India on March 16. It was Prabhupāda's eighth trip around the world in ten years.

Early in the morning of March 23, Śrīla Prabhupāda left the Calcutta temple for Māyāpur, traveling in a caravan of five cars. Prabhupāda was in the first car, three following cars carried his *sannyāsī* disciples, and the last car carried his sister, Bhavatāriṇī, and other ladies. As usual, Prabhupāda asked to stop at the mango orchard.

Daivi-śakti dāsī: *They all sat around together, just like cowherd boys, Prabhupāda in the center taking his breakfast fruits. It was* Ekādaśī, *and I had made a cake for Prabhupāda out of dates and coconut—very fancy. When Prabhupāda opened his* tiffin *and saw it, he said, "Oh, what is this? Who has made this?" So Acyutānanda Swami told him I had made it, and he started eating it right away. Prabhupāda said he liked it. Then they washed their hands, and we were on our way again to Māyāpur.*

Māyāpur
March 23, 1975

For this year's festival, almost five hundred devotees from around the world had gathered, and Prabhupāda—while taking his morning walks in the nearby fields, while entering the temple of Rādhā-Mādhava, or while lecturing from the *Caitanya-caritāmṛta*—was the central attractive feature. Each morning after giving the class, he would circumambulate the temple room, followed by his disciples. A brass bell hung from the ceiling on either side of the Deities' altar, and Prabhupāda, while circumambulating the Deities, would go up to one of the bells and ring it several times, pulling the rope while the *kīrtana* continued wildly. Then, with cane in hand, he would walk around the back of the Deity altar and emerge on the other side to ring the other bell.

The devotees would jump up and down close around him, singing Hare Kṛṣṇa, Hare Kṛṣṇa, Kṛṣṇa Kṛṣṇa, Hare Hare/ Hare Rāma, Hare Rāma, Rāma Rāma, Hare Hare. Smiling with great pleasure, Prabhupāda would continue the length of the temple room, past the pictures of Bhaktisiddhānta Sarasvatī, Gaurakiśora dāsa Bābājī, and Bhaktivinoda Ṭhākura, then come around and up the other side of the temple room to the first bell again and strongly ring it. After half a dozen such blissful circumambulations, he would leave the temple, while the *kīrtana* continued to roar. Coming out into the bright morning sunshine, he would walk up the broad staircase to his room.

On at least two occasions during that festival, Prabhupāda became stunned in trance while delivering the morning lecture. One time he was speaking in appreciation of the sacrifice of his disciples, who had spent so much money and come so far from their homes in America, Europe, and Australia to render service and attend the festival in Māyāpur. "You are all young," he was saying. "You have a good opportunity. But I am an old man. I have no opportunity. . . ."

And with these words he suddenly fell completely silent. Such silence before five hundred disciples produced a feeling of suspended time. Everyone waited. Finally, one of the devotees began chanting Hare Kṛṣṇa, and Śrīla Prabhupāda returned to external consciousness, uttering, "Hare Kṛṣṇa." He told the devotees, "Have *kīrtana*," and went to his room.

Prabhupāda again supervised the annual meeting of his Governing Body Commission and personally approved or modified all their decisions. ISKCON was indeed growing, but as Prabhupāda had told his friend, the aged Gopala Acarya, in Madras, "Kṛṣṇa and Kṛṣṇa's institution are nondifferent. If the devotees are thinking of Kṛṣṇa's institution, they will not forget Kṛṣṇa."

By insisting on the devotees' participation in the annual India pilgrimage, Prabhupāda was solidifying the spiritual basis of ISKCON, his transcendental institution. To gather his devotees like this was the reason he had prayed and struggled to erect centers in the *dhāmas*. He wanted to extend the purifying shelter of Māyāpur and Vṛndāvana to all his followers, now and in the future. Bit by bit, the plan was coming together; the whole world was being saved by Lord Caitanya's movement.

* * *

Vṛndāvana
April 16

When Śrīla Prabhupāda arrived to finally conduct the Krishna-Balaram Mandir opening, he was pleasantly surprised to see the three tall domes rising over the temple. The domes had been constructed entirely during the eight months since his last visit. The four-story international guesthouse had also been completely built during his absence. Surabhi had supervised workers in day and night shifts to get everything done on time.

The tall central dome and two side domes, one over each altar, were magnificent. Their graceful form led the mind to higher thoughts and suggested an existence beyond the material world. The strength and beauty of the domes reminded one that beneath resided the Deity of the Supreme Lord. A temple was to enlighten people, to remove their nescience, and the domes eloquently spoke of this purpose. They could be seen for miles, rising boldly above the landscape of Vṛndāvana, proclaiming the worship of Kṛṣṇa and Balarāma.

Each dome was topped by a copper *kalasā* consisting of three balls (representing the lower, middle, and higher planets), and at the top, the eternal Sudarśana *cakra*, the spinning wheel-weapon of Lord Viṣṇu. The

Sudarśana *cakra* was Kṛṣṇa Himself, and just to see this glorious symbol atop the *mandira* made the devotees feel victorious and satisfied. Even the guests could not help but regard it with awe. Atop the Sudarśana *cakras* were copper victory flags.

As Prabhupāda toured the completed building, he continually looked up at the domes. "Oh," he said, "the domes have come out very nice. What do you think?" He turned to the devotees accompanying him.

"They are magnificent!" said Haṁsadūta.

"Yes, Prabhupāda," said Tamāla Kṛṣṇa Goswami, "I think that Surabhi has done a nice job."

"Yes," Prabhupāda smiled, "everyone is telling how nice Surabhi is doing." Prabhupāda turned to Surabhi, who had gone with little sleep for weeks. "But I can't say that. Only me—I am criticizing you, because that is my job. I have to always criticize the disciple."

No less than six hundred devotees from ISKCON centers around the world had come to Vṛndāvana as part of the annual Indian pilgrimage. The high point was to be the installation of the Deities and the opening of the temple. Final preparations were going furiously—cleanups, decorations, cooking. Many important life members and guests had come and were staying in their private rooms in the forty-room guesthouse. Prabhupāda's vision had finally come to pass. He had created probably the most beautiful and opulent temple in Vṛndāvana—certainly the one most alive with dynamic devotion and preaching spirit—and along with it he had built one of the best local hotels, for visitors with an eye for *kṛṣṇa-bhakti*.

Touring the grounds, Prabhupāda walked into the sunken courtyard, its marble floor clean and dazzling. This was no rented house in America, something built for another purpose—it was a temple, like the temples in Vaikuṇṭha described in the *Śrīmad-Bhāgavatam*. "It is heaven on earth," Prabhupāda said. "I think it surpasses all the temples in India."

Prabhupāda stood smiling before the *tamāla* tree, its venerable branches spread throughout one corner of the courtyard, and he recounted how there had been a discussion of cutting it down and he had prevented it. *Tamāla* trees are associated with the pastimes of Śrīmatī Rādhārāṇī and are very rare. In Vṛndāvana there were perhaps only three: one here, one at Sevā-kuñja, and one in the courtyard of the Rādhā-Dāmodara temple. That the *tamāla* tree was growing so luxuriantly, Prabhupāda said, indicated that the devotees were performing genuine *bhakti*.

Convinced that the temple was actually ready, Prabhupāda entered his residence, just between the temple and the guesthouse. Many details demanded his attention, and many visiting disciples were present.

Thus in Ramaṇa-reti, in a place where there was no temple, a pure devotee desired, "Let there be a temple, and *sevā*, devotional service." And what had once been an empty lot was now a place of pilgrimage. Such is the power of the desires of the pure devotee.

* * *

EPILOGUE

Śrīla Prabhupāda would often say of his devotional service in India, "Vṛndāvana is my residence, Bombay is my office, and Māyāpur is where I worship the Supreme Personality of Godhead."

Bombay is the biggest commercial city in India. Prabhupāda's "business" was pure devotional service to Kṛṣṇa, and in Bombay he dealt more with the managerial aspects of Kṛṣṇa consciousness in India. He had incorporated ISKCON in India with the main branch in Bombay. All other branches of ISKCON in India, therefore, were legally part of the Bombay incorporation. In Bombay, Prabhupāda had cultivated more lawyers and businessmen as life members and earned more friends of his Society than in any other city in India. So whenever he was in Bombay, he often sought legal advice, not just about the Bombay center but also about his other affairs in India.

Since Bombay was a modern city with professional and office facilities on a level with many Western cities, Prabhupāda wanted to locate the Indian division of his Book Trust there, for printing Hindi translations of his books as well as English versions for the Indian market. Bombay, unlike Vṛndāvana and Māyāpur, was not a *dhāma* but a bustling, wealthy city. ISKCON's biggest donors lived there. Although Śrīla Prabhupāda's demeanor was entirely transcendental in Bombay, and his activities were often the same as elsewhere—speaking on *Bhagavad-gītā* and *Śrīmad-Bhāgavatam* and worshiping the Deity—nevertheless, Prabhupāda called it his office. And though it was his office, he wanted a temple there.

"Māyāpur," Prabhupāda said, "is where I worship the Supreme Personality of Godhead." Prabhupāda conceived of a temple to be built in Māyāpur that would be the grandest of all temples in his movement. He and his devotees would worship the Supreme Lord there in such a magnificent style that the whole world would be attracted to Prabhupāda's place of worship, the Mayapur Chandrodaya Mandir.

According to the *Śrīmad-Bhāgavatam*, the prescribed worship for this age is *saṅkīrtana*, the chanting of the holy names of God. *Saṅkīrtana* worship emanated from Māyāpur, the original *dhāma* of Lord Caitanya. "In the age of Kali," states *Śrīmad-Bhāgavatam*, "Lord Kṛṣṇa appears in a golden form, as Lord Caitanya, and His activity is to chant Hare Kṛṣṇa. People with sufficient intelligence will worship Him in this form." Śrīla Prabhupāda wanted to make the most wonderful worship of Caitanya Mahāprabhu in His birthplace and thus completely fulfill the predictions of the previous *ācāryas*, who foresaw a great Vedic city rising from the plains of Navadvīpa.

Māyāpur could also be considered Prabhupāda's place of worship because his spiritual master, Bhaktisiddhānta Sarasvatī, had preached extensively there and because his *samādhi* was there. Since Śrīla Prabhupāda's entire preaching mission was in the service of his spiritual master, he worshiped his spiritual master through preaching in Māyāpur. Māyāpur was the origin and symbol of preaching Kṛṣṇa consciousness, because there Lord Caitanya and Nityānanda actually began the *saṅkīrtana* movement that Prabhupāda was now carrying all over the world.

> Śrī Caitanya Mahāprabhu wanted to preach the *saṅkīrtana* movement of love of Kṛṣṇa throughout the entire world, and therefore during His presence He inspired the *saṅkīrtana* movement. Specifically, He sent Rūpa Gosvāmī to Vṛndāvana and Nityānanda to Bengal and personally went to South India. In this way He kindly left the task of preaching His cult in the rest of the world to the International Society for Krishna Consciousness.

Vṛndāvana is Prabhupāda's residence. Religious people in India as well as religious scholars in the West saw Prabhupāda as a Vaiṣṇava *sādhu*—from Vṛndāvana. When he began his preaching in New York City, he would often introduce himself as "coming from Vṛndāvana." "Here I am now sitting in New York," he once said, "the world's greatest city, but my heart is always hankering after that Vṛndāvana. I shall be very happy to return to my Vṛndāvana, that sacred place."

The people of Vṛndāvana also thought of Prabhupāda as their hometown success. Upon retiring from family life in 1954, Prabhupāda had gone to live in Vṛndāvana, first at a temple near Keśi-ghāṭa and then at the Rādhā-Dāmodara temple. After taking *sannyāsa* in 1959, he had continued to reside in Vṛndāvana and, when not living there, to reserve his two rooms at Rādhā-Dāmodara.

Vṛndāvana is the home of Kṛṣṇa consciousness, the place of Kṛṣṇa's childhood pastimes, the place where the six Gosvāmīs, sent by Lord Caitanya, had excavated holy places, written transcendental literature, and built temples. Any devotee could feel at home there, and thousands of Vṛndāvana's residents carried bead bags, chanted Hare Kṛṣṇa, and wore the Vaiṣṇava *tilaka* and dress. Vṛndāvana belonged to Rādhā and Kṛṣṇa, and this was still acknowledged by the residents of the present-day Vṛndāvana.

Ultimately, Vṛndāvana is revealed only to the pure devotee. Vṛndāvana is the eternal residence of all spiritual souls in their eternal relationship with Kṛṣṇa. The Vṛndāvana in India is a transcendental replica of Goloka Vṛndāvana, the eternal planet where Kṛṣṇa resides in the spiritual world. The pure devotees aspire to attain to Goloka Vṛndāvana after finishing their life in this world, and Prabhupāda, therefore, as a pure devotee of Kṛṣṇa, naturally felt at home in Vṛndāvana. He sometimes said that if he were to become very ill, he would prefer not to go to a hospital but to simply go to Vṛndāvana and there pass his last days. To spread the glories of Vṛndāvana, Prabhupāda had left Vṛndāvana, but like a traveler away from home, he always thought of returning.

Appendixes

BOOKS by His Divine Grace A.C. Bhaktivedanta Swami Prabhupāda

Bhagavad-gītā As It Is
Śrīmad-Bhāgavatam, cantos 1–10 (30 vols.)
Śrī Caitanya-caritāmṛta (17 vols.)
Teachings of Lord Caitanya
The Nectar of Devotion
The Nectar of Instruction
Śrī Īśopaniṣad
Easy Journey to Other Planets
Kṛṣṇa Consciousness: The Topmost Yoga System
Kṛṣṇa, the Supreme Personality of Godhead (3 vols.)
Perfect Questions, Perfect Answers
Teachings of Lord Kapila, the Son of Devahūti
Transcendental Teachings of Prahlāda Mahārāja
Teachings of Queen Kuntī
Kṛṣṇa, the Reservoir of Pleasure
The Science of Self-Realization
The Path of Perfection
Life Comes From Life
The Perfection of Yoga
Beyond Birth and Death
On the Way to Kṛṣṇa
Rāja-vidyā: The King of Knowledge
Elevation to Kṛṣṇa Consciousness
Kṛṣṇa Consciousness: The Matchless Gift
Search for Liberation
Geetār-gan (Bengali)
Vairāgya-vidyā (Bengali)
Buddhi-yoga (Bengali)
Bhakti-ratna-bolī (Bengali)
Back to Godhead magazine (founder)

A complete catalog is available upon request.

Bhaktivedanta Book Trust
3764 Watseka Avenue
Los Angeles, California 90034

Sanskrit Pronunciation Guide

Throughout the centuries, the Sanskrit language has been written in a variety of alphabets. The mode of writing most widely used throughout India, however, is called *devanāgarī,* which means, literally, the writing used in "the cities of the demigods." The *devanāgarī* alphabet consists of forty-eight characters, including thirteen vowels and thirty-five consonants. Ancient Sanskrit grammarians arranged the alphabet according to practical linguistic principles, and this order has been accepted by all Western scholars. The system of transliteration used in this book conforms to a system that scholars in the last fifty years have accepted to indicate the pronunciation of each Sanskrit sound.

The short vowel **a** is pronounced like the **u** in b**u**t, long **ā** like the **a** in f**a**r, and short **i** like the **i** in p**i**n. Long **ī** is pronounced as in p**i**que, short **u** as in p**u**ll, and long **ū** as in r**u**le. The vowel **ṛ** is pronounced like the **ri** in **ri**m. The vowel **e** is pronounced as in th**e**y, **ai** as in **ai**sle, **o** as in g**o**, and **au** as in h**ow**. The *anusvāra* (**ṁ**), which is a pure nasal, is pronounced like the **n** in the French word *bo***n**, and *visarga* (**ḥ**), which is a strong aspirate, is pronounced as a final **h** sound. Thus **aḥ** is pronounced like **aha**, and **iḥ** like **ihi**.

The guttural consonants—**k, kh, g, gh,** and **ṅ**—are pronounced from the throat in much the same manner as in English. **K** is pronounced as in **k**ite, **kh** as in Ec**kh**art, **g** as in **g**ive, **gh** as in di**g h**ard, and **ṅ** as in si**ng**. The palatal consonants—**c, ch, j, jh,** and **ñ**— are pronounced from the palate with the middle of the tongue. **C** is pronounced as in **ch**air, **ch** as in staun**ch-h**eart, **j** as in **j**oy, **jh** as in he**dgeh**og, and **ñ** as in ca**ny**on. The cerebral consonants—**ṭ, ṭh, ḍ, ḍh,** and **ṇ**—are pronounced with the tip of the tongue turned up and drawn back against the dome of the palate. **Ṭ** is pronounced as in **t**ub, **ṭh** as in ligh**t-h**eart, **ḍ** as in **d**ove, **ḍh** as in re**d-h**ot, and **ṇ** as in **n**ut. The dental consonants—**t, th, d, dh,** and **n**—are pronounced in the same manner as the cerebrals, but with the forepart of the tongue against the teeth. The labial consonants—**p, ph, b, bh,** and **m**—are pronounced with the lips. **P** is pronounced as in **p**ine, **ph** as in u**ph**ill, **b** as in **b**ird, **bh** as in ru**b-h**ard, and **m** as in **m**other. The semivowels—**y, r, l,** and **v**—are pronounced as in **y**es, **r**un, **l**ight, and **v**ine respectively. The sibilants **ś, ṣ,** and **s**—are pronounced, respectively, as in the German word *s**prechen*** and the English words **sh**ine and **s**un. The letter **h** is pronounced as in **h**ome.

Glossary

A

Ācārya—one who teaches by example.
Ādi-līlā—chapters in *Caitanya-caritāmṛta* dealing with the early life of Caitanya Mahāprabhu.
Ārati—a ceremony for worshiping the Deity of the Lord with offerings of food, lamps, fans, flowers, and incense.
Āśrama—a place of shelter conducive to the practice of spiritual life; a particular order in spiritual life.

B

Balarāma—the first expansion of Lord Kṛṣṇa, appearing as His elder brother.
Bhagavad-gītā—"Song of God"; the essential summary of spiritual knowledge spoken to Arjuna by the Supreme Lord, Śrī Kṛṣṇa.
Bhajana—worship of God by the chanting of His holy names.
Bhakti—devotion to the Supreme Personality of Godhead.
Bhakti-rasāmṛta-sindhu—Rūpa Gosvāmī's definitive explanation of devotional service to the Supreme Lord.
Brahmacārī—a celibate monk; the first of the four *āśramas,* or spiritual orders of life.
Brahma-muhūrta hour—an auspicious hour before sunrise.
Brahman—the Absolute Truth, the Supreme Spirit; especially the impersonal aspect of the Absolute.
Brāhmaṇa—an intelligent man who understands the spiritual purpose of life and can instruct others; the first Vedic social order, or *varṇa.*
Brahma-saṁhitā—a Vedic scripture describing Lord Kṛṣṇa, the Supreme Personality of Godhead.

C

Cādar—a blanket or cloth used to cover the upper part of the body.
Caitanya-caritāmṛta—the standard biography of Lord Caitanya Mahāprabhu, written by Kṛṣṇadāsa Kavirāja.
Caitanya Mahāprabhu—the *avatāra* of Lord Kṛṣṇa in this age whose mission is to teach love of God through the chanting of His holy names.

D

Darśana—audience with a revered personality or a Deity.
Dhāma—a holy place; an eternal abode of the Supreme Lord.
Dharmaśālā—an inexpensive residence set up especially for pilgrims.
Dhotī—the standard Indian men's garment, a simple piece of cloth wrapped around the lower body.

E

Ekādaśī—the eleventh day of the waning or waxing moon; fasting from beans and grains.

G

Gamchā—a short cloth wrapped around the lower part of the body.
Gauḍīya Vaiṣṇava—a follower of Lord Kṛṣṇa (Viṣṇu) in the line of Lord Caitanya Mahāprabhu.
Gopīs—the cowherd girls of Vṛndāvana, who are the most advanced and intimate devotees of Lord Kṛṣṇa.
Gṛhastha—one who is practicing spiritual life while living with wife and children; the second *āśrama,* or spiritual order.
Guṇḍa—a hoodlum.
Gurukula—the school of the spiritual master.

H

Halavā—a dessert made from toasted grains, butter, and sugar.
Hare Kṛṣṇa—the holy names of the Lord.
Hari Bol—"Chant the names of Lord Hari!"

I

ISKCON—International Society for Krishna Consciousness.

J

Jagannātha—"Lord of the universe"; a special Deity of Lord Kṛṣṇa, originating in Orissa on the east coast of India at Purī.

K

Kali-yuga—the present age of confusion and quarrel, which began five thousand years ago.
Karatālas—sacred hand-cymbals.

Karma—fruitive action, for which there is always a reaction, good or bad.
Kicharī—a cooked preparation made from rice and lentils.
Kīrtana—glorification of God, especially by the chanting of His holy names.
Kṛṣṇa—the Supreme Personality of Godhead.
Kṛṣṇa-bhakti—*See: Bhakti.*
Kṣatriya—the administrative and protective occupation according to the system of social and spiritual orders.

L

Lakh—the sum of 100,000 rupees.
Līlā—pastimes of the Supreme Lord.

M

Mandir—a temple.
Maṅgala-ārati—the first worship ceremony of the day, observed before sunrise.
Mantra—a sound vibration that liberates the mind.
Mlecchas—meat-eaters.
Mṛdaṅga—a sacred drum, made of clay, used in *kīrtana.*

N

Nārada Muni—the sage among the demigods, who is the son of Lord Brahmā and the spiritual master of Vyāsadeva.
Navadvīpa—the holy birthplace of Lord Caitanya Mahāprabhu, in Bengal.
Nṛsiṁha, Lord—an incarnation of Kṛṣṇa as half-man, half-lion.

P

Pāñcarātrakī-viddhi—the rules and regulations of devotional service as enunciated by the six Gosvāmīs.
Paṇḍāl—a tent.
Paramahaṁsa—a swanlike, self-realized personality.
Prabhupāda—"the spiritual master at whose feet all others take shelter."
Prasādam—food spiritualized by first being offered to the Supreme Lord for His enjoyment.
Pūjārī—a priest engaged in worshiping the Deity.

R

Rādhā(rāṇī)—the eternal consort of Lord Kṛṣṇa and manifestation of His internal pleasure potency.

Rāmāyaṇa— the epic history of Lord Rāmacandra written by the sage Vālmīki.

Ratha-yātrā—the annual cart festival of Lord Jagannātha.

S

Sādhu—a saintly person.

Samādhi—the tomb of a revered spiritual leader.

Saṅkīrtana—congregational chanting of the holy names of the Lord, the recommended process of *yoga* for this age.

Sannyāsī—one in the *sannyāsa* order.

Sārī—the standard garment of women in Indian society, a single piece of cloth covering the entire body.

Śāstra—scripture.

Śikhā—the tuft of hair remaining on the back of the shaven head of a Vaiṣṇava.

Śiva—the demigod who supervises the material quality of ignorance and the final destruction of the material cosmos.

Śrīmad-Bhāgavatam—the voluminous scripture composed by Śrīla Vyāsadeva to describe and explain Lord Kṛṣṇa's pastimes.

Subhadrā—the younger sister of Lord Kṛṣṇa and personification of His spiritual potency.

Śūdra—a laborer; the fourth *varṇa,* or social order, which is compared to the legs of society.

Śukadeva Gosvāmī—the great sage who originally spoke *Śrīmad-Bhāgavatam.*

T

Tāṅgā—a horse-drawn cart.

Tilaka—sacred clay marking the body of a devotee as a temple of God.

V

Vaiṣṇava—a devotee of Viṣṇu (or Kṛṣṇa).

Vaiṣya—a farmer or merchant; the third of the four occupational orders of Vedic society.

Vānaprastha—retirement from active family life, wherein one makes pilgrimage to holy places, prior to *sannyāsa*.

Viṣṇu—the Supreme Lord, Kṛṣṇa, appearing in His majestic four-armed form.

Vṛndāvana—the personal abode of Lord Kṛṣṇa, the inhabitants of which are all His intimate servants.

Vyāsāsana—the honored seat of the spiritual master.

Y

Yamarāja—the demigod who awards punishment to those who disobey the laws of God.

Yavana—one who does not follow the Vedic principles of life.

Index

When footnotes are referred to in the index, they are indicated by a number followed by an n.

A

D

E

F

G

H

I

J

L

M

N

O

P

Prabhupāda, Śrīla
news coverage of (continued)
in Hyderabad, 205
in London, 158
in Madras, 57, 58
in Melbourne, 216–17, 219–220
in New Vrindaban, 109
by *New York Times,* 109
in Paris, 166
in New Vrindaban, 107–11
in New York, 103, 244
in New Zealand, 90
Nityānanda's mercy extended by, 77
No-Objection Certificate obtained by, 243
at Nṛsiṁha temple, 67–69
ordered to preach in West, 2, 8
in Oregon, 103
in Paris, 103–4, 166, 212–14
Patrick McClure &, 220
as personification of Caitanya's mercy, 189
in Philippines, 118
philosophical expertise of, 159
in Pittsburgh, 111–12
in Portland, 103
potter story as told by, 4
Pradyumna dāsa &, 123–24
prasādam distribution desired by, 144
prasādam distribution directed by, 67, 79–80, 82–83
preaching by
America focus of, 169
India focus of, 169
See also: Prabhupāda, lectures by; letters by; cited; quoted
preaching to important men desired by, 6, 61–65
press conference held by, in Madras, 58
priests of Bālajī &, 207
priests visit, in England, 161–62
prophecy regarding, 189
protest meeting planned by, 201
publicity campaign in Juhu ordered by, 137, 138
Purī Mahārāja host to, 65, 66–67
Purī Mahārāja invited to West by, 70

Prabhupāda, Śrīla (*continued*)
Purī Mahārāja invites, 64
purports by
in *Caitanya-caritāmṛta,* 149, 150, 151, 152
about ISKCON, 192
quarantined in Bombay, 8
quarters of
at Bālajī temple, 206
at Bhaktivedanta Manor, 158
in Frankfurt temple, 214
at Hare Krishna Land, 83, 202
in Krishna-Balaram Mandir, 247–48
in Māyāpur, 73, 141, 145, 146, 189
at Rādhā-Dāmodara temple, 249–50
in Rome, 211
in Tokyo, 91
in Vṛndāvana, 182–83, 232–33, 249–50
quoted. *See:* Prabhupāda quoted
at Rādhā-Dāmodara temple, 26, 121, 122
Rādhā-Dāmodara temple "eternal" residence of, 122
Rādhā-Govinda Deities bathed by, 44
Rādhā-Kṛṣṇa Deities installed by. *See:* Prabhupāda, Deity installation(s) by
Rādhā-Rāsavihārī's relationship with, 131–32, 133
Rajaji &, 60
at Ramakrishna Hall, 69
at Ram Nuvas Dhandaria's, 9–11
at Ratha-yātrā
in Chicago, 225–26
in Melbourne, 217–19
in San Francisco, 226–27
Ravi Shankar &, 103
religion defined by, 14
reporters &
dvaita or *advaita* question &, 205
in Madras, 58
in New Delhi, 9–11
retiring from family life, 249
retiring from management considered by, 204, 205
Revatīnandana Mahārāja &, 155–56

R

T

U

V

W

Y

The Author

Satsvarūpa dāsa Goswami was born on December 6, 1939, in New York City. He attended public schools and received a B.A. from Brooklyn College in 1961. Then followed two years as a journalist in the U.S. navy and three years as a social worker in New York City.

In July 1966, he met His Divine Grace A.C. Bhaktivedanta Swami Prabhupāda, and he became his initiated disciple in September of that year. Satsvarūpa dāsa Goswami began contributing articles to *Back to Godhead,* the magazine of the Hare Kṛṣṇa movement, and later became its editor in chief. In August 1967 he went to Boston to establish the first ISKCON center there. Satsvarūpa dāsa Goswami was one of the original members selected by Śrīla Prabhupāda to form the Governing Body Commission of ISKCON in 1970. He remained as president of Boston ISKCON until 1971, when he moved to Dallas and became headmaster of Gurukula, the first ISKCON school for children.

In May 1972, on the appearance day of Lord Nṛsiṁhadeva, he was awarded the *sannyāsa* (renounced) order by His Divine Grace Śrīla Prabhupāda and began traveling across the United States, lecturing in colleges and universities. In January 1974 he was called by Śrīla Prabhupāda to become his personal secretary and to travel with him through India and Europe. In 1976 he published *Readings in Vedic Literature*, a concise account of the Vedic tradition. The volume is now being studied at various American universities. In 1977 Śrīla Prabhupāda ordered him to accept the duties of initiating *guru*, along with ten other senior disciples. He is presently working on a long-term literary project, preparing further volumes of the biography of His Divine Grace A.C. Bhaktivedanta Swami Prabhupāda.